Counterfeit medicines

Survey report

TO BE
DISPOSED
BY
AUTHORITY

Council of Europe Publishing

Counterfeit medicines

Harmonised provisions, legislation and administrative structures and procedures applicable to counterfeit medicines: stakeholders' views and experiences

in the framework of the activity "Minimising the public health risks posed by counterfeit medicines to the European citizen"

Jonathan Harper, MB, ChB, BSc (Hons), MBA

Bertrand Gellie (Consultant, Chapter 10 – Intellectual property rights)

Editor's note: the presentation of some tables, of the questionnaire and of the glossary may have been slightly adjusted to suit publishing requirements. However, neither the emphasis nor the content have been changed.

Cover design: Graphic Design Workshop, Council of Europe
Layout: SAG+ / Saverne

Council of Europe Publishing
F-67075 Strasbourg Cedex
http://book.coe.int

ISBN 92-871-5863-0
© Council of Europe, January 2006
Printed at the Council of Europe

Contents

Executive summary

This report has been commissioned by the Council of Europe Committee of Experts on Pharmaceutical Questions and its multisectoral Ad hoc Group on Counterfeit Medicines on the basis of an ongoing project to minimise public health risks posed by counterfeit medicines. The report is based on the results of several important surveys of Council of Europe member states and European pharmaceutical sector stakeholders (manufacturers and wholesalers of medicinal products) conducted by the ad hoc group in 2003 and 2004 on the subject of legislative and administrative procedures applicable to counterfeit medicines.

The goals of the surveys and the consequent report are:

- to provide a comprehensive overview of the current situation of counterfeit medicines in the territory of the Council of Europe member states to the Partial Agreement in the Social and Public Health Field;

- to identify potential gaps in legislation and administrative procedures;

- to propose models for best co-operation practices and information exchange between member states' authorities and involved stakeholders (when faced with suspected/detected counterfeit medicines);

- to propose procedures for concerned authorities and stakeholders to prevent and deal with medicines counterfeiting. These goals support the ultimate objectives of increased public health protection. The report takes into consideration pharmaceutical enterprise and stakeholder risks related to medicines counterfeiting in Council of Europe member states. It is important to note that the goals and objectives of the surveys and report are supported fully by the Council of Europe Parliamentary Assembly, as highlighted in its Recommendation 1673 (2004) on counterfeiting: problems and solution.

The report presents detailed results from the various surveys that address the following areas:

- the known current and estimated future market for counterfeit medicines (new national cases brought to the attention of the authorities and stakeholders since 1999, estimations of counterfeit medicine market growth trends, types of medicinal product affected by counterfeiting, and evidence for and extent of the impact of counterfeit medicine on public health);

- trade issues concerning counterfeit medicines (types of medicine counterfeiting practices identified, distribution of counterfeit medicines, parallel import/trade, recent extension of EU borders and their influence on counterfeit medicines reaching the market, brokers/traders – are there reasons to suspect they play a role in counterfeit medicine trading? – organised crime involvement with the counterfeiting of medicines);

- the status of pharmaceutical regulation with respect to manufacture, distribution, storage, import, export and transit for active pharmaceutical ingredients (APIs), and bulk (BPs) and finished medicinal products (FPs);

- analytical testing procedures for suspected counterfeit medicines (designated responsible laboratories, payment of analytical testing costs for suspected counterfeit medicines, and national compilation of analytical test results provided by official and private laboratories);

- national regulatory authority co-operation (legal provisions for reporting counterfeiting practices and counterfeit medicines, and national authority co-operation to tackle medicines counterfeiting);

- international regulatory authority co-operation (WHO anti-counterfeit medicine network and database system, known existence and usage of database systems concerning counterfeit medicines by authorities and stakeholders, and rapid alert systems for reporting suspected counterfeit medicines);

- regulatory authority, industry and wholesaler co-operation (industry's and wholesalers' knowledge of regulatory authorities responsible for the control of medicines counterfeiting, essential elements of good co-operation practices among regulatory authorities and the pharmaceutical and chemical (API) manufacturing industry and disclosure of covert and overt medicinal product features to investigators by the pharmaceutical and chemical (API) manufacturing industry);

- authorities, systems and procedures for detection of counterfeit medicines (existence of specialised police forces or other enforcement bodies that investigate offences concerning medicines counterfeiting, authority involvement in actions against medicines counterfeiting, active and systematic searching for suspected counterfeit medicines, customs risk analysis concerning medicinal products, coercive measures and special investigation methods nationally authorised and applied to combating counterfeit medicines, and industry's, wholesalers', traders' and pharmacists' knowledge of (i) who should be informed domestically in case of suspected counterfeit medicines and (ii) which notification procedures should be followed);

- legal provisions, enforcement, sanctions, and judicial and intellectual property procedures concerning unlicensed and counterfeit medicines (including the extent of powers of enforcement related to suspected counterfeit medicines, judicial procedures and legal action against medicine counterfeiters and industrial (intellectual) property rights (IPR) relating to medicines counterfeiting);

- adequacy of legal, judicial and administrative systems for dealing with counterfeit medicines (authority, industry and wholesaler perspectives, are the concerned authorities' current awareness, initiatives and systems adequate to prevent/fight medicines counterfeiting, what is needed to implement and improve communication between industry/wholesalers/trade firms and authorities so that action can be taken against counterfeit medicines, and what should be improved in the current systems and provisions to effectively fight medicines counterfeiting, to share information more effectively between health and customs authorities, and manufacturer and wholesaler security measures);

- counterfeit medicine and pharmaceutical crime definitions (according to current national legislation);

- adequacy of professional training concerning the detection and control of counterfeit medicines for personnel employed by authorities, wholesalers and manufacturers;

- conclusions and recommendations made by survey respondents.

A number of issues are discussed and conclusions drawn concerning the following specific subjects:

- the rise of medicines counterfeiting (and factors behind the current counterfeit medicines phenomenon);

- the extent of the counterfeit medicine problem, risk of counterfeiting according to medicinal product type and types of counterfeiting practice identified;

- the impact of counterfeit medicine on public health;

- public awareness of medicines counterfeiting and its impact on the general public's perception of the health system;

- import/export/transit licensing, bonded warehouses/free zone control and cross-border trade;

- parallel trade;

- Internet pharmacy, mail order and unlicensed medicines;

- brokers/traders' role in the supply of counterfeit medicines;

- distribution chain – legal and illegal (non-regulated);

- medicinal product supply chain complexity;

- organised crime's involvement in counterfeit medicines;

- authorities' awareness of medicinal product counterfeiting, and its impact, extent and action priorities;

- definitions of "counterfeit medicine" and "pharmaceutical crime";

- legal provisions including sanctions and penalties against medicines counterfeiting;

- perceived adequacy of legal, judicial and administrative systems in controlling medicines counterfeiting;

- regulation of APIs;

- regulation of medicines packaging and labelling, and facilities for labelling and packaging;

- systems and procedures for detecting counterfeit medicines;

- customs' control of medicinal products;

- analytical testing of suspected counterfeit medicines;

- medicinal product security and traceability systems;

- industrial property rights relevant to medicines counterfeiting;

- national authority co-operation against medicines counterfeiting;

- international authority co-operation against medicines counterfeiting (information exchange, databases and rapid alert systems for counterfeit medicines);

- authority and industry co-operation against medicines counterfeiting;

- training requirements for detecting and preventing counterfeit medicines;

- justification for extending the Council of Europe's activities regarding detecting and preventing counterfeit medicines.

Finally, a number of recommendations for implementing harmonised provisions for legislative and administrative procedures are made. These can be summarised as follows:

- the need for multiple implementation measures and the allocation of appropriate resources for tackling medicines counterfeiting;
- establishment of a co-ordinating body at European level;
- the European Commission's role and responsibility concerning medicines counterfeiting in Council of Europe member states;
- anti-counterfeiting implementation framework decision – creation of a "strong instrument"
- proposal for a legislative/regulatory and administrative framework at European level dealing specifically with medicines counterfeiting (including the legislative and regulatory framework, and the roles and responsibilities of the European co-ordinating body and the national authorities);
- targeting medicinal product types at risk of being counterfeited that pose a high risk to public health;
- detailed characterisation of the official and unofficial distribution chain for counterfeit medicines and the counterfeit medicine criminal business model;
- specific definitions and rules of interpretation concerning medicines counterfeiting;
- inspection and enforcement requirements;
- appropriate sanctions and penalties against medicines counterfeiting;
- IPR and medicines counterfeiting;
- import/export/transit regulatory controls to prevent the counterfeit medicine trade;
- regulation of Internet pharmacies, medicinal product mail order and unlicensed medicines;
- regulatory measures particularly applicable to the security of the distribution chain and packaging/labelling of medicinal products;
- regulatory measures particularly applicable to APIs and excipients;
- customs' and health authorities' information sharing concerning suspected counterfeit medicines;
- medicinal product security and traceability (pedigree tracking) systems;
- active searching and analytical testing of suspected counterfeit medicines;
- rapid alert system (RAS) for suspected counterfeit medicines;
- risk management procedures/systems for suspected counterfeit medicines;
- adverse drug reaction (ADR) reporting and pharmacovigilance systems in the context of suspected counterfeit medicines;

- national authority co-ordination structures and organisational improvements;

- co-ordination/co-operation tasks – communication networks, best practices, codes, protocols, database and reporting systems, and information disclosure;

- communication strategy (awareness raising and management of the knowledge and perception of the general public, health professionals, supply chain participants and authorities);

- education requirements for an effective system dealing with counterfeit medicines (and the proposed Council of Europe 2005 seminar on counterfeit medicines).

In summary, it can be concluded that medicines counterfeiting does exist in Europe and there are no indications that it is declining. Medicines counterfeiting is criminal, life-threatening and undermines the public health system. Medicines counterfeiting and pharmaceutical crime have to be differentiated from other forms of economic crime and counterfeiting.

Several reasons exist as to why medicines counterfeiting is prevalent, including:

- regulatory gaps (particularly for API and distribution chain regulation);

- lack of co-ordination between relevant authorities, both nationally and internationally (related to an absence of recognition of the counterfeit medicine problem);

- regulatory bodies lack resources (particularly to follow up reports on suspected counterfeit medicines);

- inefficient co-operation between stakeholders;

- weak administrative structures;

- weak enforcement and penal sanctions;

- weak export/transit regulations (import regulations are generally strong except in the context of Internet/mail order pharmacy);

- disparity in the legal availability of certain types of high-value medicinal products (unlicensed medicines) between countries;

- rapid rise in Internet pharmacy trade;

- weak packaging and printing regulations;

- increasingly complex distribution chain with transactions involving many intermediaries;

- high medicinal product prices;

- recent appearance on the market of so-called "lifestyle and embarrassment" medicinal products;

- a move by organised crime into medicines counterfeiting associated with increasing sophistication in clandestine manufacture;

- corruption and conflicts of interest.

The results from the surveys indicate that both authorities and stakeholders wish to see the counterfeit medicine issue comprehensively tackled in Europe. Ideally, a multi-layered strategy and approach at European level is required (as pure

11

national approaches are likely to be far less effective and co-ordinated). It is proposed that a co-ordinating body at European level (with responsibility for co-ordinating a European strategy for Council of Europe member states) be defined and a "legal instrument" (based on the highest legal form of co-operation possible) be created between all interested Council of Europe member states.

Now is the time to "get real" with counterfeit medicines in Europe.

1. Introduction

1.1. Background to the Council of Europe counterfeit medicine initiative

Counterfeit pharmaceuticals, including medicines and source materials, are no longer just the problem of the developing countries, but a major and widespread criminal activity. According to WHO estimates, counterfeit medicines account for approximately 6% of the world market, even higher in some areas, and are also threatening developed western countries.

They represent a great threat and harm to society. The problem of counterfeiting goes beyond the health and economic context and entails important social implications. The use of counterfeit medicines undermines the confidence in health care systems, health professionals, pharmaceutical manufacturers and distributors. The medicines themselves may appear indistinguishable from the genuine product. They may carry names of widely known products or batch numbers of registered products, but are counterfeit and fake; in fact they are produced without any control or authorisation.

The Council of Europe Committee of Experts on Pharmaceutical Questions has set up a multisectorial ad hoc group (Ad hoc Group on Counterfeit Medicines) to develop measures to minimise the public health risks posed by counterfeit pharmaceuticals in the member states of the Council of Europe.

The initiative of the Council of Europe's Ad hoc Group on Counterfeit Medicines takes into account that pharmaceutical enterprises and stakeholders may suffer serious risks and losses associated with counterfeit medicines (for example, recall, shaken consumer confidence, and loss of stock value and market share).

The pharmaceutical industry, as well as the chemical industry (the latter supplying APIs) and wholesalers – as part of the distribution chain – are considered key partners in supporting this effort.

This report presents the results of important surveys, conducted in 2003 and 2004, of member states and stakeholders, together with recommendations.

The report's objectives and goals are supported fully by the Council of Europe Parliamentary Assembly, as highlighted in its Recommendation 1673 (2004) on counterfeiting: problems and solutions (see Appendix 1).

1.2. Objectives and goals of the report

The report's objectives and goals are based on those of the Council of Europe Ad hoc Group on Counterfeit Medicines and are as follows:

Objectives

- to increase public health protection in the field of counterfeit medicines through co-operation between the public and private sectors.

Goals

- to provide a comprehensive overview of the current situation regarding counterfeit medicines in Council of Europe member states;

- to identify potential gaps in legislation and administrative procedures;

- to propose models for best co-operation practices and information exchange between member states' authorities and involved stakeholders when faced with suspected/detected counterfeit medicines;

- to propose procedures for authorities and stakeholders in preventing and dealing with medicines counterfeiting.

1.3. Council of Europe surveys

1.3.1. Member state survey (2004) (questionnaire attached as Appendix 2)

This survey questionnaire was presented in five languages: English, French, German, Spanish and Russian.

Total respondents: 11 of the 18 member state signatories to the Partial Agreement in the Social and Public Health Field; and one Council of Europe member state who is not a member of the partial agreement[1] (member state numbers 1-12).

Note: a twelfth partial agreement member state responded two months after the deadline for data submission, so unfortunately the latter was not able to be included in the survey results (however, a cursory examination of the replies from this respondent does not alter the conclusions and recommendations of this report).

Part 1. Ministry of Health – Competent drug control authority (MoH/DRA)
(Questions 1-50, twelve respondents)

Part 2. Ministry of Internal Affairs – Police agencies: enforcement regarding counterfeit medicines (MoIP)
(Questions 51-76, seven respondents)

Part 3. Ministry of Justice – Jurisdiction and prosecution – Civil and penal procedures (MoJ)
(Questions 77-101, six respondents)

Part 4. Ministry of Finance – Tax and customs agencies (MoFTC)
(Questions 102-139, six respondents)

Part 5. Ministry of the Economy/Trade: commercial laws including intellectual property rights (IPR) (patent, trademark and copyright) laws applicable to counterfeit medicines (MoET)
(Questions 140-153, five respondents)

---

1. Austria, Belgium, Cyprus, Denmark, Finland, France, Germany, Ireland, Italy, Luxembourg, the Netherlands, Norway, Portugal, Slovenia, Spain, Sweden, Switzerland and the United Kingdom.

1.3.2. Stakeholder survey (2004)
(questionnaire attached as Appendix 3)

Total respondents: 30 (14 FP manufacturers, five API manufacturers and 11 wholesalers).

Stakeholder associations represented: Active Pharmaceutical Ingredients Committee (APIC), European Chemical Industry Council (CEFIC), European Federation of Pharmaceutical Industries Associations (EFPIA), European Association of Full-Line Pharmaceutical Wholesalers (GIRP) and the International Federation for Animal Health (IFAH).

1.3.3. Member state survey (2003)
(questionnaire attached as Appendix 4)

Total respondents: eight member states (member state numbers: 4, 6-8, and 12-15, corresponding to the member state numbering system employed for the 2004 member state survey).

1.3.4. Member state IPR studies (2004)

This consisted of three separate studies (two of which are ongoing) that involve all Council of Europe member states.

1.4. Full data tabulation and presentation of questionnaire responses

The full data tabulation and presentation of the responses received, as prepared by the author of this report, are maintained by the Council of Europe Secretariat and are not annexed to this report.

1.5. Data assumptions and caveats to the report analysis

Some 66% of member states party to the partial agreement replied to the 2004 member state survey (although only a cursory analysis of the responses from one member state were made as these were received after the data lock point). It is assumed that a 66% representativeness allows conclusions to be drawn at the European level.

The member state and stakeholder surveys largely concern those from west European countries (EEA and EU) by original design. It is proposed that a further survey involving respondents from central and eastern European member states be conducted later.

It is assumed that the surveys conducted are representative of the sector's authorities and stakeholders (industry and wholesalers). The surveys have not covered brokers/traders and retail pharmacy associations, and the latter may need to be covered in any future Council of Europe survey.

Although extensive details were provided on legislation, this report does not carry a thorough legislative review. This task will need to be carried out in the near future.

The potential role of international and European level institutions was not covered in any great detail by the surveys presented in this report, although some certain broad conclusions can be drawn.

The main focus of this report has been to present and analyse the extensive data obtained in the surveys conducted in 2003 and 2004 and thus minimal reference is made to external, currently valid studies and reports (except those which are known and are deemed to be of most relevance). It would have been useful to put this report into the context of other reports on the issue and include conclusions and recommendations made by the latter in this report; but time and resource constraints have not made this possible.

It is assumed that the reader of this report has some familiarity with the EC pharmaceutical regulatory framework and thus minimal reference is made to existing EC regulations and directives on pharmaceutical regulation.

The use of the terms "drug", "medicine", "medicinal product" and "pharmaceutical" in this report should be regarded as interchangeable.

The term "pharmaceuticals" describes the following components of an FP: API, BP and packaging materials.

2. Known current and estimated future market for counterfeit medicines

2.1. New national cases brought to the attention of the authorities (since 1999)

Council of Europe member state survey: Q9 (MoH/DRA), Q58 (MoIP), Q84 (MoJ), Q110 (MoFTC) and Q147 (MoET)

See Appendix 5: Council of Europe member state counterfeit medicine case reports.

Since 1999, 58% of member state MoH/DRAs had new cases brought to their attention, 25% stated that the situation was unknown, while 17% stated that there were no cases. In addition, counterfeit medical devices (for example, contact lenses) have been identified in 2003/04.

A large number of other ministries stated that the situation was unknown. This may suggest a lack of awareness of the problem and the relative absence of priority dedicated to this issue. Only one member state where counterfeit medicine cases were reported indicated that all relevant ministries were aware of the problem.

Table 1: New national counterfeit medicine cases brought to the attention of the authorities

Member state	MoH/DRA	MoIP	MoJ	MoFTC	MoET
1	Yes	Yes	Yes	Yes	Yes
2	Yes	Unknown	Unknown	Yes	Unknown
3	Yes				
4	Yes				
5	No				
6	Yes	Yes	Unknown	Yes/unknown	Missing
7	No				
8	Unknown	Unknown	Unknown	Unknown	Unknown
9	Yes	Unknown	Unknown	Unknown	
10	Unknown	Unknown			
11	Yes	Yes	Unknown	Yes	Unknown
12	Unknown				

Chart 1: *Number of new national counterfeit medicine cases reported to individual respondent authorities*

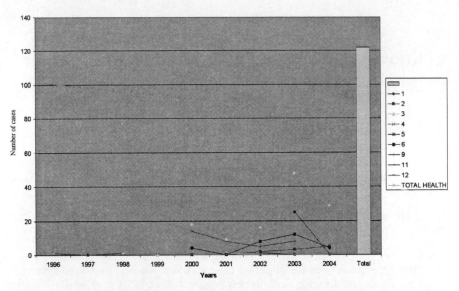

Chart 2: *Total number of new cases of counterfeit medicines reported to authorities in all respondent member states*

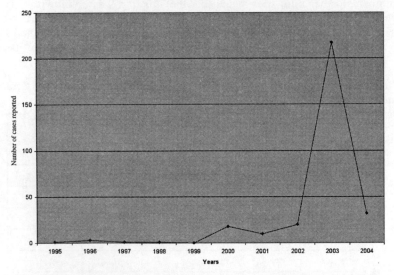

2.2. Known and estimated counterfeit medicine cases reported by manufacturers and wholesalers

Stakeholder survey: Q1

2.2.1. Known counterfeit medicine cases reported by manufacturers and wholesalers (since 1999)

See Appendix 6: Stakeholder counterfeit medicine case reports.

FP manufacturers: 11 of 14 (79%)
API manufacturers: 4 of 4 (100%)
Vet API manufacturer: 1 of 1 (100%)
Wholesalers: 5 of 11 (45%)
Total manufacturers: 16 of 19 (84%)
Total: 21 of 30 (70%)

Summary of results:

- a significant number of counterfeit medicine cases were reported by respondents;
- of the "Yes" respondents, only two reported data from other companies in the case where there were no known counterfeit medicine cases from their own product ranges;
- 100% of API manufacturers reported significant counterfeiting of their products;
- compared to a figure of 84% for all manufacturers, only 45% of wholesalers reported cases;
- the geographic location of reported cases was diverse.

Chart 3: Total number of new cases of counterfeit medicines reported by the stakeholders from their own product portfolios

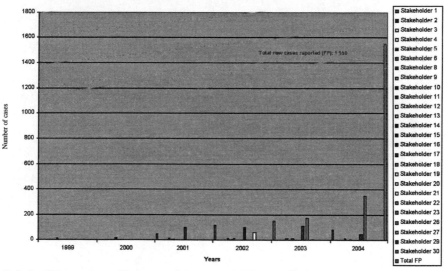

2.2.2. Current estimate of counterfeit medicine cases reported by manufacturers and wholesalers

Combining results from the stakeholder survey Q1 and Q2a

Acknowledgement of the existence of counterfeit medicines on the market:

Yes = 73%; No or no estimate provided = 27%.

Summary of results:

- positive estimates ranged from a few cases to hundreds of thousands, with one respondent (an API manufacturer) estimating that perhaps more than 33% of FPs in the EU may be counterfeit;

- where no estimates were provided, several respondents indicated that they could not make an estimate because of a lack of information.

(NB. Some responses relate only to the respondents' products, while others make an estimate of all products.)

2.2.3. Estimated proportion of counterfeit medicines on the market by region

Stakeholder survey: Q3

Table 2: Estimated proportion of counterfeit medicines on the market by region

Summary of results

	(i) API					(ii) FP				
	Region					Region				
	EU	Europe (non EU)	Asia	Africa	Other[a]	EU	Europe (non EU)	Asia	Africa	Other[a]
	Yes = 6 (6%, 1%, ≥33%, 5%, 10%, 5%)	Yes = 4 (3%, ↑, 10%, 10%)	Yes = 5 (10%, ↑, 10%, 15%, 20%)	Yes = 5 (3%, ↑, 20%, 20%, 35%)	Yes = 3 (<5-10%, 6%, 10%)	Yes = 9 (2%, 6%, 5%, <10%, 2-3%, 20%, 10%, 5-6%, 5%)	Yes = 8 (>2%, 10%, 4-5%, <10%, 25%, 20%, 8-10%, 20%)	Yes = 10 (30%, 20%, >20%, ~ , 40%, ~1%, 25%, ≤ 25%, 30%, 10-20%)	Yes = 10 (70-80%, 10%, >20%, ~50%, 50%, 1-10%, 30%, ≤25%, 35%, 20-40%)	Yes = 5 (25-40%, 20%, <5%, ~40%, 6%)
	No = 0	No = 0	No = 0	No = 0	No = 0	No/almost zero = 4 (0%, almost 0%, <0.01%, <0.0%)	No/almost zero = 3 (0%, <0.1%, <0.1%)	No = 0	No = 0	No = 1 (~0.1%)
	U/K = 4	U/K = 4	U/K = 4	U/K = 4	U/K = 3	U/K = 2	U/K = 2	U/K = 2	U/K = 2	U/K = 3
	Missing = 20	Missing = 22	Missing = 21	Missing = 21	Missing = 24	Missing = 15	Missing = 18	Missing = 18	Missing = 18	Missing = 21

a. Other regions mentioned were: South America, China, United States, Australia and total world market.

Complete tabulation of results for Table 2

Respondent	API					FP (including lookalike products)					Comments
	EU	Rest of Europe	Asia	Africa	Other	EU	Rest of Europe	Asia	Africa	Other	
1	–	–	–	–	–	–	–	–	–	–	–
2	?	?	?	?	?	?	?	?	?	?	As a rough estimate, we assume that, globally, the major part of the illegal black market of steroids and androgens consists of counterfeits
3	–	–	–	–	–	–	–	–	–	–	–
4	–	–	–	–	–	–	–	–	–	–	–
5	?	?	?	?	?	~2%	>2%	~30%	70-80%	25-40%	Asia = excluding Japan Africa = Third World Other = Latin America
6	–	–	–	–	–	–	–	–	–	–	No data available, biggest problems in China, Pakistan, East Africa, Latin America
7	6%	–	–	–	–	6%	–	–	–	–	–
8	–	–	–	–	–	5%	10%	20%	10%	20%	Other = South America For non-EU (rest of Europe), especially Belarus
9						<10%	<10%	>20%	>20%	<5%	Other = USA Asia and Africa – in some locations Depends on drug and location
10	–	–	–	–	–	–	–	–	–	–	–

Respondent	API					FP (including lookalike products)					Comments
	EU	Rest of Europe	Asia	Africa	Other	EU	Rest of Europe	Asia	Africa	Other	
11	–	–	–	–	–	2-3%	4-5%	~40%	~50%	~40%	Other = China and also depending on definition. In China fake products containing APIs are not recognised as counterfeit
13	?	?	?	?	?	?	?	?	?	?	? for APIs – no information. ? for FPs – varies a lot in different countries of a region. Further comments, see below
14	–	–	–	–	–	<0.01%	<0.1%	~1%	1-10%	~0.1%	NB. Lookalike product is not a counterfeit. The figures relate to counterfeits only. EU – not measurable. Rest Europe – probably, no statistical data. Asia – very variable between countries. Africa – very variable between countries. Other = Latin America – very variable between countries. The only reliable estimates are based on true random sampling, but this is very costly and demanding, and only gives meaningful results where the level of counterfeits is 1% or more
15	≥33%	←	←	←	<5-10%?	–	–	–	–	–	EU – possibly at least 33% if the results of the analytical fingerprinting of gentamicin can be extrapolated. Rest of Europe, Asia, Africa, Latin America – probably widespread though API regulations are more limited in many countries in this area

Respondent	API					FP (including lookalike products)					Comments
	EU	Rest of Europe	Asia	Africa	Other	EU	Rest of Europe	Asia	Africa	Other	
16	5%	10%	10%	20%	–	10%	20%	25%	30%	–	Other = US and Australia. Could be less than 5-10% These countries inspect and enforce compliance of API manufacturing worldwide Further comments, see below
17	–	–	–	–	–	–	–	–	–	–	–
18	10%	–	15%	20%	6%	–	–	–	–	?	Other – US FDA estimate
19	–	–	–	–	–	–	–	–	–	–	Cannot provide a figure as unknown
20	–	–	–	–	–	–	–	–	–	–	Not able to give a serious estimation of percentages of counterfeit drugs and APIs
21	?	?	?	?	10%	–	–	–	–	–	Other = rest of world
22	–	–	–	–	–	0%	–	–	–	–	–
23	–	–	–	–	–	5-6%	8-10%	≥25%	≥25%	6%	EU – if similar to world market (WHO/IFPMA) Rest of Europe = in Russian Federation (AIPM/CIPR report April 2002) Asia and Africa = in developing countries (WHO fact sheet 2003) Other = world market (WHO/IFPMA) UK Department of Health issued a statement in June 2004, stating that legitimately obtained medicines in the UK are unlikely to be counterfeit.

Respondent	API					FP (including lookalike products)					Comments
	EU	Rest of Europe	Asia	Africa	Other	EU	Rest of Europe	Asia	Africa	Other	
24	–	–	–	–	–	–	–	–	–	–	No incidents had been reported since 1994
25	–	–	–	–	–	–	–	–	–	–	–
26	–	–	–	–	–	–	–	–	–	–	Most of the products are in the rest of Europe, Asia and Africa
27	5%	10%	20%	35%	–	5%	20%	30%	35%	–	Rest of Europe – 20% of drugs distributed in the Russian Federation are counterfeit (2002) Asia – 10% of drugs distributed in China in 1997 were counterfeit Africa – 80% of drugs sold in Nigeria are counterfeit, according to the WHO (2001) Other – 40% of drugs sold in Argentina, Mexico and Colombia are counterfeit Further comments, see below
28	–	–	–	–	–	–	–	–	–	–	Because of lack of information, there is no answer
29	–	–	–	–	–	Almost 0%	–	–	–	–	The problem is to maintain only legal and authorised actors in the supply chain
30	–	–	–	–	–	<0.05%	<0.1%	10-20%	20-40%	–	EU – very little Rest of Europe – little Asia and Africa – in some areas Estimates are based on single published reports from the respective areas

NB. The survey responses to this question provided many detailed comments which are included in the full tabulation and presentation of results.

2.3. Estimates of growth trends in the counterfeit medicine market

Stakeholder survey: Q1, Q2a and Q2b

Increase (that is, yes) = 60%; Possible increase = 10%; Definite no/Almost no increase = 10%; No estimate provided = 20%.

Summary of results:

- at least 60% of respondents stated that the incidence of counterfeit medicine cases will increase;
- only 10% of respondents stated that counterfeit medicine cases either do not exist or will not increase;
- no estimate was provided by 20% of respondents;
- comments where the future case estimate is either possible, little or none are appended to the table below.

Table 3: Current and future counterfeit medicine case estimates

Respond-ent	Company (country base)	Company (own products)	Countries affected	Other company products	Countries affected	Current overall case estimate	Future overall case estimate
1	United Kingdom	Yes	United Kingdom	–	–	Some	–
2	Nether-lands	Yes, several	Most countries	–	–	100s of 1 000s	Same level or increase
3	Nether-lands	Yes	Nether-lands	–	–	Some	–
4	Germany	–	–	–	–	–	–
5	Germany	Yes	South America, Africa, east Europe, USA, South East Asia, Middle East, Germany	–	–	Several	Increase
6	Germany	Yes	South America, Africa, Asia, Japan, USA, east Europe, Germany	–	–	Several	Increase 5% per year
7	Finland	–	–	–	–	Zero	Zero
8	Germany	Yes	Mexico	–	–	Some	Increase
9	US	–	–	Yes	USA	Several	Same

Respon-dent	Company (country base)	Company (own products)	Countries affected	Other company products	Countries affected	Current overall case estimate	Future overall case estimate
							level or Increase
10	France	Yes	Bulgaria, China, Russian Federation, Vietnam	–	–	Several	Increase
11	United Kingdom	Yes	Nigeria, Egypt, Domini-can Repu-blic, US, China, Mexico, Colombia, Venezuela, Taiwan, Malaysia	Yes	Worldwide	Several	Increase
12	Multi-country	Yes	Global source: China, Korea, Taiwan	Yes	United Kingdom, USA	50	Increase 7.5-10%
13	Multi-country	Yes	Asia, South America, east Europe	Yes	–	Several	Possible increase[a]
14	United Kingdom	Yes	Asia, South America, Middle East, United Kingdom, USA, Germany, Bulgaria, European Union as a transit area	–	–	Several	Signifi-cant increase
15	Nether-lands	Yes	Brazil, China, Russian Federation	Yes	EU, USA	≥33% FP in EU	Increase (in regu-lated markets, particu-larly EU)
16	Belgium	Yes	India	–	–	Some	Increase

Respon-dent	Company (country base)	Company (own products)	Countries affected	Other company products	Countries affected	Current overall case estimate	Future overall case estimate
17	Netherlands	Yes	Philippines Pakistan, Saudi Arabia	–	–	Some	–
18	France	Yes	US + ?	?	Europe, Asia, Pacific	Approx. 10%	Possible increase[b]
19	United Kingdom	Yes	United Kingdom affected, France, Ireland, USA involved	–	–	5-10%	Twofold increase
20	Austria	–	–	–	–	–	Increase
21	Germany	Yes, several	United Kingdom, Germany	–	–	Several	–
22	France	–	–	–	–	–	Probably not[c]
23	United Kingdom	Yes	United Kingdom, Spain involved	–	–	Some	Increase
24	Germany	–	–	Yes	Germany affected, Switzerland involved	Some	Increase
25	Portugal	–	–	–	–	–	[d]
26	France	–	–	–	–	–	Increase
27	Multi-country	Yes	United Kingdom	Yes	France, Netherlands, United Kingdom, Germany, USA, Cambodia, Thailand, Vietnam, Czech Republic	Several	Increase/ unknown
28	Hungary	–		–	–	–	Possible increase[e]
29	Italy	–		–	–	Almost zero	Almost zero[f]
30	Norway	Yes	United Kingdom	–	–	Some	Increase

Comments provided on where the future case estimate is either possible, little or none:

a. May get worse due to enlargement and increased grey market; however, impact on individual companies will depend on their product range (major blockbusters especially at risk).

b. Will widely depend on countermeasures taken and preventative means put in place.

c. As long as we can order our medicines from registered pharmaceutical partners, there should be no problems.

d. It is not possible to estimate (given our knowledge).

e. Theoretical possibility.

f. If the actual law is maintained and there is strong control of the authorised actors, we think that it will be the same.

2.4. Types of medicinal product affected by counterfeiting

Stakeholder survey: Q4

The following types of medicinal product were reported as being at risk from counterfeiting.

Medicinal product type
High volume (high level of prescribing)
High price
Known brand
"Lifestyle"/non-reimbursed
Blockbusters
Parenterals (in developing world)
All generics
Off-label use drugs
Every type
Drugs in short supply

Stakeholder responses indicate all medicinal product types are at risk of being counterfeited, although the degree of risk is likely to depend on particular local market characteristics. Specific drug and therapeutic class examples quoted by respondents were:

- developed world: particularly branded drugs (so-called "lifestyle" and "embarrassment" drugs) to treat, for example, erectile dysfunction, weight gain and high cholesterol. Those quoted included: Procrit, HGH, Viagra, Cialis, Reductil, Epo, Epogen, Neupogen, Lipitor, Sandimmun and Augmentin.

- developing world: antibiotics, anti-malarials, vaccines and HIV drugs.

Other known surveys/data:

- medicinal product types sold via the Internet. One Council of Europe member state (not part of the survey) determined, from a study it conducted of illegal Internet pharmacies, that the black market offers prescription drugs for erectile dysfunction, slimming drugs and anabolic steroids. They did not find any other kinds of medicines on offer. Offers for anabolic steroids greatly exceeded the number of offers for other types of drug.

2.5. Evidence for and extent of the impact of counterfeit medicine on public health

2.5.1. Number of adverse effects on individuals caused by medicinal products brought to the attention of the relevant authorities

Council of Europe member state survey: Q10 (MoH/DRA), Q59 (MoIP), Q85 (MoJ) and Q111 (MoFTC)

The definition of "adverse effect" used in the questionnaire was: "an unwanted effect produced by a medicine; it may be merely inconvenient, unpleasant, frankly dangerous or fatal".

Table 4: Adverse effects brought to the attention of authorities

Member state	MoH/DRA	MoIP	MoJ	MoFTC
1	Yes	Unknown	Unknown	Unknown
2	Yes	No	Unknown	Unknown
3	Yes			
4	No			
5	Yes			
6	Yes	Unknown	Unknown	Unknown
7	Missing			
8	Unknown	Unknown	Unknown	Unknown
9	Yes	Unknown	Unknown	
10	Yes	Yes		
11	Yes	Yes	Unknown	Unknown
12	Yes			

MoH/DRA: Yes = 67%; No = 17%; Unknown = 8%; Missing = 8%.

Other ministries: sectoral authorities outside of MoH/DRA are largely unaware of the existence of an adverse drug reaction (ADR) reporting system.

2.5.2. Number of adverse effects on individuals caused by medicinal products with quality defects brought to the attention of the relevant authorities

Council of Europe member state survey: Q11 (MoH/DRA)

Yes = 17%; No = 17%; Unknown = 58%; Missing = 8%.

2.5.3. Awareness by the health authorities of near adverse effects on individuals caused by pharmaceuticals with quality defects

Council of Europe member state survey: Q12 (MoH/DRA)

Yes = 8%; No = 50%; Unknown = 33%; Missing = 8%.

The definition of "near adverse effect" or "critical incident" used in the questionnaire was: "an incident where a patient might have suffered harm and an undesirable effect without a medical intervention or treatment".

Comments:

• no quantitative data was reported by respondents;

• the one respondent who replied yes said that there were confirmed cases but no statistics were available.

3. Trade issues concerning counterfeit medicines

3.1. Types of counterfeiting practices identified

Stakeholder survey: Q5

A wide variety of counterfeiting practices were identified, which are summarised in the following table:

Table 5: Medicinal product counterfeiting practices

Counterfeit practice type
A. Finished/intermediate medicinal product
Identical copy – Identical packaging and formulation
Pure counterfeit (altered ingredients with similar packaging) • no API/placebo; • wrong API dose (insufficient/or too much); • different API; • different excipient(s); • complete fake of solid dosage forms; • diluted drug (including sterile product dilution).
Re-use of components, for example • refill of genuine packaging with substitute or no API; • refill of vials, ampoules, syringes, or re-use of packaging material; • reuse of infusion bottles; • replacing a part (lower part of big bag) of the material by sugar.
False/illegal labelling/packaging (product falsely labelled as being from the original manufacturer) • true counterfeiting is the copying of the primary and secondary packaging of the product involved by a third party (see also the WHO definition of counterfeit), that is the product appears to be from the original manufacturer but is not. This is different from relabelling and repackaging, which is just as dangerous but not counterfeiting in the true sense of the word; • "hybrid counterfeit" (genuine bulk or packaging), manipulated labels; • products falsely claiming to be an original product (for example, use of well-known name or trademark); • printing facilities involved in the production of illegal labelling and packaging.
Illegal relabelling and repackaging • illegal relabelling and repackaging of medicines for one member state market; • fake pricing label and fake labelling in general.

Illegal diversion and illicit trade of products, whether or not through the Internet

- primary pack diversion with secondary counterfeit;
- Internet trading ("Internet trading requiring no prescription is the single largest factor").

Unpackaged medicinal products, for example

- wholesale/retail of medicinal products without the primary packaging.

Placing a non-licensed medicinal product on the market

False documentation, for example

- granting a CoS without auditing the given company;
- incorrect status on import documents.

Waste/expired product re-entering the market

- repackaging of expired products with counterfeit labels.

Combined counterfeiting, for example

- product without approval, mislabelled and containing false ingredients;
- relabelling with incorrect dosage;
- manufacturing in the Far East and relabelling, and secondary launch pad the free ports of the Middle East;
- counterfeit product and packaging;
- genuine product in counterfeit packaging (to disguise source, expired product or illegal repackaging);
- counterfeit product in counterfeit packaging that imitates the packaging of parallel imports.

B. APIs

Illegal API production/distribution/diversion

A wide variety of API counterfeiting practices is suspected to occur and/or has been observed. These are practices suspected to be also taking place within the EU market as an important target and also with the involvement of manufacturers/traders/brokers located in the EU. The most important ones are:

- use of (cheap) APIs from uncontrolled or non-GMP origin/relabelling and repacking of APIs;
- "ghost plant": the API is sold by, but not manufactured by, the "registered producer" and is therefore not produced by the registered manufacturing process. The marketing authorisation holder may be (un)aware of this. The API label mentions only the authorised manufacturer. A broker/trader may play a crucial role in these practices;
- "ghost supplier": the marketing authorisation holder purchases the API willingly and knowingly from a manufacturer other than the one(s) included in the marketing authorisation. Also in this case the manufacturing process will normally differ from what is described and authorised in the registration of the medicinal product;
- "paper curtain": the API is manufactured using a different process than the one registered in the marketing authorisation. However, a double document system is used at the manufacturing site: one hidden set containing the true

data and one other set containing fake data that comply with the requirements and regulations (registration and GMP). The latter set is shown to
GMP inspectors to mislead them into thinking that the API is produced
through the registered manufacturing process. Such documentation
systems may even be in place at a site where the API is not manufactured
at all;

- "authorised facades": a manufacturer/trader that has obtained authority
  approval (CoS or accepted DMF) supplies API material from a large
  number of unauthorised manufacturers. All labelling only mentions the
  authorised manufacturer. This practice is believed to be widespread
  regarding API material imported from China and possibly also India.
  Also, more generally, such illegal relabelling is said to occur frequently
  at certain trading companies. Of course, in addition forged certificates of
  analysis and other documents will also be used in such situations;

- unauthorised API material may also be shipped in containers labelled
  with the name of a different API;

- cases have been detected where unauthorised API materials from obscure
  sources were blended with the registered API material;

- false MAA: it is also known that entire marketing applications are sold
  and used; their contents do not have any relationship with the actual
  operations involved in the manufacture of the API (or dosage form);

- other strong indications of API counterfeiting are very small companies
  with around 50 employees that claim to manufacture hundreds of
  different APIs and sell them under their own label as if they were
  manufactured by that company;

- the veterinary market is known to be a very popular target for
  counterfeit/illegal/unauthorised APIs.

3.2. Distribution of counterfeit medicines

3.2.1. Appearance of counterfeit medicines in the "legal/official" distribution chain

*Do counterfeit medicines appear in the official/legal distribution chain?
(legal distribution chain: producer of API ➜ chemical broker ➜ pharmaceutical
company ➜ wholesaler ➜ hospital pharmacy/community pharmacy (other
outlets))*

Stakeholder survey: Q6

Yes = 60%; Yes/No = 6%; No = 30%; Missing = 3%.

The majority responded "yes" (weighted towards manufacturers; wholesalers are
less convinced).

i. Distribution chain stage where counterfeit medicines appear:

a. Manufacturer (FP) responses	Number of respondents
At any stage of the distribution chain (for example, evidence for all but genuine pharmaceutical manufacturers)	4
Highest risk is with wholesalers and pharmacies	3

Wholesalers (including via "alternative" distributors and stockists)	3
Pharmacies (for example, retail pharmacy, hospital pharmacy, e-mail/mail order service)	2
Brokers with pharmaceutical licences	1
Unknown	1

b. Manufacturer (API) responses	Number of respondents
Pharmacies	2
At all stages	1
At any stage preceding the manufacture of the dosage form (counterfeit APIs appear where the legal distribution chain starts or shortly thereafter at trader/broker level)	1

c. Wholesaler responses	Number of respondents
All stages, for example: purchasing, hospitals, pharmacists and laboratories. Potential exists at all stages within the supply chain but is more likely at the lower end of the supply chain. Also, at any stage due to accidental purchase from illegal sources	3
Pharmaceutical company and wholesaler	1
Wholesalers and pharmacies	1
Small wholesalers	1
Pharmacies	1
Importation	1

ii. Why they get there: all responses relate to the profit margin (for example, wholesale profits are higher when buying bargain offers; offers at discount price, sometimes as "parallel traded" medicines although there is no evidence of this in the EU; and counterfeiting of medicines is getting ever more popular for criminal organisations to fund their activities) (seven respondents).

iii. How counterfeit medicines appear in the official distribution chain:

	Number of respondents
Insufficient control of the distribution chain (for example, it is generally due to a lack of control and/or lack of enforcement of legislation in combination with various criminal activities, including corruption, bribery, etc. In addition, it is relatively easy to obtain a wholesalers permit and it is very profitable)	7
Multiple ownership/levels in the supply chain (for example, product trading occurs among wholesalers, wholesalers and pharmacies, and pharmacies themselves. The growth in the	

number of licensed short-line wholesalers has increased the opportunity for trade and the entry of counterfeit products into the legitimate supply chain. Increasing commercial pressures at pharmacy level also lead to increased pharmacy trading and opportunities for counterfeiters)	3
Illegal trading (for example, wholesalers and pharmacists acting illegally, illegal purchases via non-official suppliers, and direct supplies to pharmacies from the counterfeiters)	3
Repackaging (for example, tablet repackagers can lose their identity in the chain; sales representatives collect samples for doctors and repack them; and very small wholesalers repackage pharmaceuticals for foreign countries or for hospital pharmacies)	2
Substandard control practices (purchaser versus supplier and non-observance of the MAA by applicants)	2
Documentation weaknesses/forgery (use of forged documents to give the products provenance; and documentation provisions do not necessarily provide 100% security against counterfeiting)	2
Poor traceability requirements	1
Insufficient control of the Internet	1
Switching API to counterfeit API. This might be carried out by the API manufacturer themselves, at a trader/broker or at a dosage form manufacturer (MA holder) or indeed at several of these parties at the same time. So the counterfeit APIs may also enter the chain with the consent of the MA holder	1
Unknown	1
Related problem: illegal re-importation	1

3.2.2. Mail order/Internet supply of counterfeit medicines

Legal permission for the supply of medicines to users by mail order

Member state survey: Q29 (MoH/DRA)

Yes = 58%; No = 42%.

In all cases where mail order was permitted both non-prescription (OTC) and prescription only (PoM) medicinal products were allowed.

Where mail order supply was permitted, the following types of control were indicated by the respondents (six member states):

- control of quantity (five member states);
- control of the Internet (three member states);
- control of suppliers (two member states);
- other controls (three member states).

Where the Internet was controlled, only one member state indicated what type of control was exercised and this was "on the basis of exposure".

Other controls stated were: (i) random checks by customs (narcotics not allowed at all); (ii) assistance from customs that control mail; and (iii) spot tests.

"Yes" comments received were:

- yes, subject to legal provisions being met, namely a prescription signed by a registered doctor must be seen by the pharmacist; and the pharmacist must be content that a proper consultancy has taken place between doctor and patient;
- valid prescription must be presented for no more than two to three months supply;
- a prescription is always mandatory (under these circumstances), even for medicines which are available without prescription. There are sporadic controls on the imported quantities. Advertising on the Internet is controlled on the basis of denunciations (law on medicines);
- PoM: legally obtained within the EU.

"No" comments received were:

- an amendment is about to be introduced that would permit authorised non-prescription medicinal products to be supplied by mail order;
- the law on medicines prohibits all forms of indirect sale of medicines;
- not stated in regulations.

Are mail orders for medicines controlled (postal shipments of medicines to users via individual orders over the Internet)?

Member state survey: Q119 (MoFTC)

Yes = 100%.

All MoFTCs in member states that allow mail order responded that mail order of medicines by individuals over the Internet is controlled. One MoFTC indicated that mail order was controlled in a member state where mail order was not permitted.

The following types of control were indicated where responses were provided (by four member states):

- control of quantity (two member states);
- control of the Internet (no member state);
- control of suppliers (no member state);
- other controls (four member states).

Other controls included: (i) the passing on of relevant information by customs to the MoH/DRA in cases of doubt (for example, multiple small-scale importations); (ii) custom risk analysis; and (iii) normal custom control checks.

Does the Internet have a role in the sale of counterfeit pharmaceuticals?

Stakeholder survey: Q7

Yes = 88%; Yes/No = 3%; No = 6%; Missing = 3%.

i. Summary of general comments received:

- the Internet does not play a role in the legal chain;
- mainly highly priced "lifestyle" products are involved;
- dosage forms containing counterfeit APIs find a very important market outlet via the Internet;
- direct supply to customers and the possibility of buying without a prescription encourages Internet supply;

- no control of the Internet supply exists at all; there is little way of confirming identity over the Internet; and there is more possibility to buy products outside the legal distribution chain (non-official suppliers);
- cross-border/cross-country orders and delivery controls are nearly impossible; Internet pharmacies are more difficult to police, particularly across national boundaries; and there are no possibilities for intervention by customs and mail services;
- there are difficulties in prosecuting and the legal consequences are unclear.

ii. How companies are tackling this issue:

a. Manufacturers	Number of respondents
Internet surveillance (for example, for target products; active monitoring of numerous Internet websites/pharmacies that offer a company's products or counterfeit versions of a company's products from locations around the world – when instances of wrongdoing are identified, the information is given to the appropriate government or legal authorities; and further development of surveillance activity with a strategy for response to "suspect" samples)	5
Notifying/assistance from regulatory authorities (for example, asking authorities to pay more attention to material from an uncontrolled origin and for more communication on this subject)	3
Covert purchasing from suspect sites	2
Educating customers (for example, warnings on the Internet through security organisations; and communication via national associations on the dangers of buying medicines via the Internet)	2
Via complaints received from customers	1
Location and "management" of the site	1
Database screening	1
Fast registration	1
Testing a device to be placed in pharmaceutical packs (pilot study involving several pharmaceutical companies and supported by the MHRA (to be conducted in autumn 2004)	1
Our company (an API manufacturer) is not tackling the sales of dosage forms via the Internet as this is outside the scope of the company's business	1
We do not have our drugs sold over the Internet	1

b. Wholesalers	Number of respondents
Strict control of product sourcing (for example, company either does not buy from non-identified partners, only buys products from official suppliers or always uses DRA approved suppliers)	5

Applying good distribution/management practices and use of IT tools (for example, self-audit and quality management)	2
Not using Internet for parallel trade	1
Information is the best tool to limit the risk	1
Pharmaceutical legislation (for example, 12. AMG Novelle – recent German drug law revision)	2
Not currently involved with Internet pharmacy	2
No measure taken/not applicable	2
As counterfeiting is still not an issue in our country we actually do not tackle it (but we think that in the future distributing counterfeit drugs via the Internet to the customer will be easier)	1

iii. Competent authorities' regulations/actions (as perceived by manufacturers and wholesalers):

a. Manufacturers	Number of respondents
No/insufficient regulation/action • generally, the issue does not have the attention of national/ local authorities. The international situation is somewhat better, although up until now within the EU this is largely confined to talking without taking action. The FDA is tackling the issue more seriously; • insufficient – this is a key point to develop as it allows counterfeits to enter new markets for specific kind of drugs; • not much help from health authorities, so far; • evidence suggests that EU authorities are not tackling the issue.	6
Unknown	3
There needs to be a global team/authority	1
Give evidential packages to the relevant authorities governing purchase and analysis (that is, evidence from monitoring and covert purchasing from suspect Internet sites)	1
Tighter controls needed of entry points and postal routes, and greater communication and co-operation across jurisdictions, particularly among regulatory bodies responsible for enforcement	1
The information conveyed to government and law enforcement authorities should ensure that suspected counterfeiters and their intermediaries are thoroughly investigated and, where appropriate, prosecuted	1
Should ensure HIV medication is provided free of charge legally from hospitals	1
EU strategy on IP enforcement	1
The FDA are looking at Internet sites and authenticating products	1

VIPPS in the United States	1
Nigerian Government is active	1

b. Wholesalers	Number of respondents
Not permitted by national regulation	3
Not known	2
Although not permitted by national regulation, citizens are able to buy them on foreign websites. Although this is difficult to avoid, we believe that national authorities should increase their controls and inspections	1
Not sufficient	1
Authorities should help to clarify every suspected case of counterfeiting, conduct research, etc.	1
Our country's regulations will allow for Internet pharmacy and this problem is likely to grow in the near future	1
The DRA is very careful in our country (including as regards the sale of nutritional products via the Internet)	1
The DRA is investigating cases	1
Cannot avoid Internet importations by a private person	1

3.2.3. Appearance of counterfeit medicines in the "unofficial" distribution chain

Where counterfeit medicines are detected in the illegal distribution chain

Member state survey: Q60 (MoIP) and Q112 (MoFTC)

All seven MoIP respondents provided an indication of where counterfeit medicines appear in the illegal distribution chain, while three of the six MoFTC respondents stated that the situation was either unknown or a response was not provided.

The possible locations in the illegal distribution chain specified by the question were: (i) fitness clubs, (ii) the bodybuilding scene, (iii) private purchase via the Internet, (iv) sports clubs (cyclists, etc.) and (v) others.

The following responses were provided:

- fitness clubs: four MoIPs and one MoFTC;
- bodybuilding scene: four MoIPs and one MoFTC;
- private purchase via the Internet: four MoIPs and two MoFTCs;
- sports clubs (cyclists, etc.): no MoIP or MoFTC;
- others: five MoIPs and two MoFTCs.

Other locations mentioned by respondents included shops specialising in undercover (illegal) goods, sex clubs, sex shops, food supplement stores, cosmetic stores and where import/border controls are carried out.

3.3. Parallel import/trade, the recent extension of EU borders and their influence on counterfeit medicines reaching the market

3.3.1. Existence of national legal provisions governing parallel imports

Member state survey: Q30 (question addressed solely to the MoH/DRA)

Yes = 75%; No = 17%; Missing = 8%.

The types of provisions mentioned by respondents were:

• the supplier must be a licensed manufacturer/wholesaler in the country of origin;
• a certificate of analysis or certificate of free sale must be present;
• no specific provisions, but existing marketing and manufacturing regulations prohibit such activity unless authorised by the MoH/DRA in accordance with those regulations (licensing of manufacture and licensing and sales regulations);
• no specific provisions exist for counterfeit medicines (licensing of importers only);
• importation invoice endorsed by the MoH/DRA;
• every parallel import requires an MA and an activity authorisation (law on medicines and parallel import regulations);
• yes (law on medicines);
• any medicinal product on the market has to be authorised by the MoH/DRA;
• yes (law on health);
• no specific measures; parallel imported medicines must have an MA.

In several cases it was mentioned that no specific legal provisions exist regulating parallel imports (although it is known that some EU and EEA countries do have specific parallel import regulations).

3.3.2. Influence on counterfeiting due to the wavering of EU internal border controls by customs authorities

Member state survey: Q136 (question addressed solely to MoFTCs)

All replies were either "unknown" or missing, thus it can be assumed that it is too early to determine the impact of less stringent border controls on the trade in counterfeit medicines.

3.3.3. Does parallel trade of medicines facilitate the emergence of counterfeit medicines?

Member state survey: Q137 (question addressed solely to MoFTCs)

Five of the six responses were either "unknown" or missing with only one respondent stating "yes" (the respondent from eastern Europe). No specific comments on this issue were provided. This issue needs studying further.

3.4. Brokers/traders – Are there reasons to suspect they play a role in counterfeit medicine trading?

Member state survey: Q35 (MoH/DRA) and Q138 (MoFTC)

MoH/DRA: Yes = 25%; No = 67%; Unknown = 8%.

Three member states said they had reasons to suspect that brokers play a role in counterfeit trading. The reasons given were:

- general knowledge of market forces although no specific information or knowledge is available on brokers. Therefore no substantive grounds exist from investigations in the member states that brokers have been involved;
- brokers are well placed to participate in the diversion of medicines including counterfeits; they facilitate international commerce of medicines and remain invisible to the authorities; brokers are not directly subject to national legislation and they operate at an international level without being mentioned on bills; and they are not a responsible party in the strict sense of legislation;
- they are the only intermediaries in pharmaceutical distribution not subject to authorisation; and their business is of a purely commercial nature and therefore is not relevant to the pharmaceutical industry (the latter being heavily regulated for specific reasons). Therefore they do not need to be licensed and no register of brokers exists.

No reason for the "no" responses was given by any respondent.

MoFTC: No = 33%; Unknown = 17%; Missing = 50%.

No one said that there was a reason to suspect that brokers play a role in counterfeit trading. However, only two of the six respondents gave a definite "no" response. No comments were provided.

3.5. The involvement of organised crime in counterfeiting

Member state survey: Q129, Q130 and Q131 (MoFTC)

3.5.1. Are there indications that organised crime is involved in counterfeiting?

Yes = 16.66%; No = 16.66%; Unknown = 16.66%; Missing = 50%.

Only one member state replied "yes", but on the other hand only one member state replied "no" (the other responses were either missing or unknown). The specific question addressing this issue required that no confidential data need be provided, however, respondents were offered the possibility of communicating information on this subject directly to the Secretariat (although the Secretariat did not receive any such information).

Specific comments received:

- unknown; the MoH/DRA would be in a better position to comment on this issue;
- no; not from the customs service perspective.

3.5.2. Does organised crime have links with other such organisations based in other countries?

Unknown = 84%; Missing = 16%.
No comments were provided by the respondents.

3.5.3. What other forms of criminality are linked with the traffic of counterfeit medicines?

Yes = 34%; Missing = 50%; Unknown = 16%.

The forms of criminality specified by the question were: (i) fraud aimed at acquiring financial aids, (ii) anabolic steroids for equestrian sport, (iii) anabolic steroids for bodybuilding, (iv) illegal drugs, (v) threats, (vi) corruption, (vii) money laundering, (viii) terrorism and (ix) other.

"Yes" responses received:

* one member state: (i), (iii), (iv) and (vii);
* one member state: (ix) other – contraband.

"Unknown" responses received:

* one member state: MoH/DRA is in a better position to reply.

4. Pharmaceutical regulation status with respect to manufacture, distribution, storage and, import/export/transit of active pharmaceutical ingredients, bulk products and finished products

4.1. Pharmaceutical production

Member state survey: Q19, Q20, Q21, Q22 and Q23 (MoH/DRA)

4.1.1. Legal provisions concerning pharmaceutical production

(APIs, BPs and FPs)
APIs: Yes = 67%; BPs: Yes = 67%; FPs: Yes = 100%.

- APIs are regulated in eight of the twelve member states;
- BPs are regulated in eight member states;
- one member state regulates APIs and does not regulate BPs;
- one member state does not regulate APIs but regulates BPs;
- seven member states regulate both APIs and BPs;
- all member states refer to national legislation while two also refer specifically to EU legislation: Directive 2003/94/EC and Volume 4 of *Eudralex*, and Directive 2004/27/EC.

4.1.2. Is a licence required for pharmaceutical production?

(APIs, BPs and FPs)
APIs: Yes = 58%; FPs: Yes = 100%; IP: Yes = 58%; OP: Yes = 58%.

4.1.3. Legal provisions concerning pharmaceutical packaging materials production

Yes = 33%; No = 59%; Missing = 8%.
(Immediate packaging for sterile medicinal products, non-sterile medicinal products and outer packaging).

- where the response was "yes", all types of packaging were covered (namely, immediate packaging or sterile and non-sterile medicinal products and outer packaging);
- legal bases where specified: general GMP rules, and national and EU legislation;
- one member state refers specifically to EU legislation (see also Q19): Directive 2003/94/EC and Volume 4 of *Eudralex*.

4.1.4. Types of control carried out by health authorities on API manufacturing

No = 8%; Yes = 92%.

Specific "yes" comments received:

- only through inspection of manufacturers of FPs;
- inspection by the DRA for export certification of APIs;
- API manufacturers and exporters provide periodic information on their activities and substances to the MoH/DRA;
- inspection carried out according to Annex 18 of the EU GMP guidelines;
- the ones predicted by Annex 18 of Directive 2003/94/EC (ICH Q7a).
- Decree on authorisation for hormonal substances, anti-infectives, anti-parasiticals, and anti-inflammatories. Primary substances used in the manufacturing process should conform to pharmacopoeia standards;
- as carried out by the inspectorate;
- controls on intermediate stages of manufacturing carried out on all API manufacturers;
- standard periodic GMP inspections;
- control of GMP conformance in accordance with public health law;
- ordinary inspections (audits) – in principle no difference between the different kind of manufacturers.

Specific "no" comment received:

- no controls for PoMs.

4.1.5. Is repackaging of medicines an important domestic activity for manufacturers?

Yes = 33%; No = 50%; Unknown = 16%.

The following table presents the "yes" responses:

Table 6: Number of manufacturers performing repackaging and estimated number of packages repacked annually

Number of manufacturers	Estimated number of repacked packages
20	7% of all medicines distributed in the member state
89	Unknown
5	Unknown
7	–

Specific "unknown" comment received:

- there is a specific provision in the field of parallel importations (see also MoH/DRA regulation on simplified authorisation and the obligatory announcement of the medicines). No information (data) available on the frequency and the quantities repacked.

4.2. Pharmaceutical distribution

Member state survey: Q24 and Q25 (MoH/DRA)

4.2.1. Legal provisions concerning domestic pharmaceutical distribution

APIs: Yes = 58%; BPs: Yes = 67%; FPs: Yes = 100%.

4.2.2. Is a license required for domestic pharmaceutical distribution?

API: Yes = 58%; BPs: Yes = 58%; FP: Yes = 100%.

4.3. Pharmaceutical storage: bonded warehouse and free zone controls

Member state survey: Q28 (MoH/DRA) and Q127 (MoFTC)

MoH/DRA
Is the storage of pharmaceuticals in a bonded warehouse/free zone governed by medicines legislation?

No = 50%; Yes = 50%.

Specific "yes" comments received:

* in a free zone;
* covered by wholesaler licence;
* covered by law on medicines;
* bonded warehouses also need an authorisation.

Specific "no" comment received:

* the norms governing storage of pharmaceuticals are the same for all agents regardless of the warehousing agreements.

MoFTC
Do finance/customs authorities apply specific control measures in free zones and customs (bonded) warehouses?

Yes = 66%; No = 17%; Unknown = 17%.

Specific "yes" comments received:

* customs can take action on goods that are not cleared provided that an application by the rights holder is in force and that the ten-day time limit for action has not passed;
* no free zones exist in our country; normal controls as opposed to specific controls are made by customs;
* control, including testing;
* ten-day retention if a demand is made to customs by the rights holder.

4.4. Pharmaceutical importation/exportation/transit

Member state survey: Q26, Q27 (MoH/DRA) and Q116 (MoFTC)

4.4.1. Legal provisions concerning pharmaceutical importation/exportation/transit

APIs: Yes = 50%; BPs: Yes = 67%; FPs: Yes = 100%.

Importation/exportation/transit: 33%
Importation/exportation only: 33%
Importation/transit only: 17%
Missing: 17%

4.4.2. Is a licence required for pharmaceutical importation/exportation/transit?

APIs: Yes = 50%; BPs: Yes = 67%; FPs: Yes = 92%.

Importation/exportation/transit: 33%
Importation/exportation only: 25%
Importation/transit only: 17%
Missing: 25%

NB. One member state responding "no" for APIs, BPs and FPs stated that a case by case authorisation is required for import and export for all types.

4.4.3. What controls are carried out by the finance/customs authorities on APIs in case of importation/exportation/transit?

Summary of responses:

• fiscal, environmental, CITIS, IPR and narcotic regulations;
• nil by customs; controls made by the MoH/DRA and MoIP (licence department);
• no control;
• normal controls appropriate for inherent risk;
• controls to ensure compliance with legislative requirements;
• only for control of psychotropics and narcotics; in the latter case customs checks authorisations issued by the MoH/DRA.

5. Analytical testing procedures for suspected counterfeit medicines

5.1. Designated responsible laboratories

Member state survey: Q37 (MoH/DRA), Q67 (MoIP), Q92 (MoJ), Q122 (MoFTC) and Q150 (MoET)

Table 7: Designated responsible laboratories for testing suspected counterfeit medicines

Member state	MoH/DRA	MoIP	MoJ	MoFTC	MoET
1	OMCL	OMCL	OMCL	OMCL Customs laboratory	OMCL
2	OMCL	OFL	OMCL OFL	OFL Private laboratories	OFL
3	OCL OFL	–	–	–	–
4	OMCL	–	–	–	–
5	OMCL	–	–	–	–
6	OMCL	Unknown	OMCL Private laboratories	Private laboratories	Private laboratories
7	OMCL OFL	–	–	–	–
8	OMCL OFL	OMCL OFL	OMCL	Other	OMCL
9	OMCL	OMCL	OMCL	OMCL OCL OFL	
10	OMCL	OMCL	–	–	–
11	OMCL	OFL National Laboratory of Expertise Private laboratories Manufacturers' laboratories	Any laboratory	Customs laboratory Other	Unknown
12	OMCL Other	–	–	–	–

Acronym	Laboratory type
OMCL	Official Medicines Control Laboratory (MoH)
OCL	Official Control Laboratory (other sectors)
OFL	Official Forensic Laboratory

5.2. Payment of analytical testing costs for suspected counterfeit medicines

Member state survey: Q38 (MoH/DRA), Q69 (MoIP), Q93 (MoJ), Q124 (MoFTC) and Q151 (MoET)

Table 8: Who pays for suspected counterfeit medicine testing costs?

Member state	MoH/DRA	MoIP	MoJ	MoFTC	MoET
1	MoH/DRA MoJ MoFTC	MoH/DRA MoJ MoFTC	MoH/DRA MoJ MoFTC	MoH/DRA MoJ MoFTC	MoH/DRA MoJ MoFTC
2	MoH/DRA	MoIP for OFL	MoH/DRA MoIP for OFL	Rights holder[a]	MoET
3	State				
4	MoH/DRA				
5	MoH/DRA				
6	MoH/DRA or MoJ	Missing	If guilty, the author of the infraction	MA/trademark holder	Missing
7	Costs borne by the laboratory that performs the analyses. In some cases they might be charged to the author of the infraction if there is a legal procedure				
8	The state where no action is taken, otherwise the person/enterprise against which administrative measures are taken	State or convicted person	State or convicted person	Missing	MoH/DRA
9	The business agent	Missing	Person under investigation	Party under investigation and party requesting testing	

Member state	MoH/DRA	MoIP	MoJ	MoFTC	MoET
10	The agency concerned MoH/DRA (costs of destruction)	The agency concerned MoH (costs of destruction)			
11	MoH/DRA	Missing	MoFTC for criminal cases Other as determined by MoJ	Missing	Missing
12	DRA but not specified				

a. In cases where potential counterfeit samples have to be tested the relevant rights holder will undertake this process and bear the costs in accordance with EC Regulation 1383/2003.

5.3. National central compilation of analytical test results provided by official and private laboratories

Member state survey: Q39 (MoH/DRA), Q68 (MoIP) and Q123 (MoFTC)

The response was very mixed, with a lot of "unknown" responses from both member states and the various ministries.

Table 9: National compilation of analytical test results

Member state	MoH	MoIP	MoFTC
1	No	No	No
2	Yes	Unknown	Unknown
3	Yes		
4	No	Unknown	
5	Yes		
6	No		No
7	No		
8	Unknown	Unknown	Unknown
9	Yes	Unknown	Unknown
10	Yes	Yes	
11	No	Unknown	Missing
12	Unknown		

6. National regulatory authority co-operation

6.1. Legal provisions for reporting counterfeiting practices and counterfeit medicines

Member state survey: Q6 (MoH/DRA), Q55 (MoIP), Q81 (MoJ), Q107 (MoFTC) and Q144 (MoET)

6.1.1. Existence of legal provisions for reporting counterfeiting and counterfeit medicines to authorities

Some 58% of MoH/DRAs stated that legal provisions existed for reporting. As regards the other ministries, the responses were mixed with several stating that they are not aware of the legal provisions. No member state was in a position to indicate that there are legal provisions in place for each of the ministries.

Table 10: Existence of legal provisions for reporting counterfeiting and counterfeit medicines to authorities

Member state	MoH	MoIP	MoJ	MoFTC	MoET
1	Yes	No	No	No	No
2	Yes	No	No	No	No
3	No				
4	Yes				
5	No				
6	Yes	Unknown	No	Unknown	Unknown
7	No				
8	Yes	Yes	Yes	No	No
9	No	No	Unknown	Yes	
10	Yes	Yes			
11	No	No	Yes	Yes	Yes
12	Yes				

MoH/DRA: Yes = 58%; No = 42%.

Comments and relevant legal references received:

- GDP guidance (incorporated into the law on medicines);
- under standard provisions, manufacturers are responsible for reporting; under EU guidance on GDP, wholesalers are to report; under the pharmaceutical association's code of ethics and standards for pharmacists, pharmacists are to report. All information on illegal products is to be immediately passed to the MoH/DRA. The MoH/DRA subsequently informs health care professionals via the RAS, which covers EU and EEA countries and those countries with which a MRA exists such as Australia, New Zealand, Canada and Switzerland;

- pharmaceutical laboratories, wholesalers and health professionals are responsible for reporting; all information has to be reported. Information is reported to the regional authority who then informs the MoH/DRA (the law on medicines);
- in line with Regulation CEE 339/93 (8 February 1993) on conformity controls on imported products from third countries;
- all civil servants are obliged by criminal law to report to legal authorities all facts that can be considered as criminal acts. Although there is no specific form, all important details should be reported;
- no specific procedure exists, but information on counterfeit medicines is published by the usual means of market surveillance (the law on medicines);
- MoH/DRA health police refer to pharmacovigilance rules and general rules on the production of pharmaceuticals (MoH/DRA regulations);
- the distribution chain (wholesaler, pharmacies, etc.) provides information about the quality defect (if detected).

MoIP: Yes = 29%; No = 57%; Unknown = 14%.

Comments and relevant legal references received:

- manufacturers and distributors report all relevant market surveillance information to the MoH/DRA, pharmacovigilance centres, police and the instruction judge (the law on medicines concerning market surveillance in general);
- health police refer to pharmacovigilance rules and general rules on the production of pharmaceuticals (MoH/DRA regulations).

MoJ: Yes = 33%; No = 50%; Unknown = 17%.

Comments received and legal references:

- manufacturers and distributors report all relevant market surveillance information to MoH/DRA, pharmacovigilance centres, police and instruction judge (the law on medicines concerning market surveillance in general);
- if the counterfeit medicine or health product is detected after it has had an undesirable effect, the pharmacovigilance provisions will lead to the notification of the MoH/DRA, which possesses extensive powers (namely, the authority to suspend all business entering, leaving or on the territory, ban advertising, withdraw a product or a group of products from the market, order destruction, and ensure public awareness). The obligation to notify (noncompliance is subject to criminal sanctions) is on various actors, starting with health professionals. The local poisoning centres also play an important role in receiving such information and then disseminating it. There is a National Pharmacovigilance Commission for medicines for human use and another for veterinary medicines as well as, at the local level, the regional centres for pharmacovigilance, which are in charge of receiving and forwarding such information (to organisations further up the hierarchical chain) (health law). In addition, the public prosecutor may take action against acts of counterfeiting after receiving information indicating a breach of law (Penal Code).

MoFTC: Yes = 33%; No = 50%; Unknown = 17%.

Comments received and legal references:

- customs may refer cases to the MoH/DRA but this is not a reciprocal arrangement;
- yes; criminal and customs legislation;
- yes; intervention request submitted to customs authorities.

MoET: Yes = 20%; No = 60%; Unknown = 20%.

Comment received:

* no obligation to report to authorities under the IPR and unfair competition laws.

6.1.2. Legal provisions concerning confidentiality of reporting

Some 75% of MoH/DRAs replied that there were no such provisions; one indicated that there are no such provisions for all ministries. The responses from other ministries were generally split between "yes" and "no".

Where the response was "yes", the legal references referred to were specific national legislation included under either the law on medicines, criminal law, customs and excise law, official secrets law or IPR law. One reference was made to the existence of a memorandum of understanding (MoU) on this issue. Only one reference was made to EC Regulation 1383/2003, which states that application data cannot be distributed by customs authorities beyond the local office.

6.2. National authority co-operation concerning medicines counterfeiting

Member state survey: Q14, Q15 (MoH/DRA), Q61, Q62 (MoIP), Q86, Q87 (MoJ), Q113, Q114 (MoFTC), Q148 and Q149 (MoET)

The data on the existence and participation in a national network against medicines counterfeiting are presented in the following table.

Table 11: Existence of a national co-operation network against counterfeiting and counterfeit medicines

Member state	MoH/DRA	MoIP	MoJ	MoFTC	MoET
1	Yes	Yes	Yes	Yes	Yes
2	Yes	Unknown	Unknown	Unknown	Yes
3	No				
4	No				
5	No				
6	No	No	No	Unknown	No
7	Unknown				
8	No	Unknown	Unknown	Unknown	Yes
9	Yes	No	No	Yes	
10	No	No			
11	No	Unknown	Yes	Missing	Yes
12	No				

The above table clearly shows that, with the exception of one member state, there is a lack of co-ordination between national authorities on this topic.

7. International regulatory authority co-operation

7.1. WHO anti-counterfeit medicine network and database system

Member state survey: Q16 and Q17 (MoH/DRA)

WHO anti-counterfeit network membership
Yes = 33%; No = 42%; Unknown = 17%; Missing = 8%.

Only a third of respondents indicated that they are a member of the network; two MoH/DRAs stated that they did not know.

Forwarding of national reports on counterfeit medicines to the WHO database
No = 42%; Unknown = 42%; Missing = 16%.

No reports are forwarded to the WHO database by any of the member state respondents. Comments received from MoH/DRAs which do belong to the network but which do not forward reports stated that this was because of time and resource constraints.

7.2. Known existence and usage of database systems concerning counterfeit medicines

7.2.1. Authority database systems for tracking counterfeit medicines

Member state survey: Q8 (MoH/DRA), Q57 (MoIP), Q83 (MoJ) Q109 (MoFTC) and Q146 (MoET)

Table 12: Existence of authority counterfeit medicine database systems

Member state	MoH/DRA	MoIP	MoJ	MoFTC	MoET
1	No	No	No	No	No
2	No	No	Unknown	No	No
3	No				
4	No				
5	No				
6	No	No	No	Unknown	Unknown
7	No				
8	Unknown	Unknown	Unknown	Unknown	No
9	Yes	No	Unknown	Yes	
10	No	No			

Member state	MoH/DRA	MoIP	MoJ	MoFTC	MoET
11	Unknown	No	No	No	Unknown
12	No				

MoH/DRA

An almost unanimous response of either "no" or "unknown" was received to this question. The one respondent (from east Europe) who replied "yes" stated that this was co ordinated by departments of the health authorities and was conducted at the national level.

Comments received:

- whilst there is no specific database dedicated to tracking counterfeit pharmaceutical products, the MoH/DRA enforcement unit records incidents of counterfeit pharmaceuticals that are detected.

Other ministries

Comments received:

- this is an area that is a problem across all industry sectors;
- no legal obligation for a database is provided in the IPR and unfair competition laws. Neither the IPR institute nor the MoET operate such a database.

7.2.2. Stakeholder awareness of counterfeit medicine database systems

Stakeholder survey: Q8

Yes = 33%; No = 63%; Yes/No = 4%.

Table 13: Stakeholder awareness of counterfeit medicine database systems

Database type	Number of respondents
Pharmaceutical Security Institute (PSI) (counterfeit incident system)	6
WHO	3
International Chamber of Commerce (ICC)	2
General Internet[a]	2
Global Anti-counterfeiting Group (www.gacg.org)	1
Anti-counterfeiting Coalition (www.iacc.org)	1
MedWatch/FDA	1
MHRA	1
Product search in, for example, CAMindex or pakmedinet	1
Europa website	1
US National Association of Boards of Pharmacy	1
QBPC (Quality Brands Protection Committee) China	1
Council of Europe	1

a. One respondent states in particular Google.

The majority of positive respondents were manufacturers; hardly any API manufacturers or wholesalers know of the existence of a counterfeit medicines database.

7.3. RAS for reporting suspected counterfeit medicines

7.3.1. Existence of a counterfeit medicine RAS

Member state survey: Q18 (MoH/DRA), Q63 (MoIP), Q88 (MoJ) and Q115 (MoFTC)

MoH/DRA: Yes = 83%; No = 0%; Missing = 17%.

Some 83% of MoH/DRAs possess a RAS. Practically no other type of ministry possess such a system.

Table 14: Description of existing RASs

Member state	Responsible department	Official powers of responsible department in information exchange/RAS	Organisational arrangements, including administrative structures
1	MoH/DRA inspectorate	None	Informal exchange of information on counterfeit medicines between members of the PFIPC
2	MoH/DRA intelligence unit	Restricted if the information has the potential to jeopardise an ongoing legal case	PFIPC network, Council of Europe ad hoc group, EU network, WHO
3	MoH/DRA	Competent authority for medicines	Inspectorate department administer the RAS
4	MoH/DRA inspectorate	Inspection, adoption of precautionary measures, intervention and withdrawal of products	The Subdirectorate General of Inspections and Medicines Control manages the information regarding withdrawal of medicinal products: it receives information from supranational organisations (the EMEA, PIC/S, etc.) and forwards it to the regional health departments
5	MoH/DRA GMP department	–	–
6	Directorate General of Public Health Protection: Medicines Federal Public Service on Public Health, Food (Chain) Safety and Environment	Exchange of information between enterprises, member states, MRA members, PIC/S members and recalls	The RAS is situated in the manufacturer and wholesaler inspection department (quality directorate) Every type of defect initiates an appropriate action with the relevant company and information exchange. Surveillance procedures are in place Counterfeit medicines is a separate category under the RAS
7	MoH/DRA inspection department	Can only exchange information that is not considered confidential by the judicial authorities and always with the permission of the MoH/DRA management board	The RAS of the EMEA

Member state	Responsible department	Official powers of responsible department in information exchange/RAS	Organisational arrangements, including administrative structures
8	Missing	–	–
9	National Institute of Pharmacy	–	–
10	MoH/DRA	Office for authorisation of pharmaceutical producers and RAS	–
11	Missing	–	–
12	MoH/DRA	As in the EU	The MoH/DRA inspectorate takes care of the RAS

MoIP: Yes = 14%; No = 43%; Missing = 43%.

Member state 11: (i) international technical co-operation of the police service, and (ii) central department of the police judiciary, which is responsible for the exchange of information and liaison with operational services.

MoJ: No = 50%; Missing = 50%.

MoFTC: Yes = 17%; No = 17%; Unknown = 33%; Missing = 33%.

Comments received:

• not aware of any RAS, but less formalised processes of information exchange exist between EU member states;
• not actually defined;
• yes, in the framework of administrative support.

7.3.2. Proposed Council of Europe RAS notification form and information exchange MoU

A draft Council of Europe counterfeit medicine RAS reporting form has been proposed and drafted by the Ad hoc Group on Counterfeit Medicines and is attached as Appendix 6 to this report. The group has made available the form and proposed its usage to the European Medicines Evaluation Agency (EMEA) and PIC/S.

8. Regulatory authority, industry and wholesaler co-operation

8.1. Industry's and wholesalers' knowledge of regulatory entities (authorities) responsible for the control of medicines counterfeiting

Stakeholder survey: Q9

Yes = 57%; Yes/No = 3%; No = 37%; Missing = 3%.

Home country in Europe:

- where the response was "yes", the response in all cases was the country specific MoH/DRA. MoH/DRAs in Europe specifically mentioned as being actively involved in tackling the counterfeit medicine problem were the MHRA (UK), AFSSAPS (France), BfArm (Germany), BPI (Belgium) and the Dutch Health Inspectorate;
- in the case of Italy, Nucleo Anti Sofistificazione (NAS), a special department of the police, was specifically mentioned;
- the only country where it was mentioned that more than one authority was involved was France with: the AFSSAPS, customs, police and DGCCRF;
- other non-governmental organisations mentioned were Phagro and the GIRP.

Third countries/other organisations:

- the US FDA was frequently mentioned as being active in the control of counterfeit medicines. It was noted that the FDA has a counterfeit branch that deals with testing (of suspected counterfeit medicines) and an inspection division that goes into the field to investigate counterfeit medicine incidents. It was stated by another respondent that the FDA is ahead in terms of the functioning of its forensic laboratory and that the FDA Office of Criminal Investigations is responsible; another stated that "it seems that the FDA is more active on this issue and does not rely only on paper";
- China: one respondent named the CSFDA, whilst another stated that the QBPC in China is perhaps the only specific body working with local government and other organisations to tackle counterfeiting;
- other countries specifically mentioned were: Colombia (INVIMA), Brazil (ANVISA), Nigeria (NAFDAC) and Switzerland (SwissMedic);
- non-governmental organisations specifically mentioned were: international co-operation in the form of the PFIPC.

Other comments received:

- one respondent stated that "in our experience the pharmaceutical authorities in the EU are hardly interested in pharmaceutical and API counterfeiting and the fight against it (DG Enterprise, EMEA, national authorities/inspectorates) with a few exceptions".

NB. No response was made to the survey by traders, therefore it is difficult to assess their knowledge of pharmaceutical regulatory control measures.

8.2. Essential elements of good co-operation practices between regulatory authorities and the pharmaceutical and chemical (API) manufacturing industries

Member state survey: Q47 (MoH/DRA), Q73 (MoIP), Q99 (MoJ) and Q133 (MoFTC)

This question was addressed to all relevant ministry types in the member state survey.

MoH/DRA
Respondent replies are summarised as follows:

*   there are no good practices in this field;
*   recognition of the counterfeit medicine problem;
*   co-operation in the area of drug registration;
*   active support in analysing and providing (pre-)clinical data on substances found;
*   adherence to principles of GMP;
*   better control of API imports susceptible to diversion (and better control of imports from third parties);
*   obligatory for industry to provide communication about counterfeit medicine problems;
*   open exchange/discussions of information particularly concerning the analytical results of counterfeit medicines; divulgence of counterfeit medicine characteristics known by industry;
*   efficiency and rapidity of action; just-in-time reports about counterfeiting problems; and quick access to information regarding production and anti-counterfeiting features;
*   periodic meetings between MoH/DRAs and national manufacturing associations on this problem;
*   creation of a strong network between national and international entities involved with counterfeit medicines;
*   centralisation of knowledge of all the diversion phenomena and trends;
*   a forum for discussion on disclosure of counterfeiting information amongst the industry is essential and an agreement with national governments on the reporting of such instances supported by any relevant general information is needed. There is also a need for confidence-building measures for anti-counterfeiting issues beyond current good working regulatory arrangements. Manufacturers should proactively carry out post market surveillance on their own products and share common information with the manufacturing and enforcement authorities. There needs to be a system of reporting, either voluntary or mandatory, for manufacturers and distributors of suspected counterfeit pharmaceutical products.

MoIP
Respondent replies are summarised as follows:

*   recognition of the problem;
*   open exchange of information, information exchange on medicines susceptible

to counterfeiting, communication and common public/private responsiveness;
- active support in analysing and providing (pre-)clinical data on substances found;
- national inter-authority co-operation supervised by the MoH/DRA;
- necessary to have one or more contact persons;
- efficiency and rapidity of action, just-in-time reports about counterfeiting problems, and quick access to information regarding production and anti-counterfeiting features.

MoJ
Respondent replies are summarised as follows:

- open exchange of information, recognition of the problem, and active support in analysing and providing (pre-)clinical data on substances found;
- regular contact between competent authorities and the pharmaceutical industry.

MoFTC
Respondent replies are summarised as follows:

- open exchange of information, recognition of the problem, and active support in analysing and providing (pre-)clinical data on substances found;
- it is essential that producers of pharmaceutical products who believe that their goods are susceptible to counterfeiting should register their rights with the customs authorities under EC Regulation 1383/2003. In applying for action against counterfeit activity, the rights holder should include as much relevant information as possible to enable the goods in question to be readily recognised by the customs authorities and increase the likelihood of a seizure being achieved. Additionally, participation in an EU-sponsored initiative, such as the 4IPR project aimed at developing a pan-European information sharing system between rights holders and law enforcement agencies within a secure environment, would also be of huge benefit to the pharmaceutical industry.

8.3. Disclosure of covert and overt medicinal product features to investigators by the pharmaceutical and chemical (API) manufacturing industries

Member state survey: Q48 (MoH/DRA), Q74 (MoIP), Q100 (MoJ) and Q134 (MoFTC)

Table 15: Disclosure of covert and overt features of counterfeit medicines to authorities

Member state	MoH/DRA	MoIP	MoJ	MoFTC
1	Yes	Yes	Yes	Yes
2	Yes	Yes	Yes	Yes
3	No			
4	Yes			
5	Yes			
6	No	No	Unknown	No
7	Missing			
8	Unknown	Unknown	Missing	Missing
9	No	No	Missing	Yes
10	Yes	Yes		
11	Yes	No	Missing	Missing
12	Unknown			

MoH/DRA: Yes = 50%; Yes/No = 8%; No = 17%; Unknown = 17%; Missing = 8%.

"Yes" comments received included:

- on a "need-to-know" basis;
- sometimes;
- if not strictly confidential;
- the covert character must be in the MA dossier if they modify the composition of the product, otherwise also the packaging forms part of the MA product dossier.

"Yes/No" comment received:

- overt features may be more readily disclosed. Trade name protection is a major concern to the industry. No voluntary covert features have been disclosed to date. The issue has probably not been sufficiently tested. The industry has indicated that it was willing to be forthcoming with information.

"No/Unknown" comments received:

- industry prudence concerning covert characteristics is understandable in order to avoid their divulgence among counterfeiters. Education of personnel in the official distribution sector concerning overt characteristics demands serious efforts;
- no cases of investigation of counterfeit medicines by the local pharmaceutical industry;
- have little experience.

MoIP: Yes = 43%; No = 43%; Unknown = 14%.

"Yes" comments received:

- on a need-to-know basis;
- sometimes;
- if not strictly confidential.

"No/Unknown" comment received:

- until now there has been no contact between the police service and the pharmaceutical industry.

MoJ: Yes = 33%; Unknown = 17%; Missing = 50%.

"Yes" comments received:

- on a need-to-know basis;
- sometimes.

MoFTC: Yes = 50%; No = 17%; Missing = 33%.

"Yes" comments received:

- on a need-to-know basis;
- sometimes. In many cases, details are not disclosed because of fears that the details of such product ingredients may be disclosed to competitive rivals within the industry. Once again this is not uncommon throughout all industrial and agricultural sectors and is to some extent understandable. However, an environment based upon mutual trust needs to be cultivated to ensure that good detailed information is available to investigators. Similarly, it is vital that covert and overt features are understood as those investigating products have

a better "feel" for which products are genuine without having to analyse the item further.

No comments were received from respondents stating "no".

Comments on cross-correspondence between answers from the relevant member state internal agencies/authorities/ministries:

• two member states have a policy of open disclosure of details to all relevant ministries; for the other member states the picture is mixed.

9. Authorities, systems and procedures for detection of counterfeit medicines

9.1. Existence of specialised police forces or other enforcement bodies that investigate offences concerning medicines counterfeiting

Member state survey: Q42 (MoH/DRA) and Q65 (MoIP)

MoH/DRA: Yes = 67%; No= 33%.

Where a "yes" response was provided the particular bodies specified were:

- MoH/DRA (two member states);
- MoH/DRA inspectorate and MoFTC;
- MoH/DRA penal section and regional police;
- MoH/DRA, MoH/DRA health police and MoIP;
- MoH/DRA and MoJ;
- MoIP;
- MoIP (police environmental and consumer protection department).

Comments provided:

- there are police forces specialised in counterfeiting but not counterfeit medicines;
- the normal medicines inspectorate and enforcement officers carry out this activity as part of their ordinary duties.

Table 16: Number of investigations and prosecutions concerning counterfeit medicines

	Member state							
	1	2	3	4	7	8	9	10
Number of investigations resulting in prosecutions	100-150	3 (7 ongoing)	0	U/K	0	U/K	U/K	U/K
Number of prosecutions resulting in convictions	U/K	3	0	U/K	0	U/K	U/K	U/K

MoIP: Yes = 86%; No= 14%.

Where a "yes" response was provided the particular bodies specified were:

- MoH/DRA;
- MoH/DRA inspectorate and MoFTC;
- MoH/DRA penal section and regional police;
- MoH/DRA health police, MoH/DRA and MoIP;
- MoH/DRA and MoIP (central brigade for prevention of industrial and art counterfeiting);

- MoIP (counterfeit service and hormone service).[1]

Concerning information on the number of investigations resulting in prosecutions and the number of prosecutions resulting in convictions, all responses were either "unknown", missing or the same as for Q42.

NB. Concerning responses to this question:

- one member state: MoH/DRA states "yes" while MoIP states "no";
- two member states: MoH/DRA states "no" while MoIP states "yes".

9.2. Authority involvement in actions against medicines counterfeiting

Member state survey: Q43a (MoH/DRA) and Q120 (MoFTC)

MoH/DRA: Yes = 92%; No = 8%.

Contact details of MoH/DRA authorities involved in counterfeit medicine actions were provided.

Specific comments received included:

- "yes": a member state highlighted the medicines testing surveillance scheme whereby the pharmaceutical society purchase random medicinal products from pharmacies and send them to the MoH/DRA to test in their OMCLs for authentication;
- "no": a member state said that whenever necessary MoH/DRA inspectors can technically help police forces.

MoFTC: Yes = 66%; No = 17%; Unknown = 17%.

A member state commented that in the case of a customs infraction, customs undertake fiscal action according to the Customs Code.

9.3. Active and systematic searching for suspected counterfeit medicines

Member state survey: Q43b (MoH/DRA), Q66 (MoIP) and Q121 (MoFTC)

Some 58% of MoH/DRAs, 42% of MoIPs and 33% of MoFTC respondents stated that they did not actively or systematically search for counterfeit pharmaceuticals. There was a degree of incongruence in responses across the ministry types.

Active searching occurs in one member state that has a specialised health police force and in the east European country respondent (the latter probably because it has a recognised counterfeit medicine problem).

Specific comments received:

- "yes": annual sampling plan by the OMCL, existence of a specialised health police force, violations of IPR and the process of customs control;
- "no": authorities only act at the time of discovery of defects and intervention occurs only in response to a signal or suspicion.

---

1. Neither of these services is currently working with counterfeit medicines.

9.4. Customs risk analysis concerning medicinal products

Member state survey: Q125 and Q126 (MoFTC)

9.4.1. Do customs authorities apply the methodology of customs risk analysis to medicinal products?

Yes = 84%; Unknown = 16%.

NB. One member state placed a question mark against each specified risk factor.

The specific affirmative answers concerning the risk factors specified by the survey were:

(i) public health (if "yes", which counterfeit pharmaceuticals are considered high risk) = 33%;

(ii) customs tariff codes (if "yes", which tariff codes do you consider "risky") = 50%;

(iii) description of good in trade documents that arouses suspicions = 50% of which:

- country of origin (sender based in) = 100%;
- destination country (consignee based in) = 100%;
- suspicious transport means = 100%;
- risk factors associated with the set up and activities of companies = 67%;
- suspicious packaging and/or marking = 100%;

(iv) Other risk factors = 33%.

Of the two member states that consider public health a risk factor in customs risk analysis, one stated that antivirals, antibiotics, anti-malarials were particular drug classes for risk analysis.

Two of the three respondents who replied that custom tariff codes were a risk factor stated that codes 3003 and 3004 were receiving particular attention.

Other risk factors mentioned were: (i) previous consignments involving the same or similar methodologies that are on record, and (ii) according to circumstance (suspicious personal behaviour, documentation and provoked suspicions).

9.4.2. If one or more of the above-mentioned risk factors are present and known for an individual importation/ exportation/transit, does this give rise to controls?

Yes = 67%; Unknown = 33%.

There was almost unanimous (four out of five) agreement from the respondents that controls are applied following risk factor identification for an individual importation/exportation/transit.

One comment stated: "in many cases yes but there are a myriad of risk factors which may result in customs applying a control and some of those included above may be present. Very often customs will also be heavily reliant upon information or intelligence which is provided by the rights holder or the rights holder's representative. This information is used by customs to create what are known as customs profiles. These are programmed into the customs electronic entry processing system and any matches generated against entered information will result in a full documentary check and possible physical examination."

9.5. Coercive measures and special investigative methods nationally authorised and applied to combating counterfeit medicines

Member state survey: Q71 (MoIP)

This question was addressed exclusively to the MoIP.

Table 17: Coercive measures and special investigative methods nationally authorised and applied to combating counterfeit medicines

Member state	Coercive measures/special investigative methods											AiG[a]	Specific[b]
	A	B	C	D	E	F	G	H	I	J	K		
1	Yes	Yes	No	No	No	Yes	No	No	No	Yes	No	Yes for all marked "yes"	Yes for all marked "yes"
2	Yes	Yes	No	No	No	Yes	Yes	Yes	Yes	Yes	No	Yes for all marked "yes"	Yes for all marked "yes"
6	Yes	Yes	Yes	Yes*	Yes	Yes*	Yes*	Yes*	Yes*	Yes*	No	Yes for all marked "yes"	Yes* = only allowed for certain medicines like narcotics (illegal drugs) and hormones
8	Yes	Yes	Yes*	Yes*	Yes	Yes	Yes	Yes/ no	No	Yes/ no	No	Yes for all marked "yes"	Yes* = permitted only in case of fraud H, J = no
9	Yes	Yes	Yes	Yes	Yes	Yes	Yes	Yes	Yes	Yes	No	Yes for all marked "yes"	Yes for all marked "yes"
10	Yes	Yes	Yes	Yes	Yes	Yes	Yes	Yes	Yes	Yes	No	Yes for all marked "yes" (see note)	Yes for all marked "yes" (see note)

Member state	Coercive measures/special investigative methods											AiG[a]	Specific[b]
	A	B	C	D	E	F	G	H	I	J	K		
11	Yes	Yes	Yes	Yes	Yes	Yes	Yes/ no	No	No	No	No	Yes for all marked "yes" (see note)	G = no (see note)

a. AiG: authorised in general.
b. Specific: used specifically to combat counterfeit pharmaceuticals.

* although the MoH/DRA in this country has reported several counterfeit medicines cases according to the member state survey.

Table code

Code	Type of coercive measure/special investigative method
A	Search warrant
B	Seizure
C	Telephone recording
D	Wiretap
E	Detention
F	Observation, with or without technical resources
G	Informants
H	Infiltration
I	Controlled deliveries, pseudo-purchase, confidential purchase
J	Proactive investigation
K	Other

NB. Member state 10: a counterfeiting case may cause a police investigation to be opened (under the Penal Code), so all the measures under Q70 and Q71 may be authorised.

Member state 11: infiltration is not authorised and not used. Informants are authorised but not used.

9.6. Industry's, wholesalers', traders' and pharmacists' knowledge of (i) who should be informed domestically in case of suspected counterfeit medicines and (ii) which notification procedures should be followed

Stakeholder survey: Q10

9.6.1. Knowledge of who should be informed

Yes = 73%; No = 13%; Yes/No = 7%; Missing = 7%.

"Yes" comments received:

• MoH/DRA mentioned in several cases;

- company address (namely, informing manufacturer);
- criminal investigators;
- in the United States the FDA is notified. They have been active in this area;
- distribution system of pharmaceuticals in this country is very well controlled and no counterfeits of pharmaceuticals have reached the distribution channel, "but if they do is another question";
- "yes, but wholesalers and pharmacists report to different regulatory bodies";
- "the MoH/DRA is the regulatory body responsible for actioning recalls in our country. The MoH/DRA then cascades this information through to all potentially affected parties";
- "all the actors in the supply chain know who the health police are because they control patent and business activity".

"No" comments received:

- "this is not known/formalised in any way. The same applies for many other EU countries";
- "especially not with regard to counterfeit APIs";
- "no confidence anything will be done".

"Yes/No" comments received:

- "big pharmaceutical companies yes, but smaller enterprises and probably the majority of distributors and retailers no".

9.6.2. Knowledge of notification procedures

Yes = 50%; Yes/No = 3%; Yes/Missing = 3%; No = 27%; Missing = 17%.

"Yes" comments received:

- additional education through pharmaceutical associations is necessary; however, it is questionable whether all cases found would be reported in practice (see analogy of counterfeited money);
- call the local offices or our country's MoH/DRA (which has a well-known counterfeit medicine reporting system);
- (i) own: control of stock and deliveries, stop supply to pharmacies; (ii) association Phagro: pharmaceutical return report, standard procedure;
- recall of products after notification by the MoH/DRA;
- wholesalers tend to be the link between manufacturers and pharmacists when reporting faulty/counterfeit products;
- there is no specific procedure, but everybody knows which health authority should be informed, and it is very easy to contact the appropriate authority;
- it would be a simple procedure: contact and inform;
- same established routines as for "stop sales" routines. Fixed routine with a complete information system;
- the MoH/DRA recall directive;
- call the MoH/DRA and explain the problem;
- direct contact with inspectorate. Forms filled in if required.

"No"comments received:

- there is no procedure. This is the case for most EU countries;
- there is no specifically defined notification procedure for counterfeit products; they should be handled like complaints, so the procedure differs depending on the impact of the "deviation";
- should be the same globally, for example as for serious adverse events;

- the problem of API counterfeiting receives hardly any attention in the EU, so authorities do not communicate about the aspects mentioned in this question;
- not publicised to stakeholders.

"Yes/No" comments received:

- "big pharmaceutical companies yes, but smaller enterprises and probably the majority of distributors and retailers no".

9.6.3. Cross-correspondence of answers from 9.6.1 and 9.6.2

Yes/Yes = 50%
No/No = 10%
Yes/No = 17%
No/Yes = 0%
No/Missing = 3%
Yes/Missing = 7%
Yes/No and Yes/No = 3%
Yes/No and Yes/Missing = 3%
Missing/Missing = 7%

10. Legal provisions, enforcement, sanctions, and judicial and intellectual property procedures concerning unlicensed and counterfeit medicines

10.1. Legal provisions and sanctions concerning unlicensed medicines

2004 member state survey results

10.1.1. Existence of legal provisions governing importation of unlicensed medicines in an amount adequate for personal use

Member state survey: Q31 (MoH/DRA) and Q117 (MoFTC)

MoH/DRA: Yes = 75%; No = 25%.

Of "yes" responses: PoMs and OTC products = 56%, PoMs only = 22%, not specified = 22%.

"Yes" comments received and legal references:

- both are not allowed; in practice a personal import policy applies (law on medicines);
- medicinal products (licensing and sale) regulations;
- only possible to do with authorisation from the MoH/DRA and via foreign medicinal product services of MoH/DRAs (law on medicines);
- there must be a demonstrable patient-doctor-pharmacist relationship; delivery can only be made by the pharmacy (law on medicines);
- small quantities for private use, which are determined on a case by case basis and according to the type of medicine; the amount should correspond to a defined treatment course (law on medicines and MA regulation);
- law on pharmaceutical activities;
- "compassionate use" – regulation related to clinical trials;
- via hospital pharmacy, temporary authorisation for nominative use given by the MoH/DRA on demand by the prescriber (health law).

"No" comments received:

- only for narcotics and psychotropics, and when people are travelling with a medical prescription for the medicines; cannot be imported directly.

MoFTC: Yes = 50%; No = 50%.
All the "yes" responses cover both PoM and OTC medicinal products.

"Yes" comments received and legal references:

- both PoM and OTC products are not allowed; in practice a personal import policy applies (law on medicines);
- legal reference provided in law on medicines;
- medicines can be imported in a quantity compatible with personal therapeutic use; no authorisation required if person carries the medicines themselves (health law).

"No" comments received:

- the importation of medicines for personal use, provided their importation is not prohibited under the misuse of drugs law, breaks no laws. However, in cases of doubt (for example, multiple small-scale importations) customs will pass the relevant information to the MoH/DRA.

NB. Concerning responses to this question by member state 6 and member state 9: the MoH/DRA responded "yes", while the MoFTC responded "no".

10.1.2. Existence of legal provisions governing unlicensed medicines other than for personal use

Member state survey: Q32 (MoH/DRA)

Yes = 92%; No = 8%.

"Yes" comments received:

- it is illegal to produce, import, possess, sell or distribute any unlicensed medicines;
- legal provision under the law on medicines;
- importations are permitted for the purpose of export or by a registered medical practitioner or dentist for use by a patient under his care. Such importations do not require authorisation (medicinal products – licensing and sale – regulations);
- medicinal products for human use (GCP) regulation that regulates investigational medicinal products;
- parallel import, import with a view to export and international commerce (invoicing without import) (law on medicines, manufacture, distribution and dispensation regulations, MA regulations and parallel import regulations);
- for certain medicinal products that do not exist domestically and are considered essential for the treatment of certain diseases; can only be obtained by health institutions and must be authorised case by case (MoH/DRA regulations);
- importation by health professionals in small quantities for their patients and distribution and delivery of non-authorised medicines for the treatment of life-threatening conditions (law on medicines and MA regulations);
- law on pharmaceutical activities;
- clinical trials regulations;
- temporary authorisation for use allowed in cohorts after submission of an MA application or if there is a delay in granting an MA (health law);
- medicinal products to be used inside a hospital department (law on medicines).

10.1.3. Existence of specific sanctions for offences relating to legal provisions governing unlicensed medicines

Member state survey: Q33 (MoH/DRA)

Yes = 92%; Unknown = 8%.

"Yes" comments received:

- six years imprisonment and/or fine of up to €45 000;
- legal provision under the law on medicines;
- summary conviction for each offence results in a maximum fine of €1 927 and/or one year in prison; on indictment for each offence the fine is €127 000 for the first conviction, or a maximum of €315 000 for each offence, and/or a maximum prison term of ten years in both cases (MoH/DRA regulations);
- the law on medicines prohibits any form of indirect sales (mail, Internet, etc.);
- offenders reported to police;
- (i) one month to one year imprisonment and/or a fine of between €2 500 and €75 000; and (ii) where the offence concerns hormonal, anti-infective, anti-parasitical or anti-inflammatory substances: one month to five years' imprisonment and/or a fine of between €15 000 and €500 000 (law on medicines and the law on the traffic of poisonous, soporific, stupefying, disinfectant or antiseptic substances).
- administrative fees and recall of product (national law);
- defined under the law on medicines;
- fine of €3 750 (health law);
- prison up to three months and/or penalties. Withdrawal of licences, that is wholesaler licence; the law does not specify any particular offence (law on medicines).

10.1.4. Existence of national institutions/dependent bodies of health authorities with responsibility to prevent the occurrence of unlicensed medicines in the national market

Member state survey: Q34 (MoH/DRA)

Yes = 67%; No = 25%; Unknown = 8%.

Of the "yes" responses:

- prevention of production, importation, placing on the market and exportation of unlicensed medicines = six of the eight member states;
- prevention of production, importation and placing on the market of unlicensed medicines = one member state;
- prevention of importation and placing on the market of unlicensed medicines = one member state.

"Yes" comments received:

- one member state declared that the MoH/DRA regulates control of unlicensed medicines by issuing "special" licences for production/importation whereby control is exerted (that is, it is not an outright ban of unlicensed medicines).

Details of responsible bodies were provided by the respondents. The majority of responsible bodies are MoH/DRAs. One member state drew attention to the specialised health police; one member state stated that customs and economic activities inspection (and border customs) often play an important role in this area (by inspecting thoroughly all kinds of sales point commercial activity); one member state also mentioned the role of the customs service (which includes a special medicinal products section); and one member state replied that regional inspection was responsible for commercial surveillance of pharmacies, drug stores, doctors' surgeries and other medicinal product sale points.

10.2. Legal provisions and sanctions concerning counterfeit medicines

2004 Council of Europe member state survey

10.2.1. Legal provisions concerning prevention of counterfeit medicines

Member state survey: Q36 (MoH/DRA), Q51 (MoIP), Q77 (MoJ), Q102 (MoFTC) and Q140 (MoET)

Table 18: Legal provisions concerning prevention of counterfeit medicines (summary of responses)

Member state	MoH/DRA	MoIP	MoJ	MoFTC	MoET
1	No	Yes	Yes	Yes	Yes
2	No	No	No	No	Yes
3	No				
4	No				
5	Yes				
6	Yes	Yes	Yes	No	Yes
7	No				
8	No	Yes	Yes	No	Yes
9	Yes	No	Yes	No	
10	Yes	Yes			
11	No	Yes	Yes	Yes	No
12	No				

MoH/DRA (medicines legislation): Yes = 33%; No = 67%.

"Yes" comments received:

- qualified person releases batches from third countries in the EU market after he sends a sample for analysis;
- one member state: the law on medicines has a provision for seizure and taking samples of suspected counterfeit products and the national GDP document states "if found the counterfeit medicine must be labelled and put into quarantine; the MA holder or owner must be informed";
- one member state (from east Europe): all APIs and FPs for manufacture, distribution and import/export/transit are under state control;
- numbered labels on pharmaceuticals and provisions on tamper-proof packaging proscribed in GMP.

NB. Where legal provisions are said to exist they tend to concern distribution and are for finished products only.

"No" comments received:

- only the provisions of existing medicinal product legislation, which require products to be licensed for marketing and manufacture, importation and distribution also to be licensed. There is no specific counterfeit legislation for medicinal products enacted in this member state;

- see comments for counterfeit medicines definition.

Description of preventive provisions and resulting obligations:

- one member state provided the following comment: There are no preventive measures. The counterfeit medicines identified in the distribution network have to be put in quarantine. They must be labelled. The minister, the holder of the MA, or the rights holder of the genuine product must be informed.

MoIP (criminal law and specific laws concerning counterfeits and counterfeiting)
Some 71% of member states replied "yes" and such provisions were provided for under either criminal law, the Penal Code or commerce/trademark law.

MoJ (criminal law and specific laws concerning counterfeits and counterfeiting)
Some 83% of member states replied "yes" and such provisions were provided for under either criminal law, the Penal Code, the Code of Administrative Offences, IPR law or health law.

MoFTC (criminal law and specific finance/customs laws)
Some 67% of member states replied "no". Of the two member states replying "yes", one specified criminal law and the other specified IPR law and EC Regulation 1383/2003 (Article 2.C.i and ii).

MoET (commercial laws)
Some 80% of member states replied "yes". Comments provided for "yes" responses were supplementary protection certificate, (IPR) legal provisions, trade-mark law, unfair competition law and the law on medicines.

10.2.2. Legal powers of administrative inspectorates and enforcement, judicial, financial/customs and economy/trade authorities concerning counterfeit medicines

Member state survey: Q5 (MoH/DRA), Q54 (MoIP), Q80 (MoJ), Q106 (MoFTC) and Q143 (MoET)

MoH/DRA
Summary of comments received concerning legal powers:

- inspection: search, take samples and seizure;
- enforcement: seize products and documents, notification of authorities, bring cases to court via public prosecutor and licence withdrawal;
- one member state: health authorities have same legal powers as police officers;
- no specific powers relating to counterfeit medicines were indicated by any respondent;
- three member states: counterfeit medicines are generally considered to be non-authorised medicinal products and consequently come under legal manufacturing and MA requirements.

Legal obligation to prosecute cases: Yes = 25%; No = 58%; Unknown = 16%.

"No/unknown" comments received:

- decisions to prosecute are taken in "the public interest";
- prosecution at summary jurisdiction is at the discretion of the MoH/DRA. It also has discretion to seek prosecution on indictment, but the final decision on trial on indictment rests, as in all criminal cases, with the Director of Public Prosecutions;

- the Attorney General may prosecute if findings warrant such action;
- counterfeit medicines will be under judicial investigation which may lead to prosecution according to the judge's decision;
- prosecution is not brought about by the public health authorities, but is generally the responsibility of legal authorities.

"Yes" comments received:

- counterfeiting of medicines is considered by criminal law as a crime. Any activities or facts suspected as being a crime must be disclosed to the legal authorities;
- one member state: health authorities have same legal powers as police officers;
- one member state: the MoH/DRA has a penal section.

MoIP
Summary of comments received concerning legal powers:

- three member states: comments largely equivalent to comments for Q5;
- one member state: the MoH/DRA has a health police unit (therefore MoH/DRA and MoIP powers coincide);
- launch penal prosecution;
- administrative responsibility is provided for in the Code of Administrative Offences;
- investigation, statement (*constatation*).

Legal obligation to investigate cases: Yes = 43%; No = 43%; Missing = 14%.

"No" comments received:

- decisions to prosecute are taken in "the public interest".

"Yes" comments received:

- from the moment a complaint has been lodged.

MoJ
Summary of comments received concerning legal powers:

- seize products, bring cases to court via the public prosecutor;
- it is an offence to sell/produce counterfeit products under trademark law, copyright, design and patents, and trade descriptions law;
- seizure, sampling and confiscation ordered by judge if risk to public health. In the case of condemnation, the means for the crime can also be confiscated even if they are not in the possession of the condemned;
- launch penal prosecution;
- examine cases according to the Code of Administrative Offences (administrative committees) and Criminal Code (judicial bodies);
- seizure, prohibit activity, confiscate and apply fines (health law) (NB. A very detailed answer was provided by this respondent).

MoFTC
Summary of comments received concerning legal powers:

- entry, search, seize, detain products and documents, sampling/copying, arrest and destroy;
- EC Regulation 1383/2003: the rights holder has the ability to lodge an application to prohibit entry of counterfeit goods into the EU. Suspect counterfeit goods detained at borders by customs are inspected by the relevant rights holder who provides a witness statement confirming that the goods infringe their rights. On the basis of this statement, customs may seize the goods and

destroy them on completion of the case. The rights holder may prosecute the offender. If customs encounter suspect goods during the course of their checks, then the regulation also makes provision for them to contact the rights holder who does not hold a valid application inviting them to apply;

- stop the goods and notify the MoH/DRA;
- detention, test, bring administrative/criminal prosecution, confiscation and destruction.

Legal obligation to investigate cases: Yes = 33%; No/Not applicable = 50%; Missing = 17%.

"No/not applicable" comments received:

- customs will never prosecute an offender for an IPR crime. This is left to the rights holder.

"Yes" comments received:

- powers to bring prosecution and investigate administrative/crime cases.

NB. Where the response provided was "yes", the member state is not an EU member state.

MoET
Summary of comments received concerning legal powers:

- search premises, vehicles and ships; require information, copy documents, take samples, seize products, and bring cases to court via the public prosecutor;
- since counterfeiting and piracy are criminal offences, the police often join with trading standards officers (TSOs) and customs to develop co-ordinated approaches. Counterfeiting and piracy are arrestable offences and therefore the police have a duty to enforce the law. Trademark law imposes a duty on every local authority to enforce breaches. Trade descriptions law – TSOs have powers to make test purchases and to enter premises to inspect and seize goods and documents. These powers also apply under trademark law. Trademark law introduced a system of notification which allows trademark owners to notify customs of potentially suspect goods being imported into the country. This system continues under the revised trademark law. Similar provisions exist for other types of IPR infringement in the copyright, designs and patent law;
- concerning IPR issues, the Office of IPR elaborates/adapts regulations to fight counterfeiting;
- the national IPR institute in the cases of damage resulting from counterfeiting does not have the possibility of initiating a lawsuit. The MoET can only initiate a lawsuit if there is damage to the image of the nation and those responsible are foreign residents;
- the IPR code confers no powers on the administration, only the judiciary has powers.

10.2.3. Official powers of health authorities concerning counterfeit medicines

Member state survey: Q13 (MoH/DRA)

This question was directed only at the relevant MoH/DRAs.
Yes = 92%; No = 8%.

"Yes" comments received:

- as per Q5 – inspection: search premises, vehicles and ships; and request information, copy documents and take samples; enforcement: seize products and bring cases to court via the public prosecutor. Counterfeit pharmaceuticals are medicinal products by definition;
- yes, but not specific to the counterfeiting of a pharmaceutical product. We would use powers to tackle unlicensed manufacture, import and wholesale, etc. Copyright and patent laws could also be brought to bear by other ministries;
- yes, as defective medicinal products come under standard legislation relating to the control of the manufacture and marketing of medicinal products Otherwise, there are no specific counterfeiting crimes for medicinal products;
- investigation, adoption of precautionary measures, intervention, product withdrawal and application of administrative sanctions;
- law on medicines (control of quality, supply and prices) and pharmacy and poisons law;
- counterfeit medicines found in the official distribution chain or on the black market constitute medicines without a marketing authorisation. Consequently, seizure and judicial proceedings come under the legislation on medicines.
- member state 8 – see Q3 (law on medicines);
- OMCL, state pharmaceutical inspectorate;
- the MoH/DRA acts via specific health police who have official powers;
- the MoH/DRA inspectors and public health pharmacist inspectors are skilled at searching and identifying infractions of health product regulations. The MoH/DRA head can take all the necessary measures for sanitary policing (health law);
- stop the marketing of the products.

10.2.4. Sanctions for counterfeit medicine offences

Member state survey: Q4 (MoH/DRA), Q53 (MoIP), Q79 (MoJ) Q105 (MoFTC) and Q142 (MoET)

Table 19: Sanctions for counterfeit medicine offences (summary of responses)

Member state	MoH/DRA	MoIP	MoJ	MoFTC	MoET
1	Yes	Yes	No	No	Yes
2	No	No	No	No	Yes
3	No				
4	Yes				
5	No				
6	Yes	Unknown	Yes	No	No
7	No				
8	Yes	Yes	Yes	No	Yes
9	No	No	No	No	
10	Yes	Yes			
11	No	Yes	Yes	Yes	No
12	Yes				

MoH/DRA (medicines legislation): Yes = 50%; No = 50%.

"Yes" comments received:

- six years' imprisonment and/or penalty of up to €45 000 (law on financial offences);

- administrative sanctions of up to a fine of €1 million, product withdrawal, closure of premises, other sanctions (law on medicines);
- product seizure, imprisonment (from one month to one year) and/or a fine of between €2 500 and €75 000 (law on medicines);
- administrative and penal measures (law on medicines);
- if the risk to public health is proven, a prison term of between three and ten years for manufacture or distribution; and a fine of between €100 and €1 000 for selling and distributing (risk to public health article in Penal Code);
- prison term of up to three months and/or penalties. Also, the withdrawal of licences, that is wholesaler licences (the law on medicines – counterfeit medicines are not mentioned in particular, but the law can be used in cases involving them).

"No" comments received:

- no specific counterfeit offences exist under the law on medicines. The offences in relation to manufacturing of medicinal products also cover any illegal manufacture, into which category such counterfeiting would fall;
- no specific sanctions under the law on medicines but sanctions exist in the Code of Administrative Offences.

Result summary

- sanctions may apply specifically to counterfeit medicines in half of the member states (or may apply to counterfeit medicines if sanctions not specifically directed at them);
- where sanctions exist they are wide ranging and cover both administrative and penal sanctions;
- concerning legal bases, where legal sanctions apply they can be specified in the laws on medicines or the penal codes or both (sometimes the two different types of legislation cross-refer, sometimes not);
- product seizure is specifically mentioned in a few cases, but should be a minimal legal requirement;
- licence withdrawal may not be particularly relevant to offences involving counterfeit medicines;
- one law specifically refers to the "risk to public health" as a basis for imposing a level of sanctions.

MoIP (specific legislation (for example, police laws)): Yes = 58%; No = 28%; Unknown = 14%.

"Yes" comments received:

- the Penal Code and the law on medicines;
- as for Q4: if the risk to public health is proven, between three and ten years' imprisonment for manufacture and distribution; and a fine of between €100 and €1 000 for selling and distributing (risk to public health article in the Penal Code);
- three to five years' imprisonment and a fine of between €300 000 and €500 000 (IPR code, Penal Code and health law).

No comments were received in the case of either a "no" or "unknown" response.

MoJ (specific laws pertaining to courts): Yes = 50%; No = 50%.

"Yes" comments received:

- a prison term of between one month and one year and/or an administrative fine

of between €2 500 and €75 000;
* as for Q53: Penal Code and the law on medicines;
* as for Q53: imprisonment for between three months and five years, and a fine of between €300 000 and €500 000 (IPR code, Penal Code and health law).

No comments were received in the case of a "no" response.

MoFTC (specific finance/customs laws): Yes = 16%; No = 84%.

"Yes" comment received:

* customs code and common law.

"No" comment received:

* need to specify them in the customs code and make them applicable to all counterfeit goods.

MoET (commercial laws, including IPR and copyright laws, in particular patent law and trademark law): Yes = 60%; No = 40%.

"Yes" comments received:

* four years' imprisonment and/or a fine of up to €45 000;
* maximum sentence of ten years and/or unlimited fine (copyright and trademark law);
* up to three years' imprisonment, a fine of €65 000 (patent, trademark and unfair competition laws).

No comments were received in the case of a "no" response.

10.3. Legal provisions and sanctions concerning counterfeit and unlicensed medicines

2003 member state survey

10.3.1. Specific national legislation applicable to protect the patient against counterfeit medicinal products

2003 member state survey: Q1

The following table summarises the relevant specific national legislation.

Table 20: Specific national legislation applicable to protect the patient against counterfeit medicinal products (2003 member state survey)

Member state	Specific national legislation
4	The falsification of medicinal products is considered a crime and several articles in the Penal Code are related to this issue, in particular: "punished with imprisonment from six months to three years, penalty from six to eighteen months and disqualification from profession from one to three years ..."; and "those, that with the intention of dispensing or using counterfeit medicines in any way, giving them a truthful appearance and in this way put in danger human life or health".
6	Application of parts of national legislation (laws and regulations) and surveillance of the distribution chain prevents counterfeits from entering it. EC Regulation 2309/93, Directive 2001/83/EC and Directive 2001/82/EC have been implemented into national legislation: (i) law on medicinal products (definition of a medicinal product,

Member state	Specific national legislation
	compliance with pharmacopoeia, basis for regulation of importing, exporting, manufacturing, packaging, labelling, content, distribution, transport, advertising, etc);
	(ii) regulation on registration of medicinal products; (iii) regulation on manufacturing, wholesaling and dispensing of medicinal products (activity licence for manufacturing, (wholesale) distribution, storage, marketing, export; GMP, GDP, GCP and GLP); (iv) ministerial decision on GDP (1995): counterfeit products found in the distribution network (separate from other medicinal products and inform the MA holder and competent authority); (v) regulation on parallel importation of medicinal products for human use and parallel distribution of them for human and veterinarian use (2001): definitions and authorisation; (vi) regulation concerning hormonal, anti-hormonal, anabolic, beta-adrenergic, anti-infectious, anti-parasitic and anti-inflammatory substances (1974): authorisation for importation, exportation, manufacture, transport, sale, offer for sale, possession and dispensation of API; (vii) customs instructions based on EC Regulation 339/93 of 8 February 1993 on checks for conformity with the rules on product safety in the case of products imported from third countries; (viii) customs instructions based on Directive 89/104/EEC of 21 December 1988 to approximate the laws of the member states relating to trademarks; (ix) customs instructions based on EU Council Regulation 3295/94 of 22 December 1994 laying down measures concerning the entry into the Community and the export and re-export from the Community of goods infringing certain IPR.
7	There is no specific provision in legislation relating to medicines that mentions the recall of counterfeit products. However, medicines are always recalled based on protection of public health. The specific reasons for recall are based on the national law that adopted Articles 117 and 118 of Directive 2001/83/EC.
8	Law on Medicinal Products and Medicinal Devices: (i) manufacture: manufacturing licence (exceptions for magistral formula, officinal formula, own formula and manufacturer's own formula conforming to recognised pharmacopoeia); (ii) marketing authorisation: no MA needed for magistral formulations, individual preparations in accordance with the pharmacopoeia or any other recognised formula, individual dispensed preparations, clinical trial preparations, and medicinal products that cannot be standardised (small quantities of pharmacists' specialities of all categories and of preparations for hospital use are now exempt from MA); (iii) parallel imports: parallel imports or re-imports of medicinal products are possible and a provision exists for a simplified MA procedure for such products. This country is the first to create the preconditions for importing medicinal products in parallel from other countries without any corresponding rights. Nevertheless, certain clearly described requirements have to be met. The medicinal product must be already authorised in the country, the importation must come from an equivalent MA system, the labelling and medical information must comply with national regulations, safety and quality requirements have to be met and patent protection of the original applicant's preparation must have expired. Countries regarded as having comparable MA systems are EU member states, United States, Canada, Japan, Australia and New Zealand; (iv) importation, exportation and foreign trade: DRA approval is required

Member state	Specific national legislation
	for commercial importation and exportation of FPs and commercial trading of medicinal products in foreign countries. Exceptions are allowed for medical personnel engaged in cross-border work, international organisations and the importation of small quantities for personal use. Approval is granted if the necessary technical and operating conditions are met and a suitable quality assurance system is in place or if the applicant already possesses an establishment licence for manufacture or an establishment licence for the importation or for wholesale trade of medicinal products. Exportation of medicinal products or their foreign trade outside of the country is prohibited if they are prohibited in the destination country or if circumstances suggest that they could be intended for an illegal purpose; (v) mail order trade: in principle is prohibited. However, the law allows so-called direct dispatches under certain circumstances: practising direct dispatch requires a licence, a doctor's prescription must have been made out for the relevant medicinal product (even for those that are OTC) and there are no safety requirements that militate against it. Appropriate consultation and sufficient medical supervision of effectiveness must also be guaranteed; (vi) wholesale and retail: an establishment licence is required both for wholesaling and for retailing of medicinal products except for those freely on sale. The DRA issues wholesale approvals if the necessary technical and operating conditions are met and a suitable quality assurance system exists. Recognised GDP rules must be respected and these include not only compliance with the conditions of distribution and storage, but a system of traceability and recall of defective products.
12	In general, legislation is harmonised with EU regulations. To protect patients: all medicines legally sold have to have an MA or be produced in a pharmacy. If a wholesaler or a pharmacy detects a counterfeit medicinal product, they are obliged to report this to the DRA. The DRA will prohibit further sale of this product, and presumably send out a public warning regarding the potential hazard. Customers are allowed to bring medicines from other members of the EEA/EU or buy medicines by mail order or over the Internet from these countries. The premise is that the medicines are legally obtained, which means that the national legislation relies on the control in other member states.
13	Relevant sections of the law on medicines: (i) prohibitions to prevent deception (see Annex A); (ii) prohibition in respect of unsafe drugs (see Annex A); (iii) prohibition on placing it in the market; (iv) participation of customs offices; (v) supervision; (vi) penal provisions; (vii) obligation to obtain an MA; (viii) obligation to notify variations and renewal of the MA.
14	It is the intention of many of the provisions of the Act on Medicines to protect the patient against illegal, counterfeit or harmful medicinal products. Therefore, specific legislation is not needed.
15	There is no specific national legislation concerning counterfeit medicines. Drug law makes no provisions for such cases.

10.3.2. Specific national legislation concerning sanctions applied against responsible criminal persons or organisations for potential or proven health risks from counterfeit or unlicensed medicinal products

2003 member state survey: Q2

The following table summarises the relevant specific national legislation:

Table 21: Specific national legislation concerning sanctions against criminal persons/organisations for health risks from counterfeit or unlicensed medicinal products (2003 member state survey)

Member state	Specific national legislation
4	Administrative sanctions could be imposed, for example, on distributors obtaining medicines from non-authorised sources. Faults and sanctions are specified in the law on medicines.
6	Penalties: one month to one year's imprisonment and/or a fine of between €2 500 and €75 000 plus seizure (secondary packaging and leaflet counterfeiting); one month to five years' imprisonment and/or a fine of between €15 000 and €500 000 plus seizure (pure counterfeiting).
7	In order to protect public health, it is stated in the criminal law that whoever corrupts, falsifies, or reduces the therapeutic value of medical substances, and by doing so creates a life or physical integrity threatening condition, can be subjected to imprisonment from one to eight years. Negligent behaviour is also punished, up to three years. However, it is necessary to prove health risks, which means that, for example, the absence of compliance with GMP is not considered automatically to be subject to criminal punishment. On the other hand, the Law on Industrial Propriety Rights, which regulates patents and trademarks, punishes counterfeiting including the non-authorised reproduction or copy of registered medicines. This illegal behaviour is subject to imprisonment up to three years, to assure the protection of property rights.
8	The law on medicines makes the same distinction between offences and infringements as are made in the Penal Code. Offences are actions that endanger human health, and can lead to a penalty under the law as soon as human health is endangered. It is not necessary to show that anyone's health is endangered.[1] If anyone's health was touched, the provisions of the Penal Code and not the provisions of the law on medicines take effect, particularly those that cover causing death by negligence or with malice aforethought and those on assault and battery.[2] According to the law on medicines, possible penalties for offences include imprisonment or fines of up to €130 000.

---

1. Offences are criminal acts for which the Penal Code provides the penalty of imprisonment for periods of between three days and three years.
2. Other provisions of the Penal Code that could be relevant to the law on medicines are: the articles on dissemination of human illnesses, on falsification of goods and on falsification of official documents.

Member state	Specific national legislation
	If the responsible person acts in his professional capacity,[1] the level of the maximum penalty rises accordingly (imprisonment of up to five years and a fine of up to €330 000). As a violation of the provisions of the law on medicines can have serious consequences for public health, acting by negligence is also considered as an offence and the punishment shall be imprisonment for up to six months or a fine of up to €65 000. If the violation of the law is less serious, this is considered as an infringement which is punished by arrest or a fine of up to €33 000.[2] In case of adulteration of medicinal products, the Penal Code can also be applicable: its article on adulteration of merchandise and the penal provisions of the law on medicines on manufacturing, marketing and importing are applicable simultaneously. The law on medicines protects the patient's health and the Penal Code the patrimony. Under the title "Adulteration of merchandise", the Penal Code provides for imprisonment or a fine for anyone, who in order to deceive another in business dealings, manufactures merchandise whose actual market value is less than its appearance leads one to believe, particularly by counterfeiting or adulterating such merchandise, and importing, storing or distributing such merchandise. If the responsible person acts in his professional capacity, the sentence shall be imprisonment, on condition that that the offence does not fall under a more severe provision (for example, fraud).
12	Offences against the law on medicines can be prosecuted and a fine or prison sentence for three months or, in more serious cases, up to two years can be handed down. Attempted offences will be punished as if they had been committed. If a counterfeit medicinal product has caused health damage the responsible criminal can be punished according to penal law.
13	The penal provisions of the law on medicines. Administrative penalties are provided by the law on medicines and criminal penalties in certain cases that are defined in the criminal law are possible (for example, "danger to the public").
14	MoH regulation regarding the conditions and order for blocking and withdrawal of medicinal products from manufacturers, wholesalers, pharmacies, drugstores and health institutions.
15	The law on medicines stipulates only administrative measures (fines). Anyone who manufactures, distributes or sells counterfeit products could be made liable under the Penal Code.

10.3.3. Specific national legislation applicable in preventing the spread of counterfeit or unlicensed medicinal products to other countries

2003 member state survey: Q3

The following table summarises the relevant specific national legislation:

---

1. A person acting in his professional capacity, according to the Supreme Court, is a person who has already committed the crime several times with the intention of achieving a steady income from it, and when the conclusion has to be drawn from his activities that that he is prepared to commit a large number of crimes of the same kind.
2. Infringements are criminal acts for which the Penal Code provides the penalty of imprisonment for periods of between one day and three months, or a fine.

Table 22: Specific national legislation applicable in preventing the spread of counterfeit or unlicensed medicinal products to other countries (2003 member state survey)

Member state	Specific national legislation
4	There is no specific legislation. Customs pharmaceutical inspectors review all medicinal product exports verifying authenticity and legality of the source. In relation to sending medicines to other member states (not exports) it can only be done by legally authorised entities, which are obliged to be supplied from legitimate sources, verifying this legality.
6	In our country, exports of medicinal products are submitted for authorisation. Medicinal products for export fulfil the same requirements as medicinal products for the domestic market. If there is no MA then they should meet the requirements of the importing country (simplified procedure). All medicinal products without an MA have to be declared. The monitoring of certain APIs prevents diversion for illegal manufacturing and is based on: • Article 68 of Directive 2001/82/EC: only empowered persons in the member state possess or have under their control VMPs or substances which may be used as VMPs that have anabolic, anti-parasitic, anti-inflammatory, hormonal or psychotropic properties. The member state shall maintain registers of manufacturers and dealers permitted to be in possession of these substances, which may be used in the manufacture of VMPs. Registers for all in/out transactions; • Directive 96/22/EC concerning the prohibition of the use in stock farming of certain substances having a hormonal or thyrostatic action and of beta-agonists: Article 8: substances having thyrostatic, oestrogenic, androgenic or gestagenic action and beta-agonists: import, manufacture, storage, distribution, sale and use; possession restricted to authorised persons. Article 9: substances having thyrostatic, oestrogenic, androgenic or gestagenic action and beta-agonists: undertaking buying, producing, and marketing, and buying or producing VMPs. Registers for all in/out transactions.
7	Community Procedure for Handling Rapid Alerts and Recalls Arising from Quality Defects which includes not only quality defects but also recalls stemming from counterfeiting or fraud. There is a specific field on the template for these cases. This procedure is being adopted not only by the EU/EEA, but also by parties to MRAs. NB. It is, however, difficult to establish a balance between the secrecy involved in an investigational process and the assurance of public health when deciding to recall a medicine. In the case of a health risk involved, the "official" reason for recall may always be announced not as a counterfeit problem, but by identifying the specific quality defect involved.
8	See Q1 – paragraph concerning foreign trade.
12	The DRA can call a halt to all further sales, including exports to other countries. It is not obvious that the authorities can seize such products. But as long as the products are inside the legal sales channels we consider stopping further sales to be adequate in preventing the spread of the products.
13	The law on medicines: section on export.

Member state	Specific national legislation
14	As soon as the existence of counterfeit or unlicensed medicines is known the competent authority will take appropriate measures on the basis of the law on medicines to prevent the spread of these products to other countries (for example, seizure of the products, shut down of companies); but from our point of view it is also the obligation of importing countries to check incoming medicinal products in accordance with the legal requirements.
15	The DRA is not involved in the export of medicinal products. Customs deal with drug export. The DRA is fully involved in drug import. MA holder should receive a certificate in order to import medicinal products.

10.4. Extent of powers of enforcement related to suspected counterfeit medicines (concerning APIs, BPs and FPs)

Member state survey: Q44 (MoH/DRA), Q70 (MoIP) and Q128 (MoFTC)

This question was addressed to member state MoH/DRAs, MoIPs and MoFTCs, and Tables 23, 24 and 25 summarise the enforcement powers available to each type of authority respectively. The following code is provided for interpretation of the results.

Code for Tables 23, 24 and 25

Code	Type of power
A	Power of entry
B	Power of search or limited to inspection
C	Power to seize, detain products and documents
D	Power to take samples/copies (specify)
E	Power to stop imports, search for counterfeits and arrest suspected persons (state circumstances permitted)
F	Power to obtain confidential information held by other sources (for example, financial institutions, telecommunications, post and the Internet)
G	Power to initiate batch recall of pharmaceuticals which are suspected of being counterfeited (contaminated with counterfeits)
H	Power to destroy
I	Other

NB. For Q70 (MoIP) and Q128 (MoFTC) the type of power coding is the same as for Q44 except E is amended (power to stop concerns only persons) and G is omitted (power to initiate batch recall of pharmaceuticals which are suspected of being counterfeited).

The table overleaf presents the results obtained from MoH/DRAs.

Table 23: Extent of enforcement powers related to suspected counterfeit medicines (MoH/DRAs)

Member state	Powers									Basis/comments
	A	B	C	D	E	F	G	H	I	
1	Yes	Yes	Yes	Yes	Yes	No	Yes	Yes	No	E = all
2	Yes	Yes	Yes	Yes	No	Yes	Yes	Yes	No	H = through court order
3	Yes	Yes	Yes	Yes	Yes	Yes	Yes	No	No	D = by right with or without court warrant E = limited to illegal importations. Search for counterfeits at all times permitted, either by right or with court warrant. No power of arrest F = specified in medicinal product (prescription and control of supply) regulations G = standard recall protocols
4	Yes	Yes	Yes	Yes	Yes	No	Yes	Yes	No	A = solely in premises subject to health laws (manufacturers, wholesalers, community pharmacies, hospitals, etc.) B = as above C = it is possible to quarantine the products and to copy documents E = as per A and B plus detention or arrest require a warrant F = requires judicial order H = yes, albeit it is delayed until proceedings are finished
5	Yes	Yes	Yes	Yes	No	Yes	Yes	Yes	No	–
6	Yes	Yes	Yes	Yes	Yes	Yes	Yes	Yes	No	A = in all stocks, warehouses and manufacturing places (law on medicines, law on the smuggling of poisonous substances, soporifics, stupefiants, disinfectants or antiseptics) B = in all private premises only with order of the investigation judge

Member state	Powers									Basis/comments
	A	B	C	D	E	F	G	H	I	
										E = detainment of the suspected persons only by the police with order – non-authorised medicines (without an MA) or destined for companies and persons without authorisation F = by the public prosecutor except in the pre-phase of administrative investigation
7	Yes	Yes	Yes	Yes	Yes	No	Yes	Yes	No	All "yes" = national decrees A, B, C and D = on facilities not licensed by the MoH/DRA only with the IGAE or only on facilities authorised by the MoH/DRA
8	Yes	Yes	Yes	Yes	Yes	Yes	Yes	Yes	No	A = the law on medicines and MA regulations, the law on administrative penalties and regional procedures B = MA regulation C = the law on medicines, MA regulations and the law on administrative penalties D = MA regulations E = the law on medicines, and the law on administrative penalties F= the law on administrative penalties, and post and telecommunications legislation (direct telephone tap is not authorised) G = the law on medicines H = the law on medicines and the Penal Code
9	Yes	Yes	Yes	Yes	Yes	No	Yes	Yes	No	B = limited inspection C = retain products E = conduct search for false products

Member state	Powers									Basis/comments
	A	B	C	D	E	F	G	H	I	
10	Yes	No	Yes	Yes	Yes	No	Yes	Yes	No	A = Penal Code, standard police rules, ministry regulation C and D = ministry regulation G = indirect justification H = supervised control by police upon request of the MoH/DRA
11	No	Yes	Yes	Yes	?	?	Yes	?	?	B, C, D and G = public health law
12	No	Yes	No	Yes	No	No	No	No	No	B = inspection D = take samples

The table below presents the results obtained from the MoIPs.

Table 24: Extent of enforcement powers related to suspected counterfeit medicines (MoIPs)

Member state	Powers									Basis/comments
	A	B	C	D	E	F	G	H	I	
1	Yes	Yes	Yes	Yes	Yes	No	–	Yes	No	–
2	Yes	Yes	Yes	Yes	No	Yes	–	Yes	No	H = through court order
6	–	–	–	–	–	–	–	–	–	Competences authorised by the Penal Code
8	Yes	Yes	Yes	Yes	Yes	Yes	–	Yes	No	A, B, C, D and E = the law on administrative penalties F = the law on administrative penalties, post and telecommunications legislation (direct telephone tap is not authorised) H = the Penal Code
9	Yes	Yes	Yes	Yes	Yes	Yes	–	No	No	–
10	Yes	No	Yes	Yes	Yes	No	–	Yes	No	Yes = a counterfeiting case may be the cause for opening a police investigation (Penal Code), so all the measures under Q70 and Q71 may be authorised
11	Yes	Yes	Yes	Yes	Yes	Yes	–	No	No	–

The table overleaf presents the results obtained from the MoFTCs.

Table 25: *Extent of enforcement powers related to suspected counterfeit medicines (MoFTCs)*

Member state	Powers									Basis/comments
	A	B	C	D	E	F	G	H	I	
1	Yes	Yes	Yes	Yes	Yes	Yes	–	Yes	No	See Q44
2	No	Yes	Yes	Yes	Yes	Yes	–	Yes	No	B = examine goods and search premises sections of customs law requires writ or search warrant C = import and export sections of customs law D, F and H = customs law E = customs law, including section on arrest
6	Yes	Yes	Yes	Yes	Yes	Yes	–	Yes	No	–
8	No	No	Yes	Yes	Yes	No	–	No	No	Yes = in the framework of import/border controls
9	Yes	Yes	Yes	Yes	Yes	Yes	–	Yes	No	A = where goods are kept B = in the case of criminal activity investigation. E = criminal case
11	Yes	Yes	Yes	Yes	Yes	Yes	–	Yes	No	A = Articles 63 and 64 of the Customs Code (access to private and professional premises). In all cases the powers do only permit the search and the verification of a customs delict of a counterfeit mark/brand If the medicine is protected by a patent or supplementary protection certificate: –detainment, EU Council Regulation 1383/2003 –denunciation of the case to the judicial authorities B = Article 64 of the Customs Code: power to visit and seize at home/in premises – see above comments C = Article 323, paragraph 2, of the Customs Code (seizure of goods) – see comments above D = Article 9-3 of EC Regulation 1383/2003. However, the modalities of the sampling are not

Member state	Powers									Basis/comments
	A	B	C	D	E	F	G	H	I	
										specified; a decree is being elaborated E = Article 323, paragraph 3: power to arrest the offender where an offence of brand counterfeiting is under way F = Article 65 of the Customs Code: communication rights of the customs agents H = if there is brand counterfeiting and the goods have been confiscated for the benefit of the state or if they have been abandoned

10.5. Judicial procedures and legal action against medicine counterfeiters

The questions under this section were addressed solely to MOJs.

10.5.1. Existing procedures outside judicial proceedings for settling counterfeit medicine offences

Member state survey: Q89, Q90 and Q91 (MoJ)

Yes = 84%; No = 16%.

Table 26 below summarises the situation:

Table 26: Sanctions, decision-making authorities and procedures for settling counterfeit medicines offences

Member state	Yes/no	Type of sanction/ other means	Decision-making authority	Procedure
1	Yes	Fines, confiscation of products	Public prosecutor within limits set by the Board of Prosecutors	No specific procedure
2	No	–	N/A	N/A
6	Yes	Administrative fine of between €2 500 and €75 000	Juridical official in the Ministry of Social Affairs, Public Health and Environment is designated to be the expert for this purpose	See Note 1 below
8	Yes	See the law on medicines	The MoH/DRA and regional authorities within their domain of competence	Law on medicines and law on administrative procedures

Member state	Yes/no	Type of sanction/ other means	Decision-making authority	Procedure
9	Yes	By imposition of fines	–	–
11	Yes	None specified	These procedures are relevant to the competence of the director general of customs	

Note to Table 26: one respondent provided the following detailed reply on this subject:

In case of offences against the medicines legislation, or its regulations to enforce the legislation, the appointed judge to the Ministry of Social Affairs, Public Health and Environment may fix a sum the voluntary payment of which may allow the avoidance of public legal action. In case of refusal to pay and also in the case where the appointed judge does not set out any proposal for a payment, the file will be submitted to the public prosecutor.

There will be an annual report on the results of the activities requested in the preceding paragraph.

The sum of money the payment of which permits an avoidance of public legal action must neither be lower than the fine foreseen for the breaking of the concerned law nor higher than the defined maximum.

In the case of the occurrence of further offences (breaking of the law), the sum of money, the payment of which permits an avoidance of public legal action, accumulates, without it being allowed to exceed twice the maximum foreseen in the preceding paragraphs.

In the case of further offences within three years after the payment of the sum (which permits avoidance of public legal action and which was set out for breaking the law and its enforcing regulations), the sum may be doubled. The sum of these payments is higher for additional proportions, which are also foreseen by the Penal Code and increased where necessary for reimbursing the costs of expertise.

The sum is transferred to a particular account of the Ministry of Social Affairs, Public Health and Environment. This account serves to support the costs of general pharmaceutical inspection, the rules of which are set out by the state. In as much these rules are not established, the provisions of the state for accounting are in force.

10.5.2. Legal action (criminal proceedings and penalties) against medicine counterfeiters

Member state survey: Q94, Q95, Q96 and Q97 (MoJ)

Table 27: Authority and decision-making body responsible for criminal proceedings

Member state	Responsible authority	Decision-making body
1	Office of Public Prosecution	Individual public prosecutors
2	The MoH/DRA for the law on medicines and the police for other proceedings	The MoH/DRA use in-house lawyers on behalf of the MoH, and the police use the state prosecution service on behalf of the Minister of the Interior
6	The public health minister and the public prosecutor. In all cases of the non-payment of the administrative fine as well where the juridical official has not formulated a proposal for payment	The public health minister and the public prosecutor
8	The MoH/DRA or regional authority instruction judges for the counterfeit	
9	Criminal investigation bodies of the Ministry of the Interior	Specified in the Code of Criminal Procedure

Member state	Responsible authority	Decision-making body
11	Public prosecutor and rights holder Following the initiation of a civil action by the owner of the patent (IPR code), the public prosecutor initiates penal procedures (Penal Code). In the field of counterfeit trademarks, the rights holder may also make his claim before the correctional tribunal	Public prosecutor and investigational judge The public prosecutor (Penal Code) and the investigational judge (Penal Code) are both qualified to take decisions on penal prosecution

Existence of a specific prosecution policy for counterfeiters of medicines:

No = 67%; Unknown = 33%.

As regards whether counterfeiting of medicines is considered and prosecuted as an organised crime, one member state responded "yes" and one member state responded "yes" depending on the scale and context.

Is forfeiture incorporated in the national prosecution policy?

Yes = 84%; No = 16%.

"Yes" comments received:

- forfeiture of proceeds of crime, for example, bank accounts, cars, boats, houses, etc.;
- the law on proceeds of crime and the forfeiture clause of the law on medicines;
- in the case of condemnation, the judge may pronounce a confiscation order on the objects of the infraction that either served or were destined for the crime or that resulted in it, even if they are not the property of the condemned;
- Penal Code;
- Criminal Code (on crime committed by officials).

Which general principles apply concerning the burden of proof?

Table 28: Types of principle applying concerning the burden of proof

Member state	Type of principle					Comment
	A	B	C	D	E	
1	No	No	No	No	No	None
2	No	No	No	Yes	No	Yes = burden of proof on the prosecution
6	No	No	No	Yes	No	Yes = burden of proof is on the prosecution
8	No	No	No	Yes	–	Yes = Maxime of investigation and official maxime
9	–	–	–	–	–	–
11	Yes	No	No	Yes	No	A = articles of the Law on Intellectual Property Rights refer to the possibility to revert the burden of proof in the field of the counterfeiting of a product applying to the procedures to obtain a patent. More generally, the jurisprudence assumes the validity of a patent. In customs matters the person who holds a counterfeit commodity is held liable for fraud (Customs Code) D = the burden of proof is on the plaintiff/ prosecutor

Table code

Code	Type of principle
A	Inverted burden of proof
B	Shared burden of proof
C	Protection of whistleblowers
D	Other principles
E	Exceptions

10.6. IPR relating to medicines counterfeiting

Three related sequential studies were conducted to examine IPR and criminal law in the context of medicines counterfeiting. They are as follows:

10.6.1. IPR and criminal law concerning counterfeit medicines comparative study

The first study commissioned by the Ad hoc Group on Counterfeit Medicines attempts to establish a synoptic view of the current situation of the sanctions existing when certain IPR are violated in the territory of each of the member states of the Council of Europe. The selected IPR are the rights resulting from patent and trademark law, as these are of greatest significance in this field and best suited to be involved in concrete judicial cases against medicine counterfeiters.

The manufacturing or the sale of counterfeit medicines call for criminal sanctions against their authors when these medicines are protected by patent or trademark rights. Violations of these rights appear to be very variably sanctioned over the whole territory defined by the 46 member states of the Council of Europe. With respect to patent rights' violations, 11 member states do not provide for any criminal sanction at all and nine for only mild prison sentences of less than one year. Only 11 member states provide for maximum fines greater than €10 000. As a whole, only 17 member states appear to possess deterrent sanctions composed of imprisonment and/or fines.

With respect to trademark violations, eight member states do not provide for such criminal sanctions at all, 18 for only mild prison sentences of less than one year. Only 14 member states provide for maximum fines greater than €10 000. As a whole, only 26 member states appear to possess deterrent sanctions composed of imprisonment and/or fines.

Chart 4: Criminal sanctions for infringement of patent and/or trademark law in the 46 member states of the Council of Europe

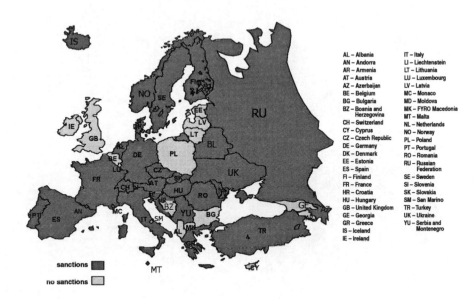

Chart 5: Criminal sanctions for infringement of patent law in the 46 member states of the Council of Europe

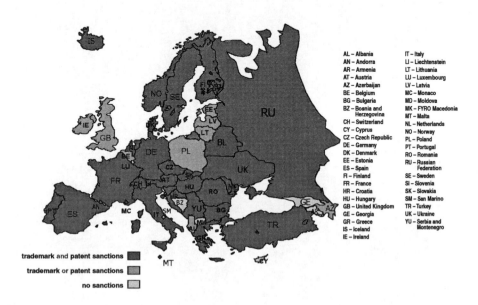

Chart 6: Criminal sanctions for infringement of trademark law in the 46 member states of the Council of Europe

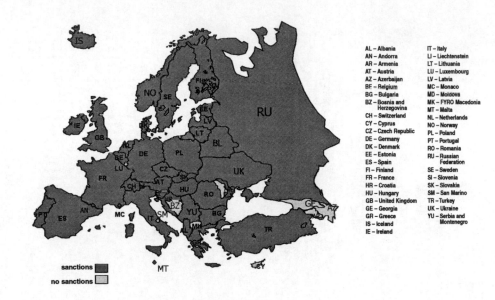

Chart 7: Prison sentences for infringement of patent law in the 46 member states of the Council of Europe

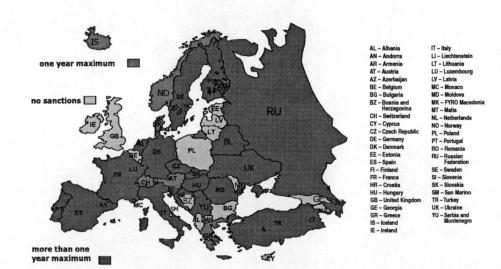

Chart 8: Prison sentences for infringement of patent law in the 46 member states of the Council of Europe

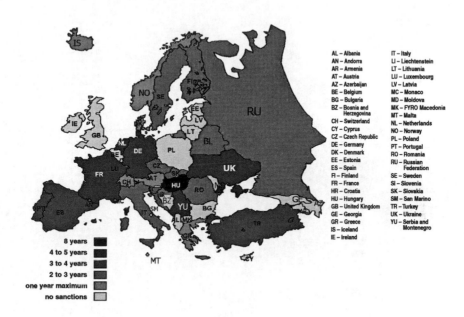

AL – Albania
AN – Andorra
AR – Armenia
AT – Austria
AZ – Azerbaijan
BE – Belgium
BG – Bulgaria
BZ – Bosnia and Herzegovina
CH – Switzerland
CY – Cyprus
CZ – Czech Republic
DE – Germany
DK – Denmark
EE – Estonia
ES – Spain
FI – Finland
FR – France
HR – Croatia
HU – Hungary
GB – United Kingdom
GE – Georgia
GR – Greece
IS – Iceland
IE – Ireland

IT – Italy
LI – Liechtenstein
LT – Lithuania
LU – Luxembourg
LV – Latvia
MC – Monaco
MD – Moldova
MK – FYRO Macedonia
MT – Malta
NL – Netherlands
NO – Norway
PL – Poland
PT – Portugal
RO – Romania
RU – Russian Federation
SE – Sweden
SI – Slovenia
SK – Slovakia
SM – San Marino
TR – Turkey
UK – Ukraine
YU – Serbia and Montenegro

8 years
4 to 5 years
3 to 4 years
2 to 3 years
one year maximum
no sanctions

Chart 9: Prison sentences for infringement of trademark law in the 46 member states of the Council of Europe

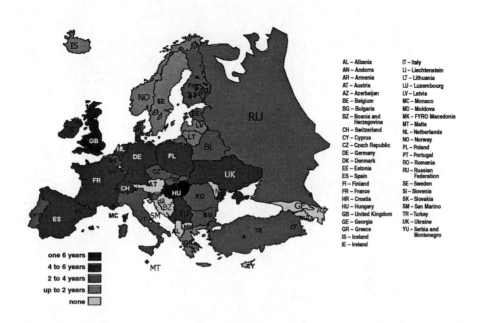

AL – Albania
AN – Andorra
AR – Armenia
AT – Austria
AZ – Azerbaijan
BE – Belgium
BG – Bulgaria
BZ – Bosnia and Herzegovina
CH – Switzerland
CY – Cyprus
CZ – Czech Republic
DE – Germany
DK – Denmark
EE – Estonia
ES – Spain
FI – Finland
FR – France
HR – Croatia
HU – Hungary
GB – United Kingdom
GE – Georgia
GR – Greece
IS – Iceland
IE – Ireland

IT – Italy
LI – Liechtenstein
LT – Lithuania
LU – Luxembourg
LV – Latvia
MC – Monaco
MD – Moldova
MK – FYRO Macedonia
MT – Malta
NL – Netherlands
NO – Norway
PL – Poland
PT – Portugal
RO – Romania
RU – Russian Federation
SE – Sweden
SI – Slovenia
SK – Slovakia
SM – San Marino
TR – Turkey
UK – Ukraine
YU – Serbia and Montenegro

one 6 years
4 to 6 years
2 to 4 years
up to 2 years
none

101

Chart 10: Fines for infringement of patent law in the 46 member states of the Council of Europe

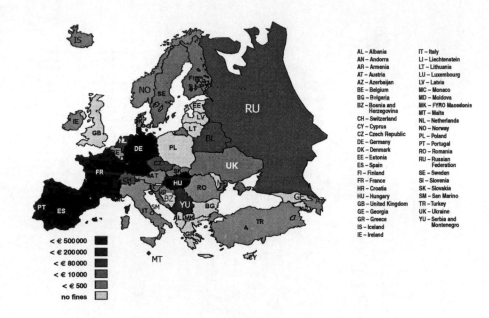

Chart 11: Fines for infringement of trademark law in the 46 member states of the Council of Europe

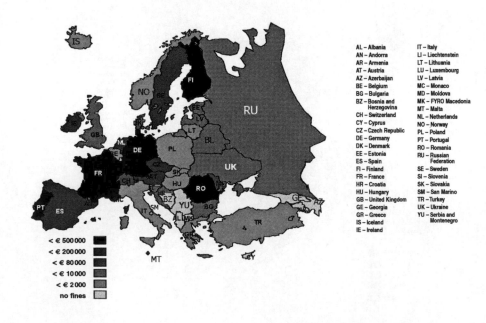

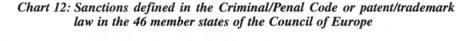

Chart 12: Sanctions defined in the Criminal/Penal Code or patent/trademark law in the 46 member states of the Council of Europe

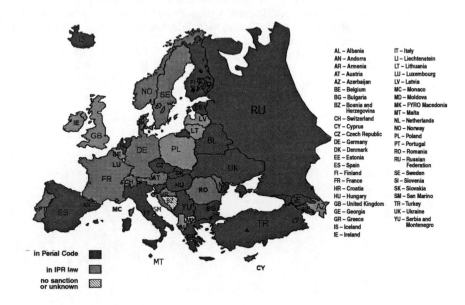

AL – Albania
AN – Andorra
AR – Armenia
AT – Austria
AZ – Azerbaijan
BE – Belgium
BG – Bulgaria
BZ – Bosnia and Herzegovina
CH – Switzerland
CY – Cyprus
CZ – Czech Republic
DE – Germany
DK – Denmark
EE – Estonia
ES – Spain
FI – Finland
FR – France
HR – Croatia
HU – Hungary
GB – United Kingdom
GE – Georgia
GR – Greece
IS – Iceland
IE – Ireland

IT – Italy
LI – Liechtenstein
LT – Lithuania
LU – Luxembourg
LV – Latvia
MC – Monaco
MD – Moldova
MK – FYRO Macedonia
MT – Malta
NL – Netherlands
NO – Norway
PL – Poland
PT – Portugal
RO – Romania
RU – Russian Federation
SE – Sweden
SI – Slovenia
SK – Slovakia
SM – San Marino
TR – Turkey
UK – Ukraine
YU – Serbia and Montenegro

in Penal Code ■
in IPR law ▨
no sanction or unknown ▨

10.6.2. Proposals for specific patent and trademark infringement claims pertaining to counterfeiting of medicines

The study presented under Section 10.6.1 does not take into consideration the quality of enforcement in member states. Some states may provide for sanctions which, however, are difficult or slow to implement by the courts.

In addition, the sanctions reported in the present study of course do not apply to counterfeit drugs which are no longer protected by a patent or a certificate of supplementary protection. Consequently, it would appear that generic drugs are particularly badly protected by IPR in their present form.

The next step could be a study of the ability of standard patent claims to be interpreted or extended in order to cope with the different types of counterfeit drugs, whenever a patent protection still exists.

If the latter study were to conclude that the patent claims system does not provide enough protection to brand name pharmaceutical companies, another study could be envisaged to set out a possible basis for a new kind of IPR to be created, providing the possibility of deterring organised criminal counterfeiters of drugs at least by appropriate criminal sanctions. This new kind of IPR could in particular relay patent rights when these expire, and benefit to and activation by generic pharmaceutical companies.

103

10.6.3. Model basis of newly proposed IPR for fighting manufacturers of counterfeit medicines

This third study attempts to define the basis of new IPR which would be expressly developed to fight against manufacturers of counterfeit drugs. This study will comprise an exploration of the different possible starting points which would justify the introduction of such new rights.

11. Adequacy of legal/judicial/administrative systems for dealing with counterfeit medicines – The authority perspective

Adequacy of the legislation and/or administrative structures to prevent and prosecute counterfeit medicines

Member state survey: Q46 (MoH/DRA), Q72 (MoIP), Q98 (MoJ), Q132 (MoFTC) and Q152 (MoET)

This question was addressed to all relevant ministry/authority types in the member state survey.

MoH/DRA: Yes = 42%; No = 50%; Missing = 8%.

Of the six MoH/DRAs who replied "yes", no answers were given as to why the current legislative and/or administrative structures were adequate, except for one respondent who stated that there was a lack of awareness of this issue in their country as the counterfeit medicine problem is relatively unknown in general.

In terms of "no" responses, the following summary of answers is provided:

- one MoH/DRA attempted unsuccessfully to get legislation changed on two occasions over the past ten years;
- there is a need for national legislation to provide for specific counterfeiting prohibitions relating to medicinal products;
- there is a need for regional legislation in this area to give a broad, effective and harmonious approach;
- one MoH/DRA has recently made proposals for amending its national legislation to include counterfeiting prohibitions; offences and penalties are under consideration;
- there is a need to introduce both tougher and specific penalties/sanctions for distributing counterfeit medicines, including imprisonment;
- a regulatory definition of counterfeit medicines is necessary, particularly as the consequences are serious;
- the shortage of personnel is a handicap for ensuring prevention and pursuit;
- there is a need to create a specific office dealing with this issue among relevant national professional associations.

MoIP: Yes = 57%; No = 29%; Missing = 14%.

As regards the "yes" responses received, no answers were given as to why the current legislative and/or administrative structures are adequate.

In terms of "no" responses received, the following summary of responses is provided:

- there is a need for a specific definition of counterfeit medicines;
- there should be a specific crime;

- specific sanctions should apply; it should be an arrestable offence with tougher penalties;
- there is a need to create a specific office dealing with this issue among relevant national professional associations.

MoJ: Yes = 66%.

One specific comment was provided by a "yes" respondent as follows:

Although legislative instruments for ensuring prevention and prosecution of counterfeit medicines exist, there is no organised and multidisciplinary co-operation between the different competent services concerning:

- information exchange;
- strategic and operational analysis of this criminal phenomenon;
- an RAS;
- regular contacts between the competent authorities and the pharmaceutical industry.

MoFTC: Yes = 17%; No = 33%; Unknown or Missing = 50%.

Comments received were:

- customs do not prosecute counterfeiters as this is left to the individual rights holders. As a department, customs "police" the movement of counterfeit goods and take appropriate action as required under EU regulations;
- there is a need to (i) identify gaps (for example, regulatory gaps as regards importation/exportation/transit/other), and (ii) modify national and international legislation and/or make changes in administrative procedures.

MoET: Yes = 60%.

The "yes" responses stated that there would seem to be a consensus that the penalties are sufficient but they are not best placed to answer a question on prevention.

The "no" responses state that a duty to report the falsification of such products should be introduced. In this respect, at the international level, co-operation, in particular concerning the exchange of information, should be strengthened.

Comments on the consistency of answers from the relevant member state's internal agencies/authorities/ministries

One member state's ministries all replied "yes" to this question, whilst another's all replied "yes" with the exception of the MoFTC. These two member states appear to have an effective legislative and administrative system in place to deal with counterfeit medicines. The situation with the other member states is very unclear.

12. Adequacy of existing countermeasures to prevent medicines counterfeiting and public health damage due to counterfeit medicines– The industry and wholesaler perspective

12.1. Are the concerned authorities' current awareness, initiatives and systems in place (for example, inspection) adequate to prevent/fight medicines counterfeiting?

Stakeholder survey: Q12

Yes = 23%; Yes/No = 3%; No = 68%; Missing = 6%.

Less than 25% of respondents consider that the current awareness of the concerned authorities, and their initiatives and systems are adequate to prevent/fight the counterfeiting of pharmaceuticals. Where a positive response was given no comments were provided as the question did not ask for them. Where a negative response was given, the following comments were provided:

- the DRA is more reactive than proactive;
- there is a lack of awareness, in particular at the national level. The EU is "looking into" the issue but not taking any concrete action. The issue is taken more seriously in the United States;
- insufficient legal basis and a lack of resources for inspections;
- health authorities are often understaffed to carry out inspections or test purchasing;
- the establishment of special "counterfeit" authorities with close contacts is required;
- co-operation with customs would improve the situation;
- they are only beginning. It will take a while for the whole supply chain to be fully analysed and remedies implemented;
- awareness does exist (first step) but the means dedicated to the fight are clearly not sufficient;
- a clear partnership between industry and the concerned authority is required – for example, shared information and best practice/guidelines for anti-counterfeit activities;
- invariably they are civil servants, you need investigators who are retired from law enforcement agencies or properly trained to look for criminality, and not waiting for it to jump up and bite them;
- awareness in countries without a problem (so far) is rising; however, up to now this is often not sufficient, but the situation seems to be improving;

- more training of law enforcement agents; liaison with law enforcement and regulatory groups; and proactive inquiries and inspection programmes by regulatory groups are required;
- as regards API counterfeiting, absolutely not. Other than in the United States, the issue is largely ignored;
- the authorities are not, or not sufficiently, involved;
- there is a lack of awareness in national and EU health authorities;
- lack of resources and legal powers mean little action;
- "we think that awareness of this problem is low because the problem still does not exist in our country. Wholesalers buy the products directly from industry. There is very little volume in the parallel market so the chance for counterfeit producers to step into the legal distribution chain of drugs is very small";
- European price levels/different prices in local markets;
- there does not appear to be a co-ordinated approach across national boundaries. Regulatory bodies appear to lack the resource to follow up reports;
- as no cases have been reported we assume that no cases have been found;
- the authorities are conscious of the counterfeiting problem but the action taken is not sufficient. They have to be very careful with the new import/export firms. They should control their supply system;
- no experiences of it;
- the issue has not been put on the national agenda.

12.2. What is needed to implement and improve communication between industry/wholesaler/trade firms and authorities so as to allow action against counterfeit medicines (suspect or proven counterfeit medicine cases)?

Stakeholder survey: Q11

Table 29: What is needed to implement and improve communication between industry/wholesaler/trade firms and authorities so as to allow action against counterfeit medicines?

	Number of respondents	
	Yes	Missing
Administrative structures	67%	33%
Co-operation agreements (best practices codes, protocols)	67%	33%
Information exchange networks	70%	30%
Communication networks	63%	37%
Other: specify measures	30%	70%

NB. There were no "no" answers provided for any means of improving communication.

Administrative structures	Number of respondents
Co-ordinating/communication structures: • establishment of a special organisation acting in close co-operation with customs authorities or even including customs functions; • a co-ordination structure comprising members of health agencies, WHO, customs and police; • across boundaries as well as within the country, and clear collaboration among regulators, health authorities, police and industry; • central associations (industry, pharmacists and wholesalers); • one authority for all federal states in Germany; • international watch unit.	7
DRAs: • use/strengthen existing structure of DRAs; • specific anti-counterfeit department in the DRA.	4
Health inspection/inspectorate	3
Reporting systems: • Internet-based reporting initiated by authorities; • established and obligatory reporting channel set out in the legal framework.	2
Investigative authorities	2
Customs and Excise	2
Local health authorities	1
Police	1
Public prosecution	1
Tax authorities	1
Trading standards	1
API inspection department(s) (of a size proportional to the extent of the regulations, making worldwide API inspection a routine matter instead of a rarity. In addition, dedicated staff that serve as a focal point for counterfeit matters/information)	1

Co-operation agreements (best practices codes, protocols)	Number of respondents
Supply/distribution agreements, quality agreements Service level agreements Delivery agreements between industry and wholesalers, and wholesalers and hospital/community pharmacies	3
To be discussed among the various stakeholders/to be defined	2
International and European co-operation agreements with all countries so as to identify and punish the source of counterfeits (deterrent sanctions), including close co-operation with pharmaceuticals firms	1
Close liaison between industry and authorities with a clear legislative framework	1
Instant quarantine of counterfeit batches and operations by customs, police and drug inspectors after notifying the genuine company and speedy follow-up of the issue. Also prophylactically (might depend on existing legislation in the countries)	1

Co-operation agreements (best practices codes, protocols)	Number of respondents
Agreements to exchange information among inspectorates all over the world regarding counterfeiting	1
At international level, for example, APIs to enjoy real application of ICH Q7a, including Article 17 (communication on the danger)	1
Respect of the best practices and new procedures	1
Among authorities of all countries (for example, Internet sites in other countries)	1

Information exchange networks	Number of respondents
As per administrative structures or co-operation agreements' (best practices' codes and protocols) survey sections	5
Use existing structure of control agencies	5
Local health authority, pharmaceutical associations and a special organisation Local health care authorities in co-operation with industry and wholesalers	2
Use industry associations. Authorities to take account of the sensitive nature of the information, by providing for confidential consultation groups Producers' associations	2
Inspectorate	1
National: for example, within the pharmaceutical association; also international, for example, via information exchange (on organisational measures, new security features and experience with anti-counterfeiting measures) between pharmaceutical associations (use ICH process guide for industry)	1
Health authorities	1
Clear structure and exchange of information among regulatory bodies and industry with a centralised database	1
Commonwealth, United Nations, World Intellectual Property Organization, WHO and World Trade Organization feeding into the European Commission	1
Transparency and public access to information on counterfeiting activities	1
Regional authorities/RPs (*Regierungspräsidium*)	1
Commission for pharmaceuticals (*Arzneimittelkommission*)	1
Creation of a specific DRA department for counterfeit medicines	1

Communication networks	Number of respondents
As per administrative structures, co-operation agreements (best practices' codes and protocols) or information exchange networks' survey sections	2
Internet database	2
Industry-wholesalers-pharmacies	2
National networks integrated into a European network, which again is part of an international network	1

Communication networks	Number of respondents
Install field alert system along the lines of the one for quality defects	1
Internet platforms with password restricted access, newsletters and guidance papers	1
Health authorities and associations of pharmaceutical industries	1
International collaboration where counterfeiting has occurred offshore, for example, the Internet	1
Mainly co-operation regarding awareness raising in public	1
Anti-Counterfeiting Group, AIM (European Brands Group), Pharmaceutical Security Institute, REACT and EFPIA	1
For example, in APIC meetings, namely within industry	1
Starting with health authorities in each country	1
DRAs	1

Other: specify measures	Number of respondents
Legislation which allows prosecution and punitive measures against counterfeiters	1
Mandatory training courses, and communication among health professionals and customers	1
Better co-operation between industry and authorities and among authorities themselves at national and international level	1
Internet pharmacy sales: clearer definition of which laws have been broken, and where	1
Assurance that cases are only made public after mutual agreement; no tort law actions and liability claims against genuine companies	1
Hotline to quickly communicate counterfeit situations to authority departments that can take immediate action	1
Stop acceptance of APIs without inspection (for example, with only a CoS and a statement of commitment without meaning)	1
Strict control of permits for production and wholesaling	1

Other comments received:

- a regulatory inspection group would be best placed to manage the situation. It could improve links with retail pharmacies;
- it is difficult at this stage to give a concrete answer to the question, for the simple reason that few or no provisions exist at the moment. To improve communication, what is generally needed is:
  - increased awareness of the problem;
  - exchange of information;
  - clarity and openness, on the one hand, whilst taking into account confidentiality where necessary, on the other hand;
  - government(s) to set up a central body (possibly within the health inspectorate) for the specific purpose of dealing with counterfeits;
  - adoption and enforcement of relevant law, and tackling the issue at European and international level. It is not a national problem, international co-operation is required;

- one respondent that provided a "no" response to the question stated that their country is a small country and interactions with the regulatory authority are excellent;

- a special authority needs to be linked with customs through, for example, random sampling of incoming products at customs via database-supported product descriptions;

- the FDA has taken a major step forward in dealing with the issue;

- public awareness of the problems of purchasing medicines over the Internet and suspicion of cheap products needs to be increased. Tighter controls are needed over pharmaceutical destruction channels. These controls need to be closely aligned with final payment mechanisms;

- what are also need are the success stories of enforcement bodies in tracing counterfeiters and penalising them severely, not only through civil but also criminal law;

- appropriate legislation is also needed to allow sharing of information among administrative bodies and rights holders, and among the different administrative bodies both at national and European level. The ability to do this is severely curtailed under current UK legislation;

- due to the almost worldwide lack of attention given to API counterfeiting (the United States is an exception), all matters relating to this question need to be developed almost from scratch. In a more general sense – also in view of the very serious nature of the criminal activity of counterfeiting pharmaceuticals and in view of the serious impact (both potential and actual) on the health of unsuspecting victims – there should be very intensive co-operation and communication on pharmaceutical counterfeiting between ministries of health and ministries of justice. This should include matters concerning the counterfeiting practices within the API market;

- for the time being, some authorities' declarations/communications are pushing in the wrong direction, for example, the French Ministry of Finances set a goal of a 50% price difference between the original drug product and the generic, stating that the current difference (an average of 28%) is not satisfactory. Such positions push in the direction of more counterfeiting, cheap but dangerous raw materials and APIs from uncontrolled origins;

- there is a need to improve communication and dissemination of information among the national regulatory bodies, and for it to be passed down through the supply chain;

- some manufacturers can be reluctant to acknowledge or act upon reports of counterfeit products, because of the potential adverse effect on their business; this reluctance needs to be overcome in the interests of all those involved in the legitimate supply of pharmaceuticals;

- due to continuing investigations, we cannot complete this answer;

- information not available;

- leave the possibility of selling medicines only to patented and controlled actors in the legal supply chain;

- it is important to be informed of known cases, in order to avoid ignorance. All parts of the distribution chain must be aware of the risks, and institute the necessary control measures.

12.3. What should be improved in the current systems and provisions to effectively fight medicines counterfeiting?

Stakeholder survey: Q13

Table 30: Desired improvements in current systems and provisions to effectively fight medicines counterfeiting (summary of responses)

Type of improvement	Number of respondents		
	Yes	Yes/no	Missing
Inspection	80%		20%
Enforcement	57%		43%
Penalisation	67%		33%
Security systems for medicines (APIs) to differentiate genuine from counterfeit medicines	67%		33%
Traceability systems for pharmaceuticals	57%	3%	40%
Other systems including systems to identify, monitor, prevent and fight the counterfeiting of pharmaceuticals	53%		47%

Recommendations to improve inspections
Increase number of inspections
Inspection of GDPs at wholesalers, distributors, etc.
Continued organised test buying, and sampling at companies/wholesalers under suspicion
Foreign manufacturers of APIs: increase number of inspections
Need to build in preventative measures as opposed to simple inspections
Systematic inspection, including some by independent international bodies
Audit within supply chain, point of sale authentication, and tighter distribution network and pedigree
Training
More testing in particular of products in focus
Proactive enquiries and inspection programmes by regulatory groups; more realistic timetable for inspection of suspect/seized goods by rights holders
Mandatory inspection of APIs worldwide
Safeguarded controlled processing flows of materials
Consider evaluating and inspecting before granting a CoS or accepting EDMF documentation
Import authorities
The smaller wholesalers in particular should be inspected more often and more thoroughly
Include other circuits (parallel)
Spot checks on imported drugs and analysis, as well as visual control of packaging. These controls should be ensured by each wholesaler
Stricter rules for production and wholesaling activities

Recommendations to improve inspections
Internet (increase the control of foreign parcels)
Control compliance with present regulations
Each actor in the legal supply chain must be controlled at least once a year
Focus on traceability documentation

Recommendations to improve enforcement
Strengthen measures
Definitions in the crime sheet should be based on the intention to introduce or sell counterfeited drugs
Clear rules for checking and reporting by distributors, and enforcement by audits/inspections
Stronger enforcement
Particularly important in Asian, African and Middle Eastern countries
Clearer definition in law and tighter control of secondary wholesalers
Training, and more powers to seize and detain
IPR enforcement
Installation of a structure that allows for very tough enforcement, proportional to the health risks involved
Unannounced visits to some producers would be very instructive (but international agreements among health authorities should be in place)
Publication of rules
Clear regulation of each party: manufacturer, importer, MAA holder and wholesaler

Recommendations to improve penalisation
Increase penalties
Should be adequate for the crime
Put appropriate legislation in place
Financial fines, industry-wide blacklisting, and exclusion from the pharmaceutical market
Tougher penalties
Raising fines and prison sanctions
Much stronger penalties
Judiciary to be offered training so as to understand that counterfeit pharmaceuticals are a health hazard and cannot be compared to a counterfeit film or a DVD
Civil and criminal law actions
Higher penalties to be regularly imposed, including custodial sentences
Each counterfeit API batch can potentially kill or seriously harm thousand of patients; penalties should be proportionate
To be effective in the countries where counterfeiting companies are located
As in place in the US – import licence withdrawal ("redlisting" made available to pharmaceutical companies)
Increased penalties to deter activities

Recommendations to improve penalisation
If someone does not buy through the legal supply chain, they must be immediately closed down
Too lenient sentences may not be a deterrent

Security systems for medicines (APIs) to differentiate genuine from counterfeit products – Recommendations for improvements
Improve systems
Security features dependent on risk and different authentication levels: overt, covert and forensic
Rules for the inclusion of covert markers in APIs and/or drug products
Trace substance and authentication of packaging
Authentication technology for rapid identification at the pharmacy level
Mixture of overt and covert anti-counterfeit features to be deployed
We use colour-shift ink which has yet to be counterfeited. Make use of new technologies but do not rely on one; adopt multi-layer anti-counterfeiting protection
Authentic packaging features according to company strategy and decision
Manufacturers should be encouraged (not obliged) to adopt security technologies appropriate to their business needs
Any technically feasible, infallible and affordable way
More unique closure systems and practices
Evaluation of imported goods (spot checks) as is in place, for example, for the importation of toys
Packaging should be more difficult to counterfeit, especially samples and clinical packages
Packaging that is extremely difficult to counterfeit and tracing included in pills
Holograms and IDs which are difficult to falsify

Traceability systems for pharmaceuticals – Recommendations for improvements
Introduce and standardise
Internet-based track and trace
If any, harmonised technical standards need to be developed
Numbering system and database. In the long term: RFID technology. Electronic track and trace would be useful
Track and trace, enforced pedigree papers and prevention of repackaging
2D bar-coding and RFID
Use of an adequate, unified, harmonised (at least European, although global would be better) system
Not RFID tagging. This has huge cost implications, and requires massive investment in infrastructure. A paper or electronic pedigree should be a mandatory requirement
Full transparency/traceability back to the manufacture of crucial, "late" API intermediates should be mandatory
For instance, application of Article 17 of ICH Q7a
Electronic batch number: unique number on each box

Traceability systems for pharmaceuticals – Recommendations for improvements
Efficient traceability systems for drugs are difficult to implement
Enable local authorities to find sources of counterfeit products
The possibility to show that an item has been bought through the legal supply chain
Clear requirements for traceability through the manufacturing and distribution chains

Other systems, including systems to identify, monitor, prevent and fight the counterfeiting of pharmaceuticals – Recommendations for improvements
Everything should be done in consultation. It is no use authorities/governments setting up a system of whatever kind to tackle (part of) the problem if it subsequently proves ineffective because of practical reasons. This can be prevented through consulting producers and those involved in the supply chain. It must be remembered that we currently stand at the beginning of a long road
Mobile mini lab for analytical authentication. Enhance customers' awareness
Maintain highly ethical retail pharmacies
Tamper evident packaging and a bar code system
Improved supply chain control, direct to consumer distribution, outlaw repackaging/over-labelling activities and global tracking systems
Allow tracer substances to be placed in the formulated product without undue impediment from registration departments
A structured programme of sampling and testing/fingerprinting pharmaceuticals to detect counterfeit APIs
Implementation of standards in each country at the correct level
European database/Internet
Suppress the quota system, which forces distributors to look for alternative suppliers
Strict regulation concerning new import/export firms and new drug distributors

Summary of other comments received:

- more stringent controls should be applied to applicants for wholesale dealer licences, as the proliferation of short-line wholesalers increases trading and potential routes of entry for counterfeit products;
- pharmacists should not be allowed to trade by way of wholesale dealing without a wholesale dealers licence;
- regulatory controls and inspection need to be applied to dispensing doctors;
- greater controls should be applied to producers of APIs;
- inspection should focus on where the APIs enter the chain and the API manufacturing sites themselves. More is needed than focusing inspection simply on registered API manufacturers: verification of whether the API present in the dosage form is indeed from that registered API manufacturer is also needed. Once APIs are in the chain they will stay in, as ingredients in the medicinal product. Thereafter, they can often only be detected through thorough analytical evaluation/fingerprinting. It is well known that, especially at certain brokers/traders, practices take place that result in the distribution of counterfeit APIs (relabelling). We also think that there should be very strict oversight of API products entering free trade zones in EU harbours to ensure that illicit API material does not enter the EU via this route;
- return to a comprehensible supply chain and at least one sales office per pharmaceutical trader/distributor/manufacturer per country which is physically

occupied by at least one legally responsible person as a link for authorities and customers (wholesalers, hospitals, retailers, consumers, etc.). It must be a qualified person with a good command of the national language, who is capable of and responsible for meeting regulations on good manufacturing, distribution and trading practice laid down in national and EU regulations and dealing with claims generated by authorities, clients and customers.

12.4. Information sharing between health and customs authorities and EC Regulation 1383/2003

12.4.1. Information sharing with health authorities in case of customs action (EC Regulation 1383/2003)

CoE member state survey: Q40 (MoH/DRA) and Q104 (MoFTC)

This question was solely addressed to the EU member states. Some 89% of the EU member state MoH/DRAs and 75% of the MoFTC respondents agreed that it would be useful for combating counterfeit pharmaceuticals for private applicants involved in customs actions, as specified in Article 5.5 (of EC Regulation 1383/2003), to authorise sharing the information contained in the application with the health authorities. A negative answer was received from only one member state MoFTC.

No specific comments on this issue were received from MoH/DRAs while one comment was received from a MoFTC: "all exchange of information is crucial in implementing controls against counterfeit goods. The applicants for customs action are best placed to produce details relating to their products which would be of immense benefit to the health authorities not only in deterring the movements of counterfeit pharmaceuticals but also educating the public against the dangers of such products using real examples. Customs is not aware of any statutory imped-iment to this type of information being exchanged with the health authorities. Certainly, in terms of producing better customs controls and achieving better seizure rates, such exchange of information as mentioned within Article 5.5 of the customs regulation is crucial."

12.4.2. Do stakeholders agree that private applicants ("rights holders") for measures specified by EC Regulation 1383/2003 should authorise and support the sharing, between the health and customs authorities concerned, of information held in the applications?

Stakeholder survey: Q14

Yes = 77%; No = 3%; Missing = 17%; Question unclear = 3%.
The significant majority replied "yes" with only one respondent replying "no".

Comments received:

• there is a preference for placing more emphasis on patient safety and the requirement for regulatory agencies (EMEA and national) to take more responsibility to uphold this aspect of medicines safety and the ability to allow the agencies to prosecute;
• this question is unclear. If it is meant that right holders/producers should be consulted beforehand and authorise the sharing of information between various authorities, such as health and customs, the answer is "yes", this

should be the case. However, this can prove impractical. It can also be envisaged, for example, that a (confidentiality) agreement is signed between relevant parties where the stakeholders with whom the information may be shared are specifically mentioned. Other solutions are possible too;
- co-operation is needed between manufacturers, distributors and agencies;
- information should be shared between interested parties;
- yes in general, but bureaucracy and cost should be minimised;
- it is questionable that health and customs, according to today's regulations, are able to be involved effectively in patent issues.

12.5. Existence or otherwise of specific manufacturer and wholesaler security personnel that have responsibility to investigate medicines counterfeiting

Stakeholder survey: Q15

Yes = 40%; Yes/No = 3%; No = 54%; Missing = 3%.

12.5.1. Nature of investigations (in the case of a "yes" response)

- preparation for litigation; independent pharmaceutical health risk assessment;
- we have a team in place but have not had to mobilise it yet;
- cross-functional product security team with corporate and regional structure. Quality assurance function plays a major role, making patient safety a priority;
- overt/covert investigations into source and major suppliers of counterfeit products;
- our security services are actively researching and monitoring the traffic of counterfeit pharmaceuticals in co-operation with the PSI and local or regional intelligence agencies, and working to identify key elements of the criminal business model that allow counterfeit medicines to thrive. Evidence of illegal operations is gathered;
- both proactive and reactive enquiries to identify the source of counterfeit manufacturing and distribution chains. Internet research and test purchases;
- alert programme, instructions and audits;
- control of sourcing;
- when drugs are received from foreign countries, they are strictly controlled;
- if needed, we have skilled pharmacists to carry out a thorough control;
- all wholesalers have pharmacists for quality assurance purposes;
- the quality manager is responsible for handling cases of potentially counterfeit products. They are handled like other cases of substandard products. Regulatory authorities and the MAA holder is notified;
- we do not have a security department as such but we do have people on the payroll who investigate, research and archive counterfeit incidents and co-operate with authorities, other security personnel and organisations where possible.

12.5.2. Summary of results achieved (in the case of a "yes" response)

- helps prosecution rather than prevention:
  – company policy and procedures being developed;
  – covert/overt anti-counterfeit features – company approach;

- Internet surveillance;
- global handling system and reporting structure;
- working party monitoring RFID and anti-counterfeit features and activities;
- support for FDA forensic lab in building product library;
- membership of the EFPIA ad hoc working party on anti-counterfeiting;
- in 2004 we successfully raided three factories manufacturing our product in China with the full support of the Chinese authorities. We continue to identify the supply routes out of the Far East and with assistance of law enforcement and regulatory authorities intercept and detain major suppliers where we can. But as we all know, counterfeiting pharmaceuticals remains big business. We do not pursue street-level dealers;
- key information is conveyed to government and law enforcement authorities and other stakeholders concerned to ensure that suspected counterfeiters and their intermediaries are thoroughly investigated and, where appropriate, prosecuted;
- since January 2004, raids have been carried out on five counterfeit manufacturing bases; about 7 million pounds worth of counterfeit products were interdicted;
- quick-acting, good information exchange with suppliers.
- quality procedures;
- counterfeit pharmaceuticals did not appear in the distribution channel;
- none as yet;
- no case detected.

12.5.3. Intention to create security personnel (in the case of a "no" response)

No = 45%; Yes = 20%; Unknown = 10%; Missing = 25%.

- the attention of each subsidiary has been drawn to the problems of counterfeiting and in sensitive countries medical representatives are trained to detect anomalies and to report them. We hire the services of private investigators on a case-by-case basis;
- various functions are involved, but at present no specific security person has been appointed. Quality assurance and the health of our customers is a fundamental value of our company. Therefore we are working on the issue of counterfeit products and are in the process of establishing the required structures and working teams within our company;
- yes, in China where it is almost done;
- yes, because of the entry of counterfeit products into the United Kingdom;
- planning of tighter control of suppliers, including references and sample surveys of products if a new or unknown supplier enters the market;
- no, investigating counterfeiting of APIs is the job of the authorities and is beyond the possibilities of the API industry;
- no, this will be primarily the authority's responsibility;
- no, it is not considered necessary at the moment;
- no, because we buy products only from official suppliers;
- no, because we do not find it relevant to our activity, as we buy mainly from laboratories (or their distributors) and we do not produce any medicine or hold any licence.

13. Counterfeit medicine and pharmaceutical crime definitions

13.1. Existence of counterfeit medicine definition in legislation

Member state survey: Q3 (MoH/DRA), Q52 (MoIP), Q78 (MoJ), Q103 (MoFTC) and Q141 (MoET)

Table 31: Existence of counterfeit medicine definition in legislation (summary of responses)

Member state	MoH/DRA	MoIP	MoJ	MoFTC	MoET
1	No	Yes	Yes	Yes	Yes
2	No	No	No	No	No
3	Yes				
4	No				
5	No				
6	No	No	No	No	No
7	No				
8	No	Yes	Yes	No	Yes
9	Yes	No	Yes	No	
10	No	Yes			
11	No	No	Yes	Yes	No
12	No				

MoH/DRA
Some 83% of MoH/DRAs stated that no such definition exists.

Specific comments received:

- the absence of a definition in medicinal products law implies that counterfeit medicines are dealt with only under the legal provisions for illegal production and commerce. The offence of merchandise falsification under the national Penal Code is an infraction against the state and is not seen as putting human or animal health in danger;
- such a definition is implied by Directive 2001/83/EC (as amended),[1] Article 1, point 2;

---

1. Directive 2004/27/EC of the European Parliament and of the Council of 31 March 2004 amending Directive 2001/83/EC on the Community code relating to medicinal products for human use (and which updates Directive 2001/83/EC, Article 1, point 2) does not specifically refer to a counterfeit medicinal product.

- no definition exists, but it is indirectly referred to by the legal definition of APIs and pharmaceuticals;
- the one member state respondent that does have a direct definition of a counterfeit medicine (in its law on medicines) is the only survey respondent from eastern Europe and is a country with a large counterfeit medicine problem.

Other ministries
The response from other ministries was mixed. References were made to indirect definitions in criminal, commercial, competition and IPR law and also EC Regulation 1383/2003 (the latter merely provides very generic definitions of all "goods infringing IPR" under the headings counterfeit, pirated and patent infringing goods).

13.2. Existence of pharmaceutical crime definition in legislation

Member state survey: Q41 (MoH/DRA) and Q64 (MoIP)

MoH/DRA
Some 83% of MoH/DRA respondents stated that there was no definition of pharmaceutical crime in their national legislation. Of these one member state responded that such a definition could be implied from infractions described under the penalties section of its national law on medicines. Of the two respondents who stated that there was a definition, the following legislative references were referred to:

- one member state (criminal law): "Corruption of food and medical substances": there is a prison sentence of between one and eight years for whoever produces, manufactures, packages, transports, treats, or has any activity regarding substances to be consumed by others, either to be eaten, drunken, or for medical or surgical activities, and who falsifies, corrupts, or changes them, or reduces their therapeutic or nutritive value or adds some ingredients, and by doing so creates danger for life or the physical integrity of others. The same penalty is reserved for those who import, hide, sell, or keep for sale the substances mentioned in the previous activities";
- one member state: several articles in the Penal Code (under the section entitled "Offences to public health") could fit the concept of "pharmaceutical crime":

One article states: "Whoever puts into circulation or retails medicinal products which are past their sell-by date or spoiled, or which do not fulfil technical requirements regarding composition, stability or efficacy, or replaces one by another, and so poses risks to human life or health shall be punished by six months' to two years' imprisonment, fines (from six to eighteen months) and professional disqualification for a period between six months to two years."

A second article states: "Whoever simulates or copies medicinal products or other substances used in therapeutics, making them seem authentic, and in so doing poses risks to human health, will be punished by six months' to three years' imprisonment, fines (from six to eighteen months) and professional disqualification for a period between six months and two years."

MoIP
All MoIP respondents stated that there was no definition. Two respondents stated that this definition might be provided for in the law on medicines.

14. Adequacy of authority/wholesaler/ manufacturer personnel training concerning detection and control of counterfeit medicines

Member state survey: Q49 (MoH/DRA), Q75 (MoIP) and Q135 (MoFTC)

MoH/DRA: Yes = 8%; No = 75%; Unknown = 17%.

Summary of "no" comments received:

- no specific training is received to detect counterfeits for both inspectors and distribution chain personnel;
- case studies should be provided;
- need greater awareness of counterfeit medicine characteristics;
- awareness of the potential problem is more important than training on how to spot a counterfeit product;
- training support could be provided by industry, professional bodies and DRAs;
- technical equipment should be provided to assist counterfeit medicine detection;
- obligation for wholesalers to notify all counterfeits as a part of GDP.

MoIP: Approximately, Yes = 50%; No = 50%.

Comments received:

- "Yes": new training always welcome, no specific training required but more experience needed;
- "No": detection, and identification and creation of a database.

MoFTC: No = 66%.

Comments provided:

- "no": awareness raising, counterfeit medicine identification and prosecution;
- "yes": not applicable to customs officers (referred to the DRA).

Comment on cross-correspondence between responses from the relevant internal agencies/authorities/ministries of the member state:

- not a single member state indicated that training is adequate across all its ministries

15. Conclusions and recommendations made by Council of Europe survey respondents

15.1. International regulatory co-operation: the viewpoint of MoH/DRAs

Member state survey: Q45 (MoH/DRA)

There was unanimous agreement by the respondents for the need for international co-operation to deal with medicines counterfeiting. The rest of this section presents the specific comments received by respondents.

15.1.1. Specific proposed areas for co-operation

(a) Exchange of information
- between competent health authorities (DRAs) on counterfeit cases;
- for all countries, not just between countries involved in their respective cases;
- between health authorities (DRAs), police and customs within the country and between countries;
- between health authorities (DRAs) and industry;
- more input from industry;
- bi- and multilateral exchange of information.

(b) Type of information to be exchanged
- on specific cases (case-by-case basis), particularly for counterfeit drugs which could be present in different markets;
- methods used by counterfeiters and periodic reports about the new typologies of counterfeiting;
- knowledge of distribution chains (need for database of distributors, wholesalers and manufacturers).

(c) Awareness raising
No specific proposals were made.

(d) Training of personnel
No specific proposals were made.

15.1.2. Proposed types of specific co-operation

- six-monthly reports from DRAs of all counterfeit medicine cases reported during that period;
- assessment of trends of supply: in particular, products and industry, types of customers, extent of brokerage activity and movement of medicinal products through free ports/zones and destinations;
- creation of a tracking system;

- permanent arrangements for exchange of information on facts between health authorities, police and customs (creation of a multidisciplinary inter-authority network);
- RAS.

15.2. Final comments and proposals from authorities concerning legislative and administrative procedures applicable to counterfeit medicines

Member state survey: Q50 (MoH/DRA), Q76 (MoIP), Q101 (MoJ), Q139 (MoFTC) and Q153 (MoET)

MoH/DRA

Legislation
- the specialist nature of medicines and the potential risks to human health posed by counterfeit medicinal products require that there be a specific legislative provision on the counterfeiting of such products and that this should be commensurate with the danger presented by the product;
- introduction of appropriate legislation requires action at a high level;
- incorporate a definition of counterfeiting into legislation;
- co-ordinate legislation inter-sectorally (import/export/transit legislation with customs legislation);
- EU regulation on counterfeit drugs needed.

Penalty provisions
- strengthen penalty provisions (including imprisonment).

Co-operation
- improve co-operation between member states;
- obligatory exchange of information between customs, public health authorities and police.

MoIP
- currently no definition of counterfeit medicines;
- medicines counterfeiting should be made a specific crime;
- medicines counterfeiting should be an arrestable offence with stronger penalties;
- there is lack of awareness of the scale of the counterfeit medicines problem by police forces (and its impact on health);
- improve co-operation between the various sectoral authorities and with the private sector;
- database needed.

MoJ
- the legislative instruments for assuring prevention and prosecution of counterfeit medicines exist. However, there is no organised and multidisciplinary co-operation between the different competent services with respect to:

  – information exchange;
  – a strategic and operational analysis of this criminal phenomenon;
  – an RAS;
  – regular contacts between the competent authorities and the pharmaceutical industry.

MoFTC
* for imported goods, a certificate should be issued for the release of medicines into free circulation.

MoET
* penalties might be sufficient; but what about prevention?
* increase international collaboration and information exchange.

15.3. Council of Europe stakeholder conclusions on industry best co-operation practices with the concerned authorities

Stakeholder survey: III. Conclusions

This section presents the specific comments received by respondents and are separated into comments on awareness, communication and co-operation, database and reporting systems, legislation and regulation, enforcement and trade practices.

15.3.1. Awareness

* a commitment to fight pharmaceutical counterfeiting at a political level is necessary to achieve results;
* the most important issue is greater awareness of the reality and seriousness of the problem;
* the problem of API counterfeiting needs to be recognised and the dangers involved need to be understood and acknowledged by the authorities as soon as possible and hopefully before a human health tragedy occurs. As soon as the authorities are ready, the European API industry will be fully prepared to enter into any form of co-operation with the authorities in order to fight the problem;
* as a full-line wholesaler, covering most of our country and serving more than 800 pharmacies daily, we have never had knowledge of any specific case of counterfeit medicines in the wholesale sector;
* counterfeit medicines are not a problem in Finland;
* there is a large risk from counterfeit medicines;
* the question has great importance, we are ready to co-operate in the future also.

15.3.2. Communication and co-operation

* best co-operation via inter-functional ad hoc working groups involving industry, associations and authorities;
* co-operation practices: need to be clear and well publicised; the company must have rapid access to the right regulator;
* a common mutual interest to share information through regular meetings, co-operation agreements, requests for intervention and training;
* the role of customs is also important in the fight;
* partnership and an industry voice to lobby relevant bodies;
* my company along with other companies based in Europe has quarterly meetings where we share best practice and criminal intelligence. Investigations costs are shared. Companies are not involved in looking at the same problem. This appears to be a very effective route in our enquiries;
* a reliable and trustful relationship;
* hold regular forums with appropriate law enforcement and regulatory groups

to discuss issues; these have given rise to a sub working group to prioritise operational and investigative opportunities; a group to co-ordinate legal/enforcement issues; and a further group for lobbying;

- is there real co-operation/transparency between the pharmaceutical industry and authorities? (See Gentamicin case.) Is the excessive pressure of authorities on prices of generics reasonable?
- share information between industry on fraudulent practices and measures to prevent their recurrence;
- regulatory bodies need to co-operate across national boundaries and disseminate information to those involved in the legitimate supply of pharmaceuticals;
- regular contacts with the national DRA and information from authorities;
- two-way information exchange;
- regulatory bodies need to co-operate across national boundaries and disseminate information to those involved in the legitimate supply of pharmaceuticals;
- as wholesalers, we consider the present co-operation adequate.

15.3.3. Database and reporting systems

- shared database of counterfeit products (objects, practices and techniques); databases (probably at national level) where all known and/or suspected cases are managed, and open to the authorities and pharmaceutical companies;
- common database system;
- install reporting (database and regulatory) systems;
- install track and trace (database and regulatory) systems;
- information on detected cases should be circulated, giving details of the products, countries and manufacturers involved.

15.3.4. Legislation and regulation

- laws and regulations detailing penalisation of counterfeiting or its support;
- stronger regulatory control of the supply chain (not only dealing with domestic manufacturers, which are a less probable source of counterfeit products);
- clear rules for distributors, pharmacists, and health care professionals requesting them to check for authenticity and to report suspected cases;
- there is an urgent need to get ICH Q7a integrated into EU regulations; the entry into Europe of APIs based solely on documents (for example, granting a CoS without auditing the given company) will not be possible anymore;
- adequate law enforcement bodies, effective pharmaceutical inspection, sufficient practical control means and a real willingness to intervene;
- greater regulatory controls are required at each level of the supply chain;
- improve legislation;
- develop guidance for industry and regulations;
- from our experiences of auditing in some Asian and East Asian countries, a clear link appears between life standards (hygiene, quality of the environment and food preparation, etc.) and GMP awareness or understanding of principles. The companies in those regions know that and site audits are well "prepared". We are willing to exchange our experience with EU auditors for more efficient audits;
- the applications (for example, for a CoS) are often well documented with the help of very expensive western consultants, but it appears to be worthwhile as once the CoS is granted the door is open to the EU;
- greater regulatory controls are required at each level of the supply chain.

15.3.5. Enforcement

- enforce legislation and prosecution;
- it is time that the authorities in the EU, in particular, recognise that by issuing such extensive regulations and requirements for APIs (which involve very high costs for industry), while at the same time completely neglecting their inspection and enforcement worldwide, they leave the door wide open to counterfeit APIs in the European market;
- if an actor does not observe these rules they must be immediately closed.

15.3.6. Trade practices

- discontinue the quota system implemented by some manufacturers, which incites distributors to buy from alternative sources. Manufacturers should be more proactive in adopting authentication technology and assisting others in the supply chain;
- strengthened and controlled co-operation between the members of the legal supply chain should be sort; each actor must sell and buy only to registered and controlled actors;
- with the growth of parallel imports (legal in France in 2005), French players will have to strengthen co-operation with authorities to prevent counterfeiting;
- counterfeiting is still a minor problem in Austria because of the fact that wholesalers buy the goods directly from industry. In countries where the parallel market has more importance, the problem is usually bigger. In economic terms, Austria is still not interesting for counterfeiting drugs. We think that the Austrian authorities' awareness of this problem is relatively low because of the situation described;
- although in recent years the media have reported some cases of printing facilities where "illegal" medicine cartons and boxes were found, we assume that most of it would be sent to the former African colonies. Eventually some of it could enter via direct sales to pharmacies or the black market, not via the wholesale circuit (although we assume that it would be residual);
- the lack of any regulations concerning EU-based printing facilities is an issue that needs attention.

16. Discussion and final conclusions

16.1. The rise of medicines counterfeiting

Counterfeiting is a common problem with several types of internationally traded products (for a good report on the impact of counterfeiting of a wide number of product types in Europe, see reference 1).[1] The consequences of counterfeiting medicinal products are considerably more severe than counterfeiting of other commonly available and high-margin product types (for example, CDs, watches, etc.), as "obviously" counterfeit medicines have a very serious public health consequence whereas, for example, a counterfeit CD does not.

The 1990s witnessed a significant rise in medicinal products counterfeiting, with a subsequent greater surge in growth since 2000. The WHO has been at the fore-front of tackling this problem and has made and continues to make major attempts to galvanise the necessary international attention and policy priorities of regula-tors and industry/distributors to tackle this potentially serious public health problem (2). The efforts made by the WHO in drawing international attention to this issue have to be congratulated; in this respect the WHO has done its task and now the onus is on the relevant authorities, producers and distributors to always remember that their primary task is to protect and deliver public health.

As a consequence, this subject is receiving greater international regulatory atten-tion; for example, a major global forum on pharmaceutical anti-counterfeiting was conducted in autumn of 2002 (3) and a major report on this topic was recently produced by an independent consulting group (4) as a response to this rapidly developing problem.

It is notable that the latter initiatives have been motivated outside of the official regulatory authority system and thus this report, based on the extensive Council of Europe surveys, must be considered timely in terms of providing a European authority response to tackling this issue.

The current counterfeit medicine phenomenon is due to a wide number of factors that are summarised in the following table:

Table 32: Factors behind the current counterfeit medicines phenomenon

- regulatory gaps (particularly for API and distribution chain regulation);
- in co-ordination with relevant authorities both nationally and internationally (related to a lack of recognition of the counterfeit medicine problem);
- lack of resources of the regulatory body (particularly to follow up reports on suspected counterfeit medicines);
- inefficient co-operation between stakeholders;
- weak administrative structures;

---

1. The numbers in brackets refer to the references at the end of the section.

- weak enforcement and penal sanctions;
- weak export/transit regulations (import regulations are generally strong except in the context of Internet/mail order pharmacies);
- disparity in the legal availability of certain types of high-value medicinal products (unlicensed medicines) between countries;
- rapid rise in Internet pharmacy trade;
- weak packaging and printing regulations;
- increasingly complex distribution chain with transactions involving many intermediaries;
- high medicinal product prices;
- recent appearance on the market of so-called "lifestyle and embarrassment" medicinal products;
- the movement of organised crime into medicines counterfeiting, associated with an increasing sophistication in clandestine manufacture;
- corruption and conflicts of interest.

A further reason why there has been a recent rise in medicines counterfeiting is that "production, distribution and consumption of counterfeits of any type (that is, cosmetics, perfume, high-tech, audio/video goods, etc.) was accepted in the past" and thus not enough attention was paid by the authorities to this problem. "Quite often, substitution of imported high-tech products by locally made copies was considered by the authorities as a patriotic action and this explains the legislative 'softness' towards infringers."

In terms of the profitability of medicines counterfeiting and the financial loss to industry, the World Customs Organisation estimates this to be 5% of world pharmaceutical trade with a value of US$20 billion, while the WHO estimates it to be 6%. The EU and EEA is (based on the responses from the surveys conducted by the Council of Europe) affected by medicines counterfeiting, although to an unknown extent.

It should also be stated that the issues raised in this report can equally apply to medical devices (some authorities are already reporting counterfeit medical devices).

16.2. Extent of the counterfeit medicine problem, risk of counterfeiting according to medicinal product type and types of counterfeiting practice identified

16.2.1. Extent of the counterfeit medicine problem in Europe

Based on the results of the surveys conducted by the Council of Europe, the counterfeit medicine problem is not insignificant in western Europe and estimates provided by several respondents indicate that the problem is not likely to go away in the foreseeable future. It affects all countries of the world. It is no longer safe to assume that the problem does not exist to any real extent in western Europe (EU and EEA) and that it can be safely ignored by authorities in the latter. Although it can be assumed that western Europe is relatively less affected by the counterfeit medicine problem than eastern Europe, it has to be borne in mind that counterfeit medicines probably regularly transit through and exit western Europe.

A lack of awareness of the full extent of the counterfeit medicine problem may be a reason why this issue has not become a European-level priority. Until recently, counterfeit medicines may not have appeared to be prevalent on the western European market. However, Council of Europe member state pharmaceutical information/inspection systems, as established, are not primarily focused on detecting counterfeit medicines. Counterfeit medicines are liable to be produced within western Europe because of the exploitation of lacunas in western European legislation and regulations.

To the extent that any specific west European member state perceives that it either does not have or has only a small counterfeit medicine problem, this does not mean that such states should not participate in any adopted recommendations, particularly as the problem is a cross-border one and one state's deciding not to adopt a recommendation potentially undermines action taken by other states.

As a reminder that the problem does exist in western Europe, it is worth restating here the well-known case in Italy in 2000 where authorities arrested participants in an international organised criminal enterprise partly based in the country. Nearly 250000 units of counterfeit medicines were seized together with 2 tonnes of raw materials. Originating from India and China, the materials were repackaged in Europe for resale in the Americas (6).

It can be safely concluded that action is now required by European authorities to prevent an avoidable human health tragedy in the future resulting from medicines counterfeiting.

16.2.2. Risk of counterfeiting according to medicinal product type

No type of medicinal product appears to be exempt from being counterfeited, although the types of medicinal products at greater risk clearly relate to the market characteristics of particular geographical regions. Although so-called "lifestyle" (including "embarrassment") and essential drugs tend to be targets for counterfeiting in developed and developing countries respectively, this distinction in terms of product type by region is becoming increasingly blurred. It cannot be safely assumed that any particular class of medicinal product is immune from potential counterfeiting.

16.2.3. Types of counterfeiting practice identified

The surveys conducted (see Section 3.1 above) show the existence of a wide variety of counterfeiting practices related to medicinal products, with counterfeiters showing no shortage of creativity. Manufacturers are more informed of counterfeiting practices than distributors – this suggests a need to create a system of communication between manufacturers and distributors on this issue as well as more involvement of distributors in informing regulatory authorities and vice versa.

There appears to be a need for a classification system of counterfeiting practices and a common terminology (for example, one comment received was that "counterfeit medicines are often considered in the restricted sense of 'falsified or fake' medicines, namely without APIs. This is an incomplete definition and omits a lot of other counterfeit practices applicable to medicinal products, such as diversion, repackaging, expired drugs, etc."). The value of a standardised classification system is that it allows both a commonality of counterfeit medicines reporting between states and a scale of penal sanctions to be applied in accordance with the level of public health risk and fraud.

16.3. Extent of counterfeit medicine's impact on public health

The direct impact of the inadvertent use of counterfeit medicines in Europe by an unsuspecting public is difficult to determine based on data currently available. The types of ADR associated with the inadvertent use of counterfeit medicines can relate to one or more of a number of problems depending on the type of counterfeiting practice employed. ADRs associated with counterfeit medicines may be due to, but not limited to, inappropriate API dosages (absent, insufficient or excessive) and quality problems (product contamination and problems with excipients).

The exact extent of the impact of counterfeit medicines on public health is hard to determine because existing reporting systems are not geared to detecting this problem. A result of this situation is that the impact on public health is under-reported and medicines counterfeiting tends to be regarded as no different in crime terms from other types of counterfeiting.

As a means of assessing the impact of counterfeit medicines on public health, more explicit incorporation of drug ineffectiveness in ADR reporting systems should be required.

16.4. Public awareness of medicines counterfeiting and the general public's perception of the health system

While there is a lack of awareness of the real extent of the counterfeit medicine problem by both the general public and health professionals, and the damage it can cause to public health, the issue does need to be presented more publicly in an objective manner. At the same time there is a danger of the public being provided with information that has been incorrectly interpreted. Several reports on this subject have already appeared in the national press (for example, see reference 7, which is provided as an example of a specific international news agency reporting its view on the subject).

The confidence of patients in good quality medicines and the health care system has been put at stake as a result of the rise in medicines counterfeiting. There is a need to raise awareness of the issue, but in such a way so as not to disrupt public confidence in the health system, namely by avoiding premature and possibly misleading information.

A distinction should be made between (i) information made publicly available concerning illegal sources of counterfeit medicines; and (ii) information on the legal manufacturing and distribution chain, where it is the authorities who need to be informed primarily.

In all these efforts it has to be kept clearly in mind that even though awareness raising is desirable and necessary, such activities should mainly focus on professionals (drug regulatory authorities, health professionals, customs, police, lawyers, etc.), since a focus on the general public could possibly endanger their confidence in appropriately and properly authorised and marketed medicinal products.

16.5. Import/export/transit licensing, bonded warehouses/free zone control and cross-border trade

Import controls are made on all FPs by each respondent, whereas this is not the case for APIs and BPs. However, there are far fewer export and transit controls on FPs, APIs and BPs. This situation suggests the existence of an important loophole in the control systems of cross-border medicines trade.

Many medicinal products that are produced specifically for the developing world in Council of Europe member states are not regulated by member state MoH/DRAs to the same degree as medicines destined for the domestic market and is thus a situation for concern.

Furthermore, several respondents indicate that existing certification schemes are often inadequate. The implication is that there is a great opportunity for document fraud. A "reliance on paper" can be said to be important, but the FDA uses this and other methods to corroborate data (for example, use of e-data, etc.).

The storage of pharmaceuticals in bonded warehouses/free zones is only governed by medicines legislation in 50% of respondent member states. This suggests that some uniformity in the legislative approach may be required, that is all states should attempt to place bonded warehouse/free zone provisions for medicinal products directly under the law on medicines.

16.6. Parallel trade

Some 75% of member state respondents indicated that they had legal provisions governing parallel imports, which rather than being specific tend to rely on existing provisions governing import licensing and marketing authorisation. Some member states have specific regulations governing parallel imports, while many do not. As this issue is not determined at EU level, there is scope for individual states to interpret their own procedures for governing parallel imports. With respect to whether parallel imports are perceived as facilitating the emergence of counterfeit medicines, all responses were either unknown or missing.

The existence of a significant level of parallel trade in the EU, in the absence of adequate controls on repackaging and relabelling, provides an opportunity for the inadvertent entry of counterfeit medicines into the market (a recent personal communication referred to a case of counterfeit tablets which had recently been introduced by a parallel trader). (Re-)exchangeable medicinal product packaging practices are highly prevalent across all European countries as a result of European directives. Furthermore, parallel trade means that any counterfeit product within the legitimate distribution chain in one member state can easily contaminate other states.

It will be necessary to examine in greater detail how parallel import practices might be linked with illegal and uncontrolled distribution sources and the increasing complexity of the distribution chain, and how parallel trade rules can be tightened with respect to pharmaceuticals, APIs and FPs. A recent study (8) on the issue of the benefit or otherwise of parallel trade in medicinal products has provided good evidence that real benefits accrue to intermediaries rather than the patient, and thus it can be reasonably argued that parallel trade of medicinal products provides a negative society benefit – particularly as it clearly allows greater opportunities for counterfeiting (personal communication). This topic is currently very controversial and urgently needs further examination.

16.7. Internet pharmacy, mail order and unlicensed medicines

The onset of the popularity of the Internet in recent years poses a large risk factor for the dissemination of medicines, as there is little regulation via this method. The Internet offers an easy way to illegally distribute medicines to consumers (that is, direct distribution of medicinal products to consumers of PoMs without a prescription, off-label use of authorised medicines, for example "lady Viagra", or non-authorised use in a given country) and there are almost no sanctions against this activity. In addition to websites dedicated to the sale of PoMs and other medicines, there are also "lifestyle" websites which offer medicines as well as advertisements for a wide range of other products.

Internet pharmacy is recognised as arguably the leading distributor of spam e-mails worldwide with an emphasis on the illegal distribution of "lifestyle" products, including, in particular, "embarrassment" drugs (for example, Viagra, Cialis, etc.). This is a good indicator of how big the counterfeit/illegal medicine business is likely to be worldwide. The dangers of purchasing such medicines via Internet pharmacy because of the high risk of purchasing counterfeits have already been reported in the general press (7).

Orders for PoMs over the Internet are both a serious threat to public health and also a means of undermining the entire drug regulatory framework.

The table below presents a good description provided by one European DRA of the Internet pharmacy situation and of the limited powers DRAs have to investigate and control it

Table 33: Example of the Internet pharmacy situation in one member state

There exists evidence that the online sale of medicines may be one of the biggest dangers for consumers and the DRA found an extensive unregulated market.

Internet medicine offers are frequently anonymous, the only contact to order goods is an e-mail address. Personal data are very strictly protected by the law and there is no possibility for the DRA to obtain the name of an e-mail address holder. Only the police have the authority to identify the seller, on the basis of a court order. Since the sale of medicines over the Internet, even PoMs, is not a criminal offence (it is only an offence under the law on medicines), the police are not authorised to inform the DRA of any name. Thus, until September 2004, the DRA had no power to take action against Internet offers because of a lack of information.

On 7 September 2004 the Act on Information Society Services (2004) came into effect. This act implements Directive 2000/31/EC on electronic commerce. It is the first act in the state laying down the responsibilities of ISPs. It means that a provider of free space on the Internet ("freeweb") is responsible for the illegal content of web pages provided that it can be proved that they are aware that the content is breaching the law and they did not remove the relevant pages from the Internet.

The DRA chose the pages that should be removed from the Internet (mainly the pages under the service "freeweb", where the offer of medicines is not very broad).

Currently, seven pages have been removed from the Internet and four others are in the process of being so. As regards other pages, the DRA has decided to order samples of medicines for laboratory testing in order to find out whether they are counterfeits or not. Unfortunately, the current legislative situation does not allow the DRA to order any samples of medicines from the Internet. That is why the DRA initiated changes in the law on medicines to make it possible for the authority to order goods from the Internet. The new law on medicines has not been passed yet.

Meanwhile, the DRA handed over cases of these infringing pages to the police and the custom office for the investigation of suspected illegal enterprise (this is a criminal offence), and it is hoped that the police will find enough evidence to prosecute. All the cases are in the investigation phase now. If there is not sufficient evidence against the seller and the police investigation is stopped, the only step the DRA can take is to ask the provider to remove the infringing web pages from the Internet. However, this means that no action is taken against the seller.

The DRA is trying every avenue available to get suspicious medicines purchased online laboratory tested because it is a way of finding out the quality of drugs offered on the black market. If counterfeit medicines are found, the DRA is ready to co-operate with pharmaceutical companies to protect their intellectual rights. The cases will also be handed over to the police.

After the first laboratory tests are completed, the DRA will have a lot of very useful information about the flow of medicines and the risks the DRA has to deal with.

The most important issue for effective minimisation of the public health risk is the legal environment. The legal situation in our state for combating the black market on the Internet is inadequate. Unfortunately, the situation is very similar in other states as well. That is why international collaboration at European level aimed at improving the current law and creating new measures and regulations against illegal sources of such sensitive goods as pharmaceuticals is so welcomed.

16.8. Brokers/traders – Do they play a role in the supply of counterfeit medicines?

Little in the way of substantive grounds exist to say that brokers do play a role in the supply of counterfeit medicines.

However, one respondent stated that "brokers are well placed to participate in the diversion of medicines including counterfeits; they facilitate international commerce of medicines and remain invisible to the authorities; brokers are not directly subject to national legislation and they operate at an international level without being mentioned on bills; and they are not a responsible party in the strict sense of the legislation".

A further respondent stated "they are the only intermediaries in pharmaceutical distribution not subject to authorisation; their business is of a purely commercial nature and therefore is not relevant to the pharmaceutical industry (the latter being heavily regulated for specific reasons). Therefore they do not need to be licensed and no register of brokers exists."

No reasons were given as to why there they are not suspected of playing a role. Furthermore, no responses to the survey were received from brokers, although they were invited to participate. In conclusion, one can assume that there would be no harm in tightening the regulatory control of brokers, as this area of trade activity currently receives little in the way of regulation.

But what is clear is that trade brokers operate largely out of the sphere of regulatory control, which has to be a point of concern.

16.9. Legal medicinal product distribution chain

The majority of stakeholders agreed that counterfeit medicines appear in the legal distribution chain (weighted towards manufacturers; wholesalers think less so). All stages of the distribution were cited.

The extent to which counterfeit medicines appear in the legal distribution chain is not entirely clear. The following reasons as to how they get there were given: insufficient control of distribution, multiple ownership/levels in the supply chain, illegal trading by legal wholesalers and pharmacies, repackaging, substandard control practices, documentation weaknesses/forgery, poor traceability requirements, insufficient control of the Internet, and switching APIs to counterfeit APIs. It was also stated that wholesalers and pharmacists report to different regulatory bodies, which makes regulation of the legal distribution chain more problematic.

16.10. "Illegal" (non-regulated) medicinal product distribution chain

The illegal distribution chain appears to play a major role in the appearance of counterfeit medicines. Sites include fitness clubs, the bodybuilding scene, private acquisition over the Internet, and others such as shops specialising in undercover (illegal) goods, sex clubs, sex shops, food supplement stores, cosmetic stores and when carrying out import/border controls.

Counterfeit medicines as "lifestyle" drugs are a particular target for counterfeiters and are targeted at locations where such "lifestyle" drugs may be desirable. For the one east European respondent, Internet orders are probably not yet an issue, and perhaps fitness clubs, etc. have not reached the level of sophistication needed for the use of "lifestyle" drugs.

16.11. Medicinal product supply chain complexity

Counterfeit medicines are a special problem since the production and distribution chain for medicinal products is ever more international and complicated; the jurisdiction of health authorities is limited to within state borders and does not fit with this strongly international oriented way of working. Criminal organisations take advantage of this situation.

There is increasing complexity of the distribution system as a result of more open trade borders, trade through free ports and more intermediaries, particularly downstream, with, for example, the proliferation of short-line wholesalers. Regulatory authorities have a problem of applying GDPs particularly to distributors below the level of the primary distributor, that is to micro-distributors, sub-entrepreneurs, import/export firms, etc. Supply chain complexity makes repackaging increasingly prevalent (and sometimes multiple for the product).

16.12. Involvement of organised crime with counterfeit medicines

There is indirect evidence for a connection between the drug trafficking trade and the recent development of the counterfeit medicines trade (for example, in the former Soviet Union and the Balkans). In many ways, illicit manufacturing and distribution of medicinal products can be viewed as a natural extension of illicit narcotic and psychotropic drug manufacturing and distribution. Experience with illicit narcotic and psychotropic production lends itself to increasing sophistication in clandestine "pseudo" manufacture of medicinal products.

It is perhaps not surprising that MoH/DRAs have a limited awareness and regulatory control of this activity, except in the area of illicit production and distribution of narcotics and psychotropics, which is well governed and regulated by the UN International Narcotics Control Board via well-established UN conventions and which involves effective co-operation and co-ordination between different sectoral authorities (police, customs and MoH/DRAs).

16.13. Authorities' awareness of medicinal product counterfeiting – Its impact, extent and action priority

Few national authorities appear to be aware of the full extent of the issues surrounding the counterfeiting of medicinal products. One respondent stated that "in our experience the pharmaceutical authorities in the EU are hardly interested in pharmaceutical and API counterfeiting and the fight against it (DG Enterprise, EMEA, national authorities/inspectorates) with a few exceptions."

However, one member state actually possesses a specific health crime police force which covers many areas of health corruption/abuse of public health expenditure and which seems to be very aware of the counterfeit medicine problem, having successfully set itself up as a inter-ministerial "unit".

The absence of a clear differentiation of medicines counterfeiting from other forms of counterfeiting dilutes enforcement, and the judiciary's and trade authority's willingness to address the problem.

In defence of the EU bodies responsible for pharmaceutical regulation, it could be said that their major focus of attention in recent years has rightly been the completion of the Pharmaceuticals Review 2001 and the satisfactory integration of the new accession states within the existing EU pharmaceutical regulatory framework. Thus, understandably, devoting attention to counterfeiting was a lesser priority at the time when compared to implementation of the aforementioned objectives. Of course, this makes no excuse now for the relevant EU authorities not to devote the necessary attention to medicines counterfeiting.

16.14. Definitions of "counterfeit medicine" and "pharmaceutical crime"

In the vast majority of European states no clear definitions of "counterfeit medicine" and "pharmaceutical crime" exist (only two respondents stated that a definition of pharmaceutical crime exists to some extent in their law – see Section 13.2 of this report). Frequently, such definitions can only be implied indirectly. The absence of such definitions reinforces the perception that there is no differentiation to be made between counterfeiting of medicines and other types of product and leads to the current difficulty in preventing medicines counterfeiting. Furthermore, the absence of a commonly agreed definition leads to inconsistencies in reporting cases of counterfeit medicines by both regulatory authorities and stakeholders.

16.14.1. Counterfeit medicine definition

The following are existing definitions of counterfeit medicine, which may provide the basis for a common European definition:

WHO definition (2)

"A product that is deliberately and fraudulently mislabelled with respect to source and/or identity. Counterfeiting can apply to both generic and branded products. Counterfeit products may include: products with the correct ingredients, with the wrong ingredients, without ingredients, with incorrect quantities of active ingredients, with fake packaging."

USA definition (9)

"The term 'counterfeit drugs' means a drug which, or the container or labelling of which, without authorisation, bears the trademark, trade name, other identifying mark, imprint, or device or any likeness thereof, of a drug manufacturer, processor, packer, or distributor other than the person or persons who in fact manufactured, processed, packed, or distributed such a drug and which thereby falsely purports, or is falsely represented, to be the product of, or to have been packed or distributed by, such other drug manufacturer, processor, packer, or distributor." (US Food, Drug and Cosmetics Act.)

Philippines definition (10)

"Counterfeit medicine refers to medicinal products with the correct ingredients but not in the amounts as provided hereunder, wrong ingredients, without active ingredients, with insufficient quantity of active ingredient, which results in the reduction of the drug's safety, efficacy, quality, strength or purity. It is a drug which is deliberately and fraudulently mislabelled with respect to identity and/or source or with fake packaging, and can apply to both branded and generic products. It shall also refer to:

(i) the medicinal product itself, or the container or labelling thereof or any part of such medicinal product, container or labelling bearing without authorisation the trademark, trade name or other identification mark or imprint or any likeness to that which is owned or registered in a state of the Council of Europe in the name of another natural or juridical person;

(ii) a medicinal product refilled in containers by unauthorised persons if the legitimate labels or marks are used;

(iii) an unregistered imported drug product, except drugs brought in the country for personal use as confirmed and justified by accompanying medical records; and

(iv) a drug which contains no amount of, or a different active ingredient, or less than eighty percent (80%) of the active ingredient it purports to possess, as distinguished from an adulterated drug including reduction or loss of efficacy due to expiration."

16.14.2. Pharmaceutical crime definition

Only a few European states possess what can be implied as a definition; it is unknown if any official definition of pharmaceutical crime is yet in existence elsewhere in the world. It can reasonably be concluded that there is a need for a commonly agreed definition given the unique public health risk of such crime compared to other types of crime.

16.15. Legal provisions including sanctions and penalties against medicines counterfeiting

Only one third of MoH/DRAs indicated that legal provisions relating to counterfeit medicines existed. Where legal provisions are said to exist they tend to concern distribution and FPs.

Legal provisions, where they exist, are non-specific to counterfeit medicines and tend to be covered by several different sector-specific laws and regulations. This leads to a lack of co-ordination and consequent difficulties for managing the counterfeit medicine problem. An indirect result of the absence of specific legal provisions for medicines counterfeiting is the perception that medicines counterfeiting is no different from other types of counterfeiting (a fallacy in view of the public health consequences).

Sanctions are in place for counterfeiting "in general" as a result of applicable IPR law (although the latter has only recently been implemented in the EU's new member states). With a few exceptions in Europe, no specific sanctions are applied against counterfeiting of medicinal products, the latter being currently regarded as an economic crime and not also a health crime. Existing sanctions for medicines counterfeiting are widely regarded as being far too lenient. However, some European states are now looking at this issue more seriously, for example Germany (11).

As a result of the need to differentiate medicines counterfeiting from other types of counterfeiting (due to its public health consequences), some states outside of Europe have tackled this problem by introducing specific regulations applicable to the counterfeiting of medicines.

16.16. Perceived adequacy of legal/judicial/ administrative systems for controlling medicines counterfeiting

Some 50% of MoH/DRAs said the situation was inadequate. Less than 25% of stakeholders consider that the current awareness of the concerned authorities, and their initiatives and systems are adequate to prevent/fight the counterfeiting of pharmaceuticals.

Areas of weakness stated by respondents included: a lack of staffing and other resources, proactivity on the part of the authorities, awareness of the problem (it was stated that the issue is taken more seriously in the United States) and co-ordination with customs, insufficient regulation of the entire supply chain, more authority-industry co-operation needed, more training needed, a lack of specific legislation and legal powers, the absence of a co-ordinated approach across boundaries, and finally that the issue has not been placed on the national agenda.

In general, legislation and regulation of the manufacture of FPs is acceptable in all states examined where the identity of the FP manufacturer is known. For APIs the situation is less tightly regulated; for example, some important gaps in inspection exist which permit diversion of APIs into the production of counterfeit FPs.

Regulation of primary distribution appears to be adequate, but this becomes more problematic below this level in view of the complexity of the supply chain (see Section 16.11).

Frequently, there is a lack of co-ordination on legislation/regulation both between the different authorities in a given state (for example, MoH/DRA, MoIP, MoJ, MoFTC and MoET) and between states.

In conclusion, it can be stated that major weaknesses are the absence of (i) a comprehensive anti-counterfeiting legal framework for medicines and (ii) a clearly designated instrument for co-ordinating/managing medicines anti-counterfeiting both at the national level and at the European level.

16.17. Regulation of APIs

Replies from stakeholder respondents and from some MoH/DRAs suggest that API regulation is an area of major regulatory weakness. For example, as was reported, it is certainly possible that legitimate FP manufacturers could unwittingly be marketing counterfeit medicines (as APIs are fake/or if not fake could have a different specification to what was originally authorised).

Regulation of the manufacture and distribution of APIs is conducted at a much less intense level than for FPs. The types of control, where they exist, are highly variable and inconsistent between MoH/DRAs. Often there are no satisfactory regulatory controls of APIs (for example, manufacturing and broker/trader licensing and inspection, documentation validation, batch traceability, import/export/transit, etc.) made whatsoever. It has been stated by some respondents that API monographs need updating, need to be made more complete (in order to permit effective analytical testing) and further efforts are required for international harmonisation of monographs.

It is strongly suggested that regulatory control of APIs needs urgent strengthening and more consistency in the regulatory approach to APIs be adopted.

16.18. Regulation of medicines packaging, labelling and facilities for printing of labelling and packaging

Regulation of medicines packaging and labelling printing is not performed consistently across all surveyed states and may be an area where, perhaps, more regulatory attention is required. Of concern is the probable existence of illegal, or more accurately unregulated, packaging and printing facilities. Lack of regulations governing repackaging, relabelling and associated printing facilities is an area requiring attention.

16.19. Systems and procedures for detection of counterfeit medicines

16.19.1. Authorities

Specialised enforcement bodies for investigation of counterfeit medicines offences

These were said to exist in most of the member states; their exact nature varying, although principally they were under the control of the MoH/DRAs. One member state MoH/DRA has a specialised penal section, another has a specialised health police service and yet another a specialised consumer protection service, whilst others have police forces specialised in counterfeit products but not specifically medicines. Given the number of counterfeit medicine cases reported by both the authorities and manufacturers/distributors, the number of prosecutions reported is comparatively low.

Active searching for counterfeit medicines

In general there is no active searching strategy by MoH/DRAs; where there was, this was done in one case by a specialised health police force and in the other case by an member state that has a recognised counterfeit medicine problem. The specific use of an annual random sampling plan was mentioned by only one MoH/DRA. In conclusion, this situation suggests that a rather reactive, as opposed to proactive, approach is employed by competent authorities to detect counterfeit medicines.

Coercive measures and special investigation methods nationally authorised and applied to combating counterfeit medicines by interior ministries/police

The use of search warrants, seizure and observation (with or without technical resources) were universally applied. Telephone recordings, wiretaps, detention, informants, infiltration, controlled deliveries, pseudo-purchases, confidential purchases and proactive investigations were employed by the majority of states, but with no consistent pattern across states. It can be concluded that the majority of recognised coercive measures and special investigation methods are available to all states. The issue seems to be rather one of being able to identify suspected counterfeit medicine cases and to mobilise the required enforcement authorities, as opposed to a lack of enforcement powers that can be brought to bear.

16.19.2. Stakeholders

Awareness of who should be informed and notification procedures

Respondents were generally clear about who should be informed (that is, the authorities) concerning suspected counterfeit medicines. However, it was stated that industry reports to different authorities compared to wholesalers/pharmacies, and that the situation was clearer for larger companies compared to smaller companies. It was further stated that the system for notification of suspected APIs was far less clear than for FPs.

Concerning the existence of clear notification procedures for suspected counterfeit medicines, some respondents said that it was clear while others said that there was no specific procedure for counterfeit medicines. It was further stated that there was no clear procedure for APIs.

Existence of specific manufacturer and distributor security personnel that have responsibility to investigate medicines counterfeiting

Some 40% of respondents indicated that they had security systems in place to investigate medicines counterfeiting. The types of investigation carried out were various and included independent pharmaceutical health risk assessment; overt/covert investigations into source and major suppliers of counterfeit products; researching and monitoring counterfeit traffic of pharmaceuticals (in co-operation with the PSI and local or regional intelligence agencies); working to identify key elements of the criminal business model; proactive and reactive inquiries to identify the source of manufacturing and distribution chains; Internet research; test purchases; audits; and control of sourcing. Investigative activity where it exists tends to reside in the company quality assurance function.

Where it was stated that no such security systems existed, 50% of respondents indicated that they were planning to implement such a system in the future. It can thus be concluded that stakeholders are increasingly taking the medicines counterfeiting issue seriously.

16.20. Customs' control of medicinal products

16.20.1. Customs' risk analysis

The actual approach and factors adopted by member states in customs' risk analysis of medicinal products varies. Risk factors applying to medicinal products (for example, specific drug classes or tariff codes) are not universally employed by authorities. This suggests that there is scope for wider utilisation of risk factors specific to medicinal products.

It was generally the case that controls are applied following identification of risk factors for a particular consignment. One respondent stated that "very often customs will also be heavily reliant upon information or intelligence which is provided by the rights holder or the rights holder's representative. This information is used by customs to create what are known as customs profiles. These are programmed into the customs electronic entry processing system and any matches generated against entered information will result in a full documentary check and possible physical examination."

16.20.2. API regulatory controls

The type of controls carried out by finance/customs authorities on APIs in cases of import/export/transit are not consistent across member states and often not specifically related to medicinal products. It is notable that specific controls are implemented by customs authorities for narcotics and psychotropics as a result of obligations under UN conventions.

16.20.3. Information sharing with health authorities in case of customs action (EC Regulation 1383/2003)

The significant majority of both health and customs authorities, and also stakeholders, agreed that information sharing was important. The one specific authority comment provided was: "all exchange of information is crucial in implementing controls against counterfeit goods. The applicants for customs action are best placed to produce details relating to their products, which would be of immense benefit to the health authorities not only in deterring the movements of counterfeit pharmaceuticals but also in educating the public against the dangers of such products using real examples. Customs is not aware of any statutory impediment to this type of information being exchanged with the health authorities. Certainly, in terms of producing better customs controls and achieving better seizure rates, such exchange of information as mentioned within Article 5.5 of the (EC) Customs Regulation [12] is crucial."

One stakeholder stated: "if it is meant that right holders/producers should be consulted beforehand and authorise the sharing of information between various authorities such as health and customs, the answer is yes, this should be the case. However, this can prove to be impractical. It can also be envisaged, for example, that a (confidentiality) agreement is signed between relevant parties where the stakeholders with whom the information may be shared are specifically mentioned. Other solutions are possible too."

16.21. Analytical testing of suspected or known counterfeit medicines

In general this is conducted by a national OMCL, although in the case where a counterfeit is detected by ministries other than the MoH/DRA, other types of laboratory may be responsible; for example, an official forensic laboratory, a customs laboratory or private laboratories. Procedures concerning payment for testing suspected counterfeit medicines vary between countries and cover either specific ministries, the state in general, the guilty party or the manufacturer. There is some scope for rationalising and standardising payment policy and procedures. A mixed response was provided concerning the existence of legal provisions for centralised reporting of test results.

A specific problem mentioned was the absence of information for interested parties on the results of tests on suspected counterfeit APIs and excipients.

16.22. Medicinal product security and traceability systems

The absence of such systems combined with an increasingly complex distribution system leads to major difficulties in identifying counterfeit medicines. Efforts are required to improve and implement medicinal product security and traceability systems.

16.23. IPR with relevance to medicines counterfeiting

It can be concluded from the Council of Europe IPR Study No. 1, Chapter 10.6.1, "Criminal law comparative study", that criminal sanctions appear to be far from being harmonised and of a strength which is probably not a deterrent when applied to counterfeit medicines manufactured by organised criminal organisations.

Due to the territorial effect of industrial property laws, it appears that counterfeiters could exploit the discrepancies which exist between member states in order to escape or minimise the risk of criminal sanctions.

Harmonisation and, where applicable, strengthening of sanctions appear to be facilitated in the majority of the member states that are signatories to the European Patent Convention, where these sanctions are defined in the Penal Code, the amendment of which may be easier to carry out than in a less frequently revised patent or trademark law.

The present study does not take into consideration the quality of enforcement in the member states. Some may provide for sanctions which, however, would be difficult or long to implement in practice.

In addition, the sanctions reported in the present study would not of course apply to counterfeit drugs which are no longer protected by a patent or a certificate of supplementary protection. It would consequently appear that generic drugs are particularly badly protected by IPR in their present form.

16.24. National authority co-operation against medicines counterfeiting

Some major gaps exist in co-ordination between national authorities in different sectors based on the survey's evidence (only one member state indicated that there was a complete co-operation network involving all relevant authorities).

If the public health and economic aspects of the counterfeit medicine problem are recognised, then serious efforts need to be made to increase national inter-sectoral co-operation, preferably on a formalised basis.

The existence of legal provisions for reporting counterfeit medicines was also highly variable. Where legal arrangements were said to exist, the type of provision cited was also highly variable as were the existence of corresponding conditions for confidentiality of reporting.

16.25. International authority co-operation against medicines counterfeiting (information exchange, databases and RASs)

Co-ordinated information exchange on the appearance of counterfeit medicines and their impact on public health is weak. This reflects a number of factors including the absence of clear reporting requirements for counterfeit medicines under existing medicinal product defect and adverse reaction reporting systems, the lack of recognition of the public health threat posed by counterfeit medicines, the absence of a commonly agreed definition of counterfeit medicines and pharmaceutical crime in Europe, the lack of regulatory resources to tackle medicines counterfeiting and the difficulties for MoH/DRAs to exchange information between themselves due to legal provisions relating to data protection.

The WHO counterfeit medicine database system clearly is not used satisfactorily by European countries (and for that matter by other countries elsewhere in the world). Perhaps part of the reason for this is that such a database is not linked to any direct regulatory response action. Almost no MoH/DRA operates a counterfeit medicine database. Several counterfeit medicine databases exist (operated by non-governmental organisations) although the extent to which they are utilised by stakeholders is highly variable.

The results of the surveys further show that there are some large data incongruences between counterfeit medicine cases known to national authorities, manufacturers and wholesalers.

Concerning RASs operated by MoH/DRAs, almost all stated that the provisions for such systems existed and where reports were forwarded they tended to be to international/European-level bodies such as the PFIPC, Council of Europe, MRA members, PIC/S members, the EMEA and the WHO – there was no consistent pattern of forwarding reports to international/European-level bodies or to national authorities. National authorities outside of the MoH/DRA were rarely involved in an RAS system.

It can be concluded that there is a major problem concerning lack of co-ordination and awareness in the reporting and registering of counterfeit medicine cases. The existence of a number of counterfeit medicine databases and RASs which have no clear linkage to regulatory enforcement causes confusion. There is thus substantial agreement among respondents on the need for a common, Europe-wide database and reporting system for counterfeit medicines and that these should involve close collaboration between all players (authorities, manufacturers, brokers, wholesalers, pharmacies and health professionals).

Related to this issue is the existence (and ongoing development) of EU-level pharmaceutical database systems (pharmacovigilance, quality defects, clinical trials, MAs, etc.). On the one hand, it would seem logical to place a counterfeit medicine database and reporting system within the existing EU pharmaceutical database system. However, this would exclude the participation of non-EU Council of Europe member states, many of which have a not insubstantial counterfeit medicine problem that also indirectly impacts on EU member states. Therefore, it would of course be an advantage to have a counterfeit medicine database and reporting system placed under the existing EU database and reporting framework, but only if participation were extended to non-EU member states. Otherwise, the only alternative would seem to be to place this under the supervision of the Council of Europe or an alternative European-wide authority.

16.26. Authority and industry co-operation against medicines counterfeiting

A mixed picture was produced by the survey. Frequently mentioned was the need for industry to divulge to the authorities known information on counterfeit medicines (including the results of analytical tests conducted on suspected counterfeits by industry and also pre-clinical data) and to do so in a timely fashion.

Generally, there was disclosure on a need-to-know basis and if not, in strict confidence. Reference was also made to what was disclosed in the MA dossier in terms of covert features, although rarely are voluntary covert features disclosed. Also non-indication of covert characteristics can be understood in terms of industry's reluctance to pass on this information to counterfeiters. The issue of what needs to be disclosed may not have been sufficiently tested as yet.

Few or no formal provisions exist for co-operation between industry and authorities on the subject of medicines counterfeiting at this time.

16.27. Training needs for the detection and prevention of counterfeit medicines

Not a single member state authority in any sector indicated that current training is adequate in order to detect, investigate and take action against counterfeiters. Based on the responses received, it can safely be concluded that there is a need to

147

provide standardised training and education for the detection and prevention of counterfeit medicines.

16.28. Justification for the extension of Council of Europe activity in the areas of detection and prevention

There is good evidence to suggest that the counterfeit medicine problem in east European and central European countries is significant. For example, a large number of cases have been reported in the Russian Federation (13). As counterfeit medicines are a cross-border trade problem, the situation in eastern Europe impacts on western Europe and it is in the interests of the latter to address the problem in the former. This can be achieved via an extension of the Council of Europe's initiative to all member states in central and eastern Europe.

17. Recommendations for the implementation of legislative and administrative measures against medicines counterfeiting

A summary of recommendations was made in a presentation to the Ad hoc Group on Counterfeit Medicines in December 2004 (see Appendix 8). This section of the report presents both strong and detailed recommendations for implementation, without in anyway proposing any fixed high-level legal agreement at this stage. The recommendations presented are for discussion only at this stage.

17.1. Need for multiple implementation measures and the allocation of appropriate resources

Action is now required to tackle the counterfeit medicine problem in order to avoid a human health tragedy in Europe (and elsewhere). A battery of measures is probably required in order to effectively tackle the problem as no single measure alone is likely to be adequate.

Of course, potentially anything is possible to implement from a regulatory perspective with the allocation of the necessary resources and/or the "undying efforts" of the very often extremely dedicated authority/regulatory staff. A long-term view to tackling the problem needs to be adopted.

Recommendation No. 1

Definition of the human, financial and system resources required to implement an effective medicines anti-counterfeiting strategy.

17.2. Establishment of a European-level co-ordinating instrument

The establishment of a European co-ordinating instrument can perhaps be viewed as one of the principal recommendations of this report, although to do so will require a detailed discussion of the necessary human and financial resources. Based on the results of the various surveys conducted, quite clearly there is a need for a European co-ordinating structure to be designated to oversee, co-ordinate and manage the medicines anti-counterfeiting issue throughout Europe, particularly as several tasks can only be managed at this level. To date, no institution has been given responsibility for managing this major emerging public health problem. The task is difficult, if not impossible, to manage solely at the national level. Furthermore, the tasks required to tackle medicines counterfeiting go beyond the purely drug regulatory function.

Several recommendations on this issue were received from respondents, which can be summarised as being based on the creation of a co-ordination structure comprising health authorities, the WHO, customs, police and industry/

distributor/pharmacy associations that operates both across boundaries as well as across sectors in the country. It would operate as an international observatory and would supervises international and European co-operation agreements between authorities and industry (which should be based on a clear legislative framework).

The relevant European/international-level bodies that potentially have a role to play in European level co-ordination include:

- the Council of Europe;
- EU institutions (see Section 17.3 below);
- the WHO;
- the INCB;
- EUROPOL/INTERPOL;
- the World Customs Organization (WCO);
- the PIC/S;
- the ICH and its Global Co-operation Group;
- other international anti-counterfeiting initiatives, for example the PFIPC.

Whichever European-level structure is determined to be best placed to oversee co-ordination, it is important that clear roles and responsibilities are defined so as to avoid unnecessary duplication of efforts made by other institutions. Two options are proposed for the management of the counterfeiting issue in Europe (with of course support from the other institutions mentioned above):

Option 1. Council of Europe via its relevant institutions – Directorate Generals of Legal Affairs, and Social Cohesion, the EDQM/OCL network, etc.

The Council of Europe, via its Directorate General of Legal Affairs, has a mandate to promote the rule of law amongst its member states, which it achieves via conventions, agreements and recommendations, in particular in the protection of citizens' security and the fight against crime (14). The Council of Europe Directorate General for Social Cohesion, via its Public Health Committee (Partial Agreement), has a mandate to promote public health protection amongst the member states. In addition the Council of Europe operates the European Directorate for the Quality of Medicines (EDQM), which co-ordinates the OMCL inspection network and the European Pharmacopoeia.

Thus, the Council of Europe with its strong and well-established legal, public health and quality of medicines mandate, based on the protection of human rights and the principles of democracy, can be seen to have several advantages if called upon to co-ordinate a medicines anti-counterfeiting initiative throughout Europe.

It should be assured that the European structures, which have the authority and the technical network to take on such a role, are assigned sufficient human and financial resources to manage it.

Option 2. UN INCB

The UN INCB has major experience in managing a related problem – that of narcotics and psychotropics, together with their precursors. At the least, the UN INCB should be an active partner in tackling this issue. Because of the obvious criminal links between illicit and counterfeit drug manufacturing and production, the UN INCB has extensive knowledge of the criminality networks involved in illicit drug manufacture and distribution (and these networks are likely to be the same as those involved with counterfeit medicine manufacture and production).

The UN INCB has a clear international mandate and has successfully promoted inter-sectoral co-operation between the relevant authorities, both nationally and internationally (which shows that it must be possible to achieve good inter-sectoral co-operation for the control of counterfeit medicines).

It is strongly recommended that discussions be conducted with the UN INCB concerning ways to tackle the counterfeiting issue.

Recommendation No. 2

Determination of the European co-ordinating body with responsibility for overseeing the implementation of the provisions of this report and their long-term management; definition of the roles of other relevant international organisations; and drafting of a report on how UN INCB practice and experience could be applied to medicines counterfeiting.

17.3. EU institutions' roles and responsibilities concerning medicines counterfeiting in the Council of Europe member states

Within the European Commission, there are several important institutions that have a potentially important supporting role to play in implementing medicines anti-counterfeiting measures in the Council of Europe member states (both EU and non-EU member states), as proposed by this report. These bodies include, amongst others:

- EC DG Enterprise (pharmaceutical trade and regulation);
- EC DG Legal (penal code, customs, etc.);
- EC DG Taxud;
- the EMEA (medicinal product registration and post-market surveillance for medicinal products approved via EU central and mutual recognition procedures).

It will be important to establish the relative roles of the above (and perhaps other) European Commission institutions in relation to the designated European co-ordinating body, with respect to the recommendations described in this report. It should also be stated that the existing good communications and relations between the legal departments of the Council of Europe and the EU provide an appropriate facility and opportunity for the development and harmonisation of existing and proposed draft legislation on medicines counterfeiting.

Recommendation No. 3

Definition of EU institutions' roles and responsibilities concerning medicines anti-counterfeiting measures.

17.4. Anti-counterfeiting implementation framework decision – Creation of strong recommendations to member states?

It is assumed that the political will exists to move forward on this issue. This report should be seen as only one tool in order to get the required administrative and legal provisions into operation. Other tools include Council of Europe Parliamentary Assembly recommendations, Ad hoc Group on Counterfeit Medicines minutes, etc. Ideally this report, combined with these other documents, should be drawn together in a formal policy document.

Having established the most appropriate institutional basis for implementation, it is advisable that strong recommendations to member states (perhaps in the form of a convention/co-operation agreement), committing the relevant parties to certain obligations, need to be created (a convention on medicines counterfeiting could perhaps be analogous to the successful UN conventions on narcotics, psychotropics and their precursors (15)). The type of instrument most appropriate should ideally be based on the highest form of co-operation possible between the Council of Europe member states, and its substance should probably be based on strong recommendations (as opposed to dictates).

The preamble to the proposed instrument needs to thoroughly spell out why it is necessary to have a European-level provision to deal with medicines counterfeiting (based on the findings in this report, the Council of Europe Parliamentary Assembly recommendations and other valid important points made in the various ad hoc group meeting minutes over the past two years).

It is recommended that the proposed recommendations to member states cover three principle areas:

(i) a legislative/regulatory framework for dealing with medicines counterfeiting in member states;

(ii) a European co-ordinating body (EU and international bodies) – roles and responsibilities;

(iii) national authorities – co-ordination, role and responsibilities.

The provisions of the proposed instrument should ideally not be placed just under the control of one sectoral authority (that is, not just under health), as a satisfactory handling of the counterfeit medicine problem requires a co-ordinated intersectoral approach.

The outline of a model instrument is presented in Appendix 9 to this report.

Recommendation No. 4

Creation of strong recommendations (that is, for example, a convention, co-operation agreement, etc.) to deal with medicines counterfeiting at the European level.

17.5. Strong recommendations to member states: proposal for a European-level legislative/regulatory and administrative framework dealing specifically with medicines counterfeiting

17.5.1. Legislative and regulatory framework

Member states' legislation and regulations contain different legal provisions to deal with medicines counterfeiting. However, the scope and type of such provisions varies considerably between member states and between sectors. It can be concluded that no single satisfactory legal provision against counterfeiting exists in any member state and that, thus, there is a need for a legislative/regulatory framework model applicable to both human and veterinary medicinal products that can be applied in member states. National authorities could be left a degree of flexibility as to how this might be implemented at national level, so long as the provisions are incorporated into national legislation.

Many of the recommendations provided under Section 17 of this report are legislative/regulatory aspects that need to be incorporated into such a legislative/regulatory framework model.

In order to finalise the framework model, it is recommended that a complete codification of existing national legal provisions that potentially apply to medicines counterfeiting should be conducted (based on the work already started in this area by the relevant surveys and this report).

17.5.2. European co-ordinating instrument – Role and responsibilities

Many of the recommendations provided under Section 17 of this report refer to European-level administrative roles and responsibilities for implementation of the anti medicines counterfeiting strategy and need to be incorporated into the proposed instrument.

17.5.3. National authorities – Co-ordination, role and responsibilities

The proposed instrument should detail a specific national inter-sectoral counterfeit medicines co-ordination strategy and procedures as well as define clearly the recommended role and responsibilities of the various national authorities. Some of these issues are covered in more detail elsewhere in Section 17 of this report.

Recommendation No. 5

Complete codification of existing member state legislation (continuation of existing Council of Europe work on this topic based on the start provided by this report and the Council's studies already conducted); definition of the European co-ordinating instrument's role and responsibilities concerning anti medicines counterfeiting; and definition of national authorities' roles and responsibilities, and co-ordinating mechanisms concerning counterfeiting.

17.6. Targeting medicinal product types at risk of being counterfeited and those that carry a potentially high public health risk

The type of medicinal product counterfeited may vary by country/geographic region and be due to specific local market factors. Survey results indicate that a broad range of medicinal product types are at risk of being counterfeited.

Efforts should concentrate on tackling those counterfeit medicines identified as being at high risk of being counterfeited together with those that carry a potentially high public health risk, in order to maximise the use of limited regulatory resources. Thus a Europe-wide database system of medicines known to be at risk of being counterfeited with weightings according to potential public health risk needs to be created. This could be made similar to that already managed by, for example, the US (NABP) website (this site lists medicinal products that are known to be at risk of being counterfeited).

> **Recommendation No. 6**
>
> Database of medicinal products at high risk of being counterfeited and those that carry a potentially high public health risk.

17.7. Detailed characterisation of the official and unofficial distribution chain for counterfeit medicines and the counterfeit medicine criminal business model

Several survey respondents have indicated that it would be extremely beneficial for a detailed characterisation of the existing official and unofficial distribution chain to be carried out, thus allowing more targeted actions to be taken by authorities, particularly with respect to inspection and registration of traders in the pharmaceutical field. A detailed and ongoing characterisation of the criminal business model for medicines counterfeiting is also vital (refer also to the PSI initiative in this area). This should be a task for the European co-ordinating body.

> **Recommendation No. 7**
>
> Characterisation of (i) the official and unofficial pharmaceutical distribution chain for counterfeit medicines; and (ii) the counterfeit medicine criminal business model.

17.8. Specific definitions and rules of interpretation concerning medicines counterfeiting

Specific agreed definitions of "counterfeit medicine" and "pharmaceutical crime" should be defined and included in the proposed convention/co-operation agreement:

17.8.1. Definition of "counterfeit medicine"

It is recommended that a common definition of "counterfeit medicine" be adopted that is acceptable to all member states; probably based on the WHO definition. The latter appears to be the most widely accepted and comprehensive international definition.

17.8.2. Definition and concept of "pharmaceutical crime"

It is recommended that a commonly agreed definition of "pharmaceutical crime" be adopted by the member states; this would go a long way in communicating to authorities, stakeholders and the general public the important essential difference in type and degree of crime relating to medicines counterfeiting as opposed to counterfeiting of other product types.

It is beyond the scope of this report to provide a recommended comprehensive definition of "pharmaceutical crime" that can be applied to all member states. However, it is recommended that the following items/conceptual points presented in the following table be included in the eventual definition of "pharmaceutical crime":

Table 34: Items/conceptual points that should be included in a definition of "pharmaceutical crime"

- formal classification of types of medicines counterfeiting, which is linked to a clear scale of regulatory violation and appropriate penalties;
- aggravated circumstances of counterfeiting and piracy;
- intent;
- health risk and damage;
- IPR;
- falsification (product, packaging and documentation);
- fraud;
- illegal trading;
- possession;
- other items to be determined and agreed upon.

Any agreed definition and explanatory notes will probably need to be updated on a regular basis to take into account evolving counterfeiting practices.

Concerning "aggravated circumstances of counterfeiting and piracy", the ad hoc group (record 3) has already recommended the following definition and explanation:

Definition: "aggravated circumstances of counterfeiting and piracy" are those that justify and necessitate special legal provisions including more stringent sanctions. Counterfeit medicines constitute an aggravated circumstance of counterfeiting requiring special attention and consideration in legal provisions including sanctions. Aggravated circumstances of counterfeiting and pirating comprise:
- all cases where individual and public health is involved;
- where confidence in medicines and authorities and subsequent compliance with therapeutic regimes are compromised;
- the willingness of industry and investors to invest in research and pharmaceutical business are compromised;
- where organised crime (for example, money laundering) and bio-terrorism are involved;
- where loss of public funds (funds for social security) are wasted.

Explanatory notes regarding the circumstances: counterfeit medicines constitute both an individual and public health danger (for example, if vaccinations of individuals do not work the community (public) is endangered) because:
- their quality is unpredictable and not subject to control (by definition);
- no recall procedures in case of defects;
- lack of specific legislation concerning counterfeit medicines in Council of Europe member states;
- lack of export control;
- lack of therapeutic action or unintended wrong action;
- not safe (toxic, non-sterile);
- no active search and investigation for quality defects caused by counterfeits in official control laboratories;
- lack of know-how in detection and recognition;
- rapidly increasing problem;
- not included in national security plans.

17.8.3. Other relevant related terminology

A number of relevant related terms (for example, traceability of a medical product and risk to public health) need to be defined and included in the proposed

155

instrument. These terms should, as far as possible, be based on existing EU regulations on medicinal products and other relevant terminology and definitions.

Recommendation No. 8

Finalisation of definitions of "counterfeit medicine" and "pharmaceutical crime" (and other relevant related definitions) and their incorporation into the proposed instrument.

17.9. Inspection requirements

It was generally agreed that increased efforts aimed at inspection are required and as such specific inspection standard operating procedures in relation to the detection of counterfeit medicines should be implemented. The specific inspection measures proposed by survey respondents are summarised in the following table.

Table 35: Summary of recommendations for improved inspection procedures concerning the prevention of counterfeit medicines

---

- adoption of a more proactive random search strategy (proactive enquiries and combined regulatory group inspection programmes);
- continuous organised test buying and sampling at companies/wholesalers under suspicion;
- focus on testing of high risk products;
- systematic inspection including some by independent international bodies;
- spot checks and analysis on imported drugs and visual control of packaging (these controls should be ensured by each wholesaler);
- improved validation of documentation (paper and electronic – anti-fraud measures);
- less reliance on documentation and certificates as a regulatory control measure (due to the relative ease of documentation fraud);
- each participant in the legal supply chain should be controlled at least every year;
- increased GDP inspections (more often and more thoroughly, especially for smaller wholesalers);
- evaluation and inspection before granting a CoS or accepting (EDMF) documentation;
- mandatory inspection of API manufacturers worldwide and increased number of inspections of foreign API manufacturers;
- increased inspection linkage with retail pharmacies;
- inspection of repackagers;
- provisions for audit of the entire supply chain;
- point of sale authentication system;
- system for accurate determination of product pedigree – focus on traceability documentation and clear rules for checking authenticity;
- controlled processing of flows of materials;
- more realistic timetable for inspection of suspect/seized goods by rights holders;
- evaluation of imported goods (spot checks) as is in place, for example, for toys;
- increase foreign parcels control (necessary due to increasing Internet pharmacy).

Recommendation No. 9

Creation of standard operating procedures for inspection of suspected counterfeit medicines (including both proactive and reactive measures).

17.10. Enforcement requirements

It was generally agreed by respondents that increased efforts (supported by allocation of appropriate powers) aimed at enforcement of counterfeit medicine violations/offences are required. These are summarised in the following table.

Table 36: Summary of recommendations for improved enforcement measures against counterfeit medicines

- more powers to seize and detain (arrest);
- IPR enforcement;
- definitions in the crime sheet should be based on the intention to introduce or to sell counterfeit drugs;
- clear rules for checking and reporting by distributors and enforcement by audits/inspections;
- tighter control of secondary wholesalers;
- installation of a structure that allows for very tough enforcement, proportional to the health risks involved;
- sample visits without previous notice to some producers would be very instructive (but international agreements among health authorities should be in place);
- publication of clear rules and regulations for each party: manufacturer, importer, MAA holder and wholesaler (namely, preventive action).

Recommendation No. 10

Creation of appropriate enforcement powers and procedures against counterfeiting.

17.11. Appropriate sanctions and penalties against counterfeiting

There is a need to have sufficient legislation that allows prosecution and punitive measures against medicine counterfeiters and distributors. It was generally agreed that sanctions and penalties should be much stronger than those that currently exist. Thus, a clearly spelled out list of sanctions specific to medicines counterfeiting should be created and included as part of any specific counterfeit medicine legislation/regulation. The level of sanction should be commensurate with the degree of infringement/violation. The following table summarises sanctions and penalties proposed by respondents (including sanction policy recommendations).

Table 37: Summary of recommendations for sanctions and penalties that should be applied against counterfeit medicines

- all existing measures should be generally increased (that is, raising fines and introducing/increasing imprisonment sanctions);
- training of judiciary to understand that counterfeit pharmaceuticals are a health hazard and cannot therefore be compared, for example, to a counterfeit film on a DVD;
- sanctions and penalties should be commensurate with the crime (for example, counterfeit APIs can potentially kill or seriously harm thousands of patients per API batch. Penalties should take account of this);
- financial fines, industry-wide blacklisting and exclusion from the pharmaceutical market;
- civil plus criminal law actions;
- sanctions should be applied in the countries where the counterfeiting companies are located;

- sanctions as in place in the US – import licence withdrawal, "redlisting" made available to pharmaceutical companies;
- if the manufacturer or the distributor does not buy through the legal supply chain he must be immediately closed down.

Recommendation No. 11

Definition of a common basic European penal code for pharmaceutical crime with sanctions commensurate with the level of the crime.

17.12. IPR and medicines counterfeiting

The next step could be a study of the ability of standard patent claims to be interpreted or extended in order to cope with the different types of counterfeit drugs, whenever patent protection still exists.

If the latter study were to conclude that the patent claiming system does not provide enough protection to brand name pharmaceutical companies, another study could be envisaged to set out the possible basis of a new kind of IPR to be created, providing for the possibility of deterring organised criminal counterfeiters of drugs by, at least, appropriate criminal sanctions. This new kind of IPR could in particular relay patent rights when these expire and benefit to and be activated by generic pharmaceutical companies.

Appropriate IPR provisions need to be clearly covered within the definition of pharmaceutical crime.

Recommendation No. 12

Completion of the ongoing studies on IPR and pharmaceutical crime, definition of a common basic European penal code for pharmaceutical crime with sanctions commensurate with the level of the crime.

17.13. Import/export/transit regulatory controls to prevent the counterfeit medicine trade

Attention is required for tightening up member states' legislative and regulatory loopholes in medicinal product/medical device licensing rules for import, export and transit, particularly the latter two areas and to ensure that such provisions are standardised across member states. Regulatory provisions for export and transit should also cover bonded warehouses and free zones. It is vital to ensure that exported medicines are regulated to the same standards as domestically utilised medicines. Regulatory standards applied should be the same for APIs as FPs. Furthermore, it is desirable to examine how parallel trade rules for medicinal products can be tightened up to minimise repackaging and relabelling practices (see Section 17.15 below).

Recommendation No. 13

Creation of standardised and tight regulatory provisions for import, export and transit (including bonded warehouses and free zones) and for parallel trade that apply equally to APIs and FPs.

17.14. Regulation of Internet pharmacy, medicinal product mail order and unlicensed medicines

This should be regarded as a priority area for attention and requires a European-level approach (particularly as frequently Internet orders are placed outside the country of destination). There is no obvious reason why Internet pharmacies should be treated any differently, in terms of regulation, to high street pharmacies. Internet pharmacy sales require a clearer definition of which laws have been broken and where. Mail order is obviously connected to Internet pharmacy, and provisions have to be made to control import/export/transit of mail order medicinal products.

A related topic is that of unlicensed medicines (compassionate use) that may or may not be legitimately imported into any particular state. Clearer and more standardised procedures need to be developed governing unlicensed medicines and their compassionate use.

Possible approaches to tackling this problem are summarised in the following table.

Table 38: Summary of recommendations for regulation of Internet pharmacy and mail order

---

- legal liability for Internet pharmacies to disclose information about the operation of their site;
- registration by MoH/DRAs of Internet pharmacy websites, the proprietor of the site, the registered pharmacist responsible for dealing with offers made by the site, and the physical location of the Internet pharmacy involved;
- publication by the MoH/DRA of a directory of such Internet sites;
- sharing such directories between the MoH/DRAs of different member states;
- sharing of information by manufacturers with MoH/DRAs of known offending Internet pharmacies offering counterfeited versions of their medicines;
- regular inspection of the premises of Internet pharmacies;
- increased spot checks on imported mail order deliveries;
- raised public awareness of the problems of purchasing medicines over the Internet and suspicion of cheap products;
- controls need to be closely aligned with final payment mechanisms.

Recommendation No. 14

Creation of Internet and mail order pharmacy regulations.

In this context, reference is made to the Council of Europe Committee of Experts on Pharmaceutical Questions model information to empower the Internet user to make a healthy and informed choice from the abundance of risky offers of medicines and medicinal services via the Internet. The model information has been made publicly available to inspire authorities concerned with the protection of public health to perform their own information campaigns. Some member states' authorities have already implemented the model for public campaigns (see Appendix 10).

17.15. Regulatory measures particularly applicable to the security of the distribution chain and packaging/labelling of medicinal products

Greater emphasis needs to be placed by authorities on the regulation of non-full-line wholesalers and brokers/traders. It is acknowledged that in order to do this, additional resources need to be allocated to MoH/DRAs. A summary of proposed regulatory control measures particularly applicable to the distribution chain is provided in the following table.

Table 39: Summary of recommendations for regulation of the distribution chain and packaging/labelling

- strengthening of existing GDP guidelines (explicit inclusion of trading under such guidelines) and applicability to non-full-line wholesalers;
- regulation and licensing of brokers;
- emphasis on adoption of secure business practices by all participants in the drug supply chain (for example, only purchasing from/supplying to registered and controlled actors);
- regulatory control, and elimination as far as possible, of repackaging and relabelling. Increased supervision of repackagers and relabellers and strengthened licensing conditions for such activities. More explicit control of repackaging and relabelling under parallel importation regulations, including maintenance of detailed repack batch records;
- return to a comprehensible supply chain and at least one sales office per pharmaceutical trader/distributor/manufacturer per country, physically occupied by at least one legally responsible person as link for authorities and customers (wholesalers, hospitals, retailers, consumers, etc.). It must be a qualified person with a good command of the national language capable of and responsible for meeting regulations on good manufacturing, distribution and trading practice laid down in national and EU regulations, and dealing with claims generated by authorities, clients and customers;
- licensing of non-full-line wholesalers – strict control of permits for production and wholesaling; more stringent controls should be applied to applicants for wholesale dealer licences, as the proliferation of short-line wholesalers increases trading and potential routes of entry for counterfeit medicinal products;
- pharmacists should not be allowed to trade by way of wholesale dealing without a wholesale dealer licence;
- regulatory controls and inspection need to be applied to pharmacists and dispensing doctors (original pack dispensing).

Recommendation No. 15

Creation of stronger regulations concerning distribution and packaging/relabelling.

17.16. Regulatory measures particularly applicable to APIs and excipients

Regulatory control measures proposed by respondents that are particularly applicable to APIs are summarised in the following table (refer also to Section 12.3).

Table 40: Summary of recommendations for regulation of APIs

- due to the almost global lack of attention given to API counterfeiting (the US is an exception), all matters relating to this question need to be developed almost from scratch – greater controls should be applied to producers of APIs;
- acceptance of APIs without inspection (for example, with only a CoS or a statement of commitment without meaning) should be terminated;
- inspection should focus on where the APIs enter the chain and at API manufacturing itself. More is needed than focusing inspection only on the registered API manufacturer: verification of whether the API present in the dosage form is indeed from the registered API manufacturer is also needed (see section on traceability below and provisions of ICH Q7a). Once APIs are in the chain they will stay in, as ingredients in the FPs. Thereafter, they can often only be detected through thorough analytical evaluation/fingerprinting. It is well known that at certain brokers/traders in parti-cular, practices take place that result in the distribution of counterfeit APIs (relabelling). There should be very strict oversight of API products entering free trade zones in EU harbours to ensure that illicit API material does not enter the EU;
- full implementation of the provisions of Appendix 18 of Directive 2003/94/EC and ICH Q7a is required in member states;
- strengthening and standardisation of international API monographs (via the ICH and European Pharmacopoeia).

Recommendation No. 16

Creation of stronger regulations concerning API control.

17.17. Customs and health authority information sharing concerning suspected counterfeit medicines

Information sharing between customs and health authorities should occur and be made more explicit, whilst confidentiality agreements should be in place. However, it is recognised that some manufacturers may be reluctant to acknowledge or act upon reports of counterfeit medicines because of the potential adverse effect on their business. This reluctance needs to be overcome in the interests of all involved in the legitimate supply of pharmaceuticals. A possible model to enhance health and custom authorities co-ordination is the creation of a specific medicines section/liaison unit within customs authorities.

It is essential that producers of pharmaceutical products who believe that their goods are susceptible to counterfeiting should register their rights with customs authorities in accordance with EC Regulation 1383/2003 (12). In applying for action against counterfeit activity, the rights holder should include as much relevant information as possible to enable the goods in question to be readily recognised by the customs authorities and increase the likelihood of a seizure being achieved. Additionally, participation in an EU-sponsored initiative, such as the 4IPR project aimed at developing a pan-European information sharing system between rights holders and law enforcement agencies within a secure environment, would also be of huge benefit to the pharmaceutical industry.

Recommendation No. 17

Creation of agreement/memorandum of understanding on information sharing between customs and health authorities.

17.18. Medicinal product security and traceability (pedigree tracking) systems

17.18.1. Security systems to differentiate genuine APIs from counterfeit medicines

It was generally agreed that security systems should be improved and specific recommendations are summarised in the following table.

Table 41: Summary of recommendations concerning medicinal product security systems

- any technically feasible, infallible and affordable way of improving security should be introduced;
- introduction of security features depending on risk (different authentication levels: overt, covert and forensic);
- make use of new technologies but do not rely on one; adopt multi-layer counterfeit protection;
- more anti-counterfeiting measures applied especially to samples and clinical packages;
- holograms and IDs which are difficult to falsify;
- tamper proof/tamper evident packaging;
- unit of use packaging;
- use of packaging that is impossible to falsify and tracing included in pills;
- more unique closure systems and practices;
- rules for the inclusion of covert markers in APIs and/or medicinal products;
- a mixture of overt and covert anti-counterfeit features should be deployed;
- use of trace substances;
- use of colour-shift ink (which has yet to be counterfeited);
- authentication of packaging features (according to company strategy and decision);
- authentication technology for rapid identification at the pharmacy level.

It was generally agreed that traceability systems should be established and improved. Specific recommendations made are summarised in the following table.

Table 42: Summary of recommendations concerning medicinal product traceability systems

- harmonised and standardised technical standards need to be developed and introduced to enable local authorities to find sources of counterfeited products;
- use of an adequate unified harmonised (at least European, better still global) system;
- clear requirements for traceability all through the manufacturing and distribution chains should be introduced (such systems should have the possibility of showing that any given item has been bought through the legal supply chain);
- 2D bar coding;
- Internet-based track and trace;
- electronic track and trace – electronic batch number: unique number on each box;
- numbering system and database;
- enforced pedigree papers and prevention of repackaging;
- paper or electronic pedigree should be a mandatory requirement;
- implementation of the provisions of Article 17 of ICH Q7a (for agents, brokers, traders, distributors, repackers and relabellers). Full transparency/traceability back to the manufacture of crucial, "late" API intermediates should be mandatory;
- RFID technology (in the long term); it was also stated that RFID tagging was not an ideal solution at this time as its introduction currently has huge cost implications, and requires massive investment in infrastructure.

Recommendation No. 18

Creation of guidelines on medicinal product security and traceability systems (based on review of best practice elsewhere and anti-counterfeiting technology used in other industries); and use of more sophisticated anti-counterfeiting measures for high risk products.

17.19. Active searching and analytical testing of suspected counterfeit medicines

Introduction of proactive sampling for counterfeit medicines based on high risk products (in terms of counterfeiting and public health risk) is required. For example, one member state has a medicines testing surveillance scheme whereby the national pharmaceutical association purchases random medicinal products from pharmacies and sends them to the MoH/DRA to test in the OMCL for authentication. Payment procedures and responsibility for testing of counterfeit medicines need to be more clearly defined.

Recommendation No. 19

Creation of random sampling surveillance system for medicinal products at high risk of being counterfeited; and definition of testing facilities and payment responsibility and procedures.

17.20. RAS for suspected counterfeit medicines

It is recommended that member states adopt the RAS for counterfeit medicines as proposed by the Ad hoc Group on Counterfeit Medicines (see Appendix 7). As far as possible, this system should be incorporated into existing medicine reporting systems (for example, quality or pharmacovigilance) so as to avoid extra/duplicative administrative burdens. The exact functioning and procedures for such a system needs to be determined. Ideally, the reporting system should be managed/co-ordinated at a central level and co-ordinated/incorporated into the EMEA and PIC/S reporting systems. In this respect, a letter on this issue has been sent to the EMEA by the Council's Secretariat. In order for such a system to work effectively it should incorporate reporting by, and provision of reports to, wholesalers and pharmacies, in addition to manufacturers and authorities.

Recommendation No. 20

Implementation of the Council of Europe ad hoc group's RAS for suspected or known counterfeit medicines.

17.21. Risk management procedures/systems for suspected counterfeit medicines

The Ad hoc Group on Counterfeit Medicines is elaborating a draft model procedure for the management of suspected counterfeit medicines that offers public health authorities a decision tree (with instructions for use in the legend). The focus of the risk management procedure is on the rapid prevention of imminent health risk, taking into account the significance of an eventual stock-out of essential medicines. The ad hoc group will look into interfaces for co-operation with stakeholders from the private sector and adequate mechanisms to increase the sensitivity of signal detection in order to apply the procedure also to those counterfeit medicines which are not easily recognised.

Recommendation No. 21

Implementation of the Council of Europe ad hoc group's recommended counterfeit medicines risk management system.

17.22. ADR reporting and pharmacovigilance systems in the context of suspected counterfeit medicines

ADR reporting and pharmacovigilance systems should be amended/upgraded to account more for medicinal product usage problems related to counterfeit medicines (for example, ineffectiveness). Perhaps a specific category of suspected counterfeit medicine problem should be added as a separate line item, as for example the FDA has now done via the MedWatch system.

Recommendation No. 22

More explicit incorporation of drug ineffectiveness in ADR reporting systems; and introduction of a separate line item for suspect counterfeit medicines.

17.23. National authority co-ordination structure and organisational improvements

The following recommendations are made for improving national authority co-ordination and organisational structures to combat medicines counterfeiting (see Section 12.2).

17.23.1. Co-ordinating and communication structural improvements

At the national level, there is an absolute need for better co-ordination/co-operation between (i) the different sectoral authorities, (ii) the authorities and pharmaceutical sector stakeholders, and (iii) pharmaceutical sector stakeholders. The following proposals based on respondent replies are made concerning possible national co-ordinating structures:

Table 43: Summary of recommendations concerning structural improvements in national co-ordination and communication

---

- national networks integrated into a European network which again is part of an international network;
- national inter-agency (authority) commission;
- a special organisation with close co-operation with customs authorities or even including customs functions; for example, carrying out random sampling of incoming products at customs via database-supported product descriptions;
- central associations (representing industry, wholesalers and pharmacists);
- co-ordination/communication structure between health authorities and pharmaceutical industry, wholesalers and pharmacy associations;
- separate co-ordination/communication structure between industry/wholesalers/pharmacy associations;
- periodic meetings between MoH/DRAs and national industry/wholesalers/pharmacy associations.

17.23.2. Available best regulatory practice models and strengthening of health/drug regulatory authorities

With specific reference to strengthening of MoH/DRAs, lessons can be learnt from the FDA as it has taken a major step forward in dealing with the counterfeit medicine issue. Much can be learnt from what the FDA has already achieved and what it is planning to implement (16). It is noted that the FDA has a counterfeit branch that deals with testing (of suspected counterfeit medicines) and an inspection division that goes into the field to investigate counterfeit medicine incidents. It was stated by one respondent that the FDA is ahead in terms of its forensic laboratory function and that the FDA Office of Criminal Investigations is responsible, whilst another stated that "it seems that the FDA is more active on this issue and does not rely only on paper". Particular recommendations received are indicated in Table 44 below.

Table 44: Summary of recommendations concerning best regulatory practice models

- an effective model appears to be the creation of a specific "health police" service that has extended powers (this already exists in one member state). Related to this is the creation of a specific medicines section within the customs authorities. The creation of a specialised health police service may for several reasons not be possible in some countries; but at the least, police and customs authorities should appoint designated liaison officers;
- creation of a specific anti-counterfeit medicine section within DRAs;
- strengthening of MoH/DRA inspectorates;
- API inspection department(s) (of a size proportionate to the extent of the regulations, making worldwide API inspection a routine matter instead of a rare exception. Plus dedicated staff that serve as a focal point for counterfeit matters/information).

17.23.3. Involvement of the following authority types in regulatory co-ordination (in addition to MoH/DRAs)

In addition to MoH/DRAs, several types of closely co-ordinated national authorities need to be involved in tackling the counterfeit medicine problem. These can be summarised in the following table.

Table 45: Types of national authority that are potentially involved in controlling counterfeit medicines

- MoH/DRAs;
- local health authorities;
- police and investigative authorities;
- justice/public prosecution authorities;
- customs and tax authorities;
- trade and commerce authorities.

It is highly recommended that the above authorities designate people who will be dedicated to the medicines counterfeiting issue. In view of the very serious criminal nature of medicines counterfeiting and the (potential and actual) serious impact on the health of unsuspecting victims, there should be very intensive co-operation and communication between the MoH and the MoJ.

Recommendation No. 23

Creation of guidelines/recommendations on national inter-sectoral co-operation in combating counterfeit medicines; learning from/adoption of good regulatory practice concerning counterfeit medicines; and definition of the authorities concerned.

17.24. Co-ordination/co-operation tasks – Communication networks, best practices, codes, protocols, database and reporting systems, and information disclosure

While some recommendations are presented here, based on respondent replies (see also Section 12.2), concerning possible types of co-operation, the exact nature of such co-operation needs ultimately to be defined between all authorities and stakeholders. It is probable that any agreed types of co-operation involving information exchange (between administrative bodies and rights holders, and between different administrative bodies inter and intra-nationally in Europe) will have to be legally provided for under the proposed instrument as described above. The types of co-operation can be classified into those that should be organised/co-ordinated at European level and those that should be conducted at a national level. Of course, the types of co-operation will overlap between European and national levels.

17.24.1. European co-ordination of anti-counterfeiting tasks

The following table summarises anti-counterfeiting tasks that ideally should be co-ordinated at the European level.

Table 46: European co-ordination of anti-counterfeiting tasks

- international collaboration where counterfeiting has occurred offshore (for example, Internet pharmacy);
- centralisation of knowledge on all the diversion phenomena and trends;
- open exchange/discussion of information, particularly concerning the analytical results of counterfeit medicines; and divulgence of counterfeit medicine characteristics known by industry;
- co-ordination of exchange of information between inspectorates (including particularly APIs – Article 17, ICH Q7a);
- co-ordination of exchanges between national pharmaceutical associations and health authorities (with a centralised database);
- co-ordination with relevant international and European organisations, for example the UN, WIPO, WHO, WTO, European Commission and the EMEA;
- co-ordination of co-operation between known anti-counterfeiting groups;
- system for permitting rapid information cascade through the supply chain;
- information provision to all parts of the distribution chain (it is important to be informed of known cases, in order to avoid ignorance; all parts of the distribution chain must be aware of the risks, and institute the necessary control measures);
- operation of relevant information (database) and reporting systems (from and to national authorities);
- co-ordination concerning public awareness raising;
- definition of best practices, codes, protocols and agreements.

17.24.2. National level anti-counterfeiting co-operation tasks (between (i) sectoral authorities and (ii) the MoH/DRA and stakeholders)

The following table summarises anti-counterfeiting tasks that should ideally be co-ordinated at the national level.

Table 47: National level anti-counterfeiting co-ordination tasks

- operation of a hotline to quickly communicate counterfeit situations to relevant authority departments so that immediate action can be taken and co-ordinated;
- instant quarantine of counterfeit batches (with co-ordination between customs and police, and inspection after the genuine company is notified);
- definition of the types of authority from different sectors that should be involved and their respective roles;
- national authority co-ordination procedures;
- co-ordination procedures between authorities and industry/wholesalers/pharmacy association;
- institution of specialised police and customs liaison officers to deal with medicines counterfeiting;
- provision of reports to the European co-ordinating body;
- national information and database systems;
- active support in analysing and providing (pre-)clinical data on substances found.

17.24.3. Data sharing: information (database) and reporting systems

There is significant agreement on the need to have common Europe-wide information and reporting systems concerning counterfeit medicines that allows for the necessary and timely data sharing between all relevant parties. Ideally, such systems would be placed under the authority of the EU as the latter already has advanced medicinal product information and reporting systems, including the existence of several databases. However, to the extent that member states that are not EU members would be excluded from participating in such systems, then this option would not be ideal and it may be more appropriate for a Europe-wide authority, such as the Council of Europe, to supervise such systems. Ideally, the exact supervising European institution(s) and types of information and reporting systems should be set out within a co-operation agreement/legal framework. The proposed systems should avoid duplication of existing EU systems.

The table below presents an outline summary of the type of information (database) and reporting systems required as a tool to combat medicines counterfeiting and to aid communication and co-ordination between authorities and stakeholders (some of these systems are mentioned elsewhere in Section 17 of this report). Most of these systems will probably be Internet-based with password restricted access. Systems should be designed to permit efficiency and rapidity of action and just-in-time reports about counterfeiting problems.

Table 48: Suggested required types of information (database) and reporting systems

- listing of responsible national authorities (all relevant sectors) and contact persons;
- medicinal products at high risk of being counterfeited (and with high public health risk);

- an RAS for suspected counterfeit medicines (analogous to that which operates for quality defects),
- case history listing of detected counterfeit medicines;
- counterfeit medicine practices identified;
- recommended anti-counterfeiting measures;
- listings of reliable and registered manufacturers, brokers and wholesalers (also blacklisting of non-reliable manufacturers, brokers and wholesalers);
- listings of registered Internet pharmacies (also blacklisting of known Internet pharmacy infringers);
- analysis and provision of (pre-)clinical data on counterfeit substances found (centralised procedure for testing of suspect counterfeit substances);
- successful legal actions implemented;
- international data on counterfeiting from outside the European area.

17.24.4. Information disclosure by industry to authorities

In many cases, details concerning suspected counterfeit medicines are not disclosed because of fears that the details of medicinal product ingredients may be disclosed to competitive rivals within the industry. A lack of disclosure is not uncommon throughout all industrial and agricultural sectors and is to some extent understandable. However, an environment based upon mutual trust needs to be cultivated to ensure that good detailed information is available to investigators. Similarly, a better understanding of what are "covert" and "overt" features is vital so that those responsible for investigating suspect counterfeit medicinal products have a better "feel" for which products are genuine without having to analyse the item further.

A forum for discussion on disclosure of counterfeiting information throughout industry and an agreement with national governments on the reporting of such instances, supported by any relevant general information, are essential. There is also a need for confidence-building measures for anti-counterfeiting issues beyond current good working regulatory arrangements. Manufacturers should proactively carry out post-market surveillance on their own products and be prepared to share information with the enforcement authorities. There needs to be a system of reporting, either voluntary or mandatory, of suspected counterfeit pharmaceutical products by manufacturers and distributors.

The issue needs to be examined in more detail by both sides in terms of what is appropriate to disclose, so as to foster an atmosphere of mutual trust.

Recommendation No. 24

Definition of

(i) European-level "anti counterfeit medicines" co-ordination tasks;

(ii) national authority "anti counterfeit medicines" co-ordination tasks;

(iii) creation of a common European information (database) and reporting system for counterfeit medicines;

(iv) agreed European-level disclosure policy concerning suspect counterfeit medicines, including a clear clarification of what are "covert" and "overt" medicinal product features.

17.25. Communication strategy – Awareness raising and knowledge/perception management of the general public, health professionals, supply chain participants and authorities

A clear and effective communication and public relations strategy for the general public, health professionals, supply chain participants and authorities is required, based on a partnership between European-level/national authorities, manufacturers, wholesalers, pharmacies, health professionals and consumer associations. As the information needs of the various stakeholders differ in terms of both technical and policy content, the communication strategy needs to be differentiated accordingly.

A reference can be made to the FDA's VIPPS programme in terms of how the US authorities are tackling public awareness of counterfeit medicines (17).

17.25.1. Audience – Recipients of communications

The communication strategy needs to be differentiated according to the type of recipient; brief suggestions of relevant issues are summarised as follows:

European co-ordination

A vital task of the proposed European-level co-ordinating body is to ensure and manage a co-ordinated communication strategy. How this can be achieved is to be determined.

National authorities

Particular attention is required for awareness raising of the counterfeit medicine issue amongst police, judicial, customs and trade authorities.

General public

There needs to be assurance that cases are only made public by mutual agreement – with no tort law actions and liability claims against genuine companies. Success stories of enforcement bodies able to trace and prosecute counterfeiters, not only through civil but also criminal law, need to be publicised.

The general public needs to be warned of the dangers of purchasing medicinal products from risk/non-authorised sources and encouraged to report medicinal product ineffectiveness to health professionals. Some basic rules can be provided to the general public to ensure that they avoid buying potential counterfeit medicines and know what to do in case they suspect having purchased a counterfeit medicine.

Health professionals

Doctors and pharmacists need to be updated on the counterfeit medicine problem in general and alerted to the need to be vigilant. Assistance in identification of suspected counterfeit medicines is required as well as detection of potential ADRs caused by counterfeit medicines. Educational campaigns may be required.

General and professional press

It is important that both the general and specialist/professional press receive accurate reports on the status of medicines counterfeiting, so as to avoid an undermining of the public health system, to provide correct guidance on necessary vigilance procedures and to provide a reasonably accurate estimate of the size of the counterfeit medicine problem and its consequences (particularly vis-à-vis counterfeiting of other product types).

17.25.2. Communication strategy components

This should consist of, but not be limited to:

* determination of relevant associative partners in the communication strategy;
* determination of relevant recipients of communications;
* monitoring of public opinion and the press on the counterfeit medicine subject and collation of all published reports;
* "management" of the general and professional press;
* determination of the most appropriate media for communication;
* issuing regular press releases;
* educational campaigns.

Recommendation No. 25

PR communication strategy and management (based on relevant association partnerships) with appropriate sensitisation of and delivery to the general public, consumer associations, health professionals, distribution chain participants, authorities and other relevant audiences.

17.26. Education requirements for an effective system dealing with counterfeit medicines and the Council of Europe 2005 seminar on counterfeit medicines

17.26.1. Education and dissemination of experience in identifying and dealing with counterfeit medicines

Training courses aimed at professionals at the MoH/DRA and other relevant authorities (ministries/authorities of the interior, police, judiciary, customs, trade and industry), together with those involved in the distribution chain should be implemented in the near future and should probably be mandatory. The objectives of such training are several fold and include:

* awareness raising of the seriousness of the medicines counterfeiting issue;
* detection and identification of counterfeit medicines;
* risk management procedures for dealing with suspected counterfeit medicines;
* technical aspects of counterfeit medicine prevention and detection;
* provision of case studies.

In addition to Council of Europe provision (see below), it is anticipated that training and education support on the counterfeit medicine issue could be provided by industry, professional associations, DRAs and other relevant stakeholder organisations as a part of ongoing general education concerning pharmaceutical regulation.

17.26.2. Council of Europe 2005 seminar on counterfeit medicines

The Council of Europe organised a seminar on counterfeit medicine issues from 21 to 23 September 2005, which was aimed at the relevant authorities and stakeholders. The seminar covered:

* the legal environment which targets counterfeiters and deters counterfeiting taking into consideration results of the studies covered by this report (legislative and administrative gaps);
* specific enforcement structures and risk management procedures;
* shaping a model for national and international co-operation;
* best practice of industry and distribution;
* training programmes for concerned officials from the different relevant authorities;
* public health challenges.

17.27. Extension of Council of Europe counterfeit medicine project to all interested member states

It is recommended that the Council's counterfeit medicines initiative (as described by this report) be extended to all interested member states in eastern Europe. The recognised disadvantage of the existing Council of Europe studies on counterfeit medicines is that they are significantly biased towards the EU (EU-15) and EEA member states. A further survey, perhaps involving at least five central/east Europe member states would be of considerable value both in terms of (i) information provision and (ii) gaining a better understanding of the counterfeit medicine issue in central/eastern Europe. With increasing free cross-border trade, counterfeiting of medicines affects all European states – and it is important to solve this problem at a general European level (that is, the authorities and stakeholders in west European countries cannot afford to ignore the counterfeit medicine problem in eastern European countries). It would also be important to conduct some type of study on the impact of the relaxation of the EU's internal borders (particularly in view of the recent accessions) on trade in counterfeit medicines.

A further survey of central or eastern European member states would be valuable, perhaps on the basis of an abbreviated version of the existing questionnaire, or focused on certain sectors, for example health, justice, police and customs.

****

Sabine Walser, Secretariat, contributed to the development of the survey questionnaire and computerised the survey using the free software EPI-Data Version 3.02.

References

1. "Impacts de la contrefaçon et de la piraterie en Europe, Rapport final", Centre d'études internationales de la propriété industrielle (CEIPI), 9 July 2004.

2. The WHO project on substandard and counterfeit medicines, World Health Organization, November 2003 (http://www.who.int/medicines/organisation/qsm/ activities/qualityassurance/cft/counterfeitinfo.shtml).

3. The Global Forum on Pharmaceutical Anti-counterfeiting, Reconnaissance International, Geneva, 22-25 September 2002.

4. Satchwell, G., "A sick business. Counterfeit medicines and organised crime", Stockholm Network, 2004 (http://www.efpia.org/2_indust/ Sickbusiness.pdf).

5. Personal communication from Dr Alexander Bykov, Sanofi-Aventis and AIPM, Russian Federation, November 2004.

6. "Counterfeit medicines", EFPIA, 2004 (http://www.efpia.org/indust/ counterfeitdrugs.pdf).

7. "Viagra bought online often fake", "Viagra spam fills mail inboxes" and "Fake prescription drugs warning", sample of BBC news reports, 2004 (http://news.bbc.co.uk).

8. Kanavos, P. et al., "The economic impact of pharmaceutical parallel trade in European Union member states: a stakeholder analysis", LSE, January 2004 (http://www.lse.ac.uk/collections/LSEHealthAndSocialCare/pdf/ Workingpapers/Paper.pdf).

9. US Federal Food, Drug and Cosmetics Act (as amended by the FDA Modernization Act of 1997), Chapter II – Definitions, 17 November 1998 (http://www.fda.gov/opacom/laws/fdcact/fdcact1.htm).

10. An act prohibiting drugs, providing penalties for violations and appropriating funds, Philippines Republic Act No. 8203, 2003.

11. Wesch, M.W., "Strafbarkeit von Arzneimittelfalschern", *Pharm. Ind.*, Vol. 66, No. 7, 2004, pp. 872-873.

12. EC Regulation No 1383/2003 of 22 July 2003 concerning customs action against goods suspected of infringing certain IPR and the measures to be taken against goods found to have infringed such rights.

13. "Pharmaceutical piracy a tough pill to swallow", *Moscow Times*, 9 April 2001, p. 12.

14. "Working together to build Europe on the rule of law", Council of Europe Directorate General of Legal Affairs, January 2003.

15. Single Convention on Narcotic Drugs 1961 as amended by the 1972 protocol; Convention on Psychotropic Substances 1971 including Final Act and Resolutions, as agreed by the 1971 United Nations Conference for the Adoption of a Protocol on Psychotropic Substances, and the Schedules

annexed to the Convention; and United Nations Convention against Illicit Traffic in Narcotic Drugs and Psychotropic Substances 1988 including Final Act and Resolutions, as agreed by the United Nations Conference for the Adoption of a Convention against Illicit Traffic in Narcotic Drugs and Psychotropic Substances, and the Tables annexed to the Convention.

16. "Combating counterfeit drugs – A report of the Food and Drug Administration", US Department of Health and Human Services, February 2004.

17. Verified Internet Pharmacy Practice Sites (VIPPS), FDA, 2004 (http://www.fda.gov/cder/consumerinfo/counterfeitdrugsLo.pdf).

Acronyms

ADR   Adverse Drug Reaction
API   Active Pharmaceutical Ingredient (active substance)
APIC   Active Pharmaceutical Ingredient Committee
BP   Bulk pharmaceutical product
CEFIC   European Chemical Industry Council
CoS   Certificate of Suitability
DRA   Drug regulatory authority
EDMF   European drug master file
EFPIA   European Federation of Pharmaceutical Industry Associations
EDQM   European Directorate for the Quality of Medicines
EMEA   European Medicines Evaluation Agency
FDA   Food and Drug Administration
FP   Finished medicinal product
GDP   Good distribution practice
GIRP   Groupement International de la Repartition Pharmaceutique (European Association of Full-Line Pharmaceutical Wholesalers)
GMP   Good manufacturing practice
ICH   International Conference on Harmonisation of Technical Requirements for Registration of Pharmaceuticals for Human Use
IFAH   International Federation for Animal Health
INCB   International Narcotics Control Board (UN)
IP   Immediate packaging
IPR   Intellectual (Industry) property rights
MA   Marketing authorisation
MAA   Marketing authorisation application
MoET   Ministry of the Economy/Trade
MoFTC   Ministry of Finance/Tax/Customs
MoH   Ministry of Health
MoIP   Ministry of Internal Affairs/Police
MoJ   Ministry of Justice
MoU   Memorandum of understanding
MRA   Mutual recognition agreement
OCL   Official control laboratory (other sectors)
OFL   Official forensic laboratory
OMCL   Official medicines control laboratory
OP   Outer packaging
OTC   Over the counter (non-prescription medicinal product)
PFIPC   Permanent Forum on International Pharmaceutical Crime
PIC/S   Pharmaceutical Inspection Convention
PoM   Prescription only medicine
PSI   Pharmaceutical security institute
QA   Quality assurance
QBPC   Quality Brands Protection Committee (China)
RAS   Rapid alert system

VIPPS   Verified Internet Pharmacy Practice Sites
VMP   Veterinary Medicinal Product

List of tables and charts

Appendices

1 Counterfeiting: problems and solutions. Council of Europe Parliamentary Assembly Recommendation 1673 (2004).

2 Survey questionnaire – Inventory of Council of Europe member states, legislation and administrative structures/procedures in place to fight counterfeit medicines. Council of Europe Partial Agreement in the Social and Public Health Field, 2004

3 Questionnaire for stakeholder survey – Views on best co-operation practices, measures and experiences applicable to counterfeit (falsified or fake) medicines. Council of Europe Partial Agreement in the Social and Public Health Field, 2004

4 Questionnaire for survey – National legislation on counterfeit and unlicensed medicines. Council of Europe Partial Agreement in the Social and Public Health Field, 2003

5 Council of Europe member state counterfeit medicine case reports (from survey – Appendix 2)

6 Stakeholder counterfeit medicine case reports (from survey – Appendix 3)

7 Counterfeit medicine RAS reporting form (as proposed by the Council of Europe Ad hoc Group on Counterfeit Medicines)

8 Major findings and recommendations concerning the Council of Europe surveys on counterfeit medicines. Presentation to the Council of Europe Ad hoc Group on counterfeit medicines by Jonathan Harper, 7 December 2004

9 Proposal for a model agreement on international and national multisectoral co-operation on counterfeit medicines

10 Council of Europe Partial Agreement in the Social and Public Health Field: medicines and the Internet – Model information for the Internet user

Appendix 1

Counterfeiting: problems and solutions.
Council of Europe Parliamentary Assembly
Recommendation 1673 (2004)

1.   The Parliamentary Assembly notes with concern the rapidly rising incidence of counterfeit goods in Europe – a phenomenon which places customers' health and well-being at risk, erodes the markets for legitimate producers, damages the reputation of brand names, distorts competition, undermines employment and reduces tax income.

2.   The image of counterfeiting as a harmless activity must be challenged. Council of Europe member states should improve data collection on the linkage between counterfeited goods and injuries or deaths, in particular as regards products such as pharmaceuticals, spare parts, toys, personal care products, household items, foodstuffs, alcoholic drinks and tobacco.

3.   Policies for better surveillance, control and prevention of counterfeit-related risks to public health and well-being should be developed, as should communication with the public and industry. Special regulations are also needed to oversee the sale of medicines and other sensitive products over the Internet.

4.   The Assembly welcomes the adoption in July 2003 by the European Union's Council of Ministers of a regulation aimed at protecting intellectual property rights against counterfeit and pirated goods entering the European Union and hopes that it can soon be supplemented by a proposed directive on the harmonisation of procedures within member states for combating counterfeiting and piracy of goods circulating in the European Union. The Assembly in this context welcomes the application of the new regulation within the enlarged European Union as from July 2004.

5.   To make anti-counterfeit laws and measures more efficient, they should be harmonised as far as possible throughout the continent. While intellectual property rights must be protected, there could also be reason to use confiscated counterfeit goods for social and charitable purposes. The Assembly therefore supports the idea that further use could be made of certain counterfeit goods – such as clothing and shoes – in exceptional circumstances and under certain conditions guaranteeing their conformity with minimum quality and safety standards of a national or European origin, and only after any distinctive brand signs on the goods in question have been removed. These items could be given to orphanages and humanitarian organisations – wherever possible via the rightful owners of the imitated brands – instead of being systematically destroyed as is the current practice in many countries, in line with countries' moral obligation to assist their most vulnerable citizens, especially when the latter cannot otherwise be given adequate living conditions.

6.   In conclusion, the Assembly recommends that the Committee of Ministers ask the member states of the Council of Europe:

i.   to further tighten national laws and measures against counterfeiting and to seek their harmonisation at European level as exemplified by European Union legislation;

ii.   to entrust the competent authorities with the gathering of statistical data on the links between counterfeits and injuries or deaths among the public, in particular for the groups of products listed in paragraph 2 above;

iii.   to shape policies for better surveillance, control and prevention of public health risks associated with counterfeit goods;

iv.   to improve communication with consumers, alerting them to the risks posed by counterfeit goods and ways of identifying such goods;

v.   to encourage industry to enhance information-sharing on counterfeit-related problems and to strengthen practical measures against counterfeiting, including consumer hotlines and improved data management systems;

vi.   to draw up special regulations to oversee the sale of medicines and other sensitive goods over the Internet;

vii.   to consider permitting the exceptional use of certain confiscated counterfeit goods for social purposes along the lines set out in paragraph 5 above;

viii.   to involve more actively local actors, inter-professional groups and consumer associations in national anti-counterfeiting efforts, in particular via information campaigns;

ix.   to ensure appropriate training of customs officials on the means and policies to detect counterfeit goods.

7.   The Assembly in this context welcomes the work carried out within the Council of Europe by the Committee of Experts on Pharmaceutical Questions (under the Partial Agreement in the Social and Public Health Field), aiming to develop and implement effective measures to minimise public health risks posed by counterfeit medicines.

8.   The Assembly also recommends that the Committee of Ministers invite the European Union to consider using certain seized counterfeit goods for social and charitable purposes in exceptional circumstances and under certain conditions, as outlined in paragraph 5 above, by making the necessary adaptations to existing or planned European Union legislation.[1]

---

1. Text adopted by the Standing Committee acting on behalf of the Assembly, on 7 September 2004 (see Doc. 10069, report of the Committee on Economic Affairs and Development, rapporteur: Mr Schreiner).

Appendix 2

Survey questionnaire –
Inventory of Council of Europe member states' legislation and administrative structures/procedures in place to fight counterfeit medicines
Council of Europe Partial Agreement in the Social and Public Health Field, 2004

1. Ministry of Health – Competent drug control authority

A. General information

1.   What is the type of legal system* under which your state operates?

2.   Which agency/agencies have the responsibility for the enforcement of the medicines legislation (control of Drug Act)?

3.   Is there a definition of counterfeit pharmaceuticals* in the medicines legislation (e.g. Drug Act/Public Health Act)?

4.   Are sanctions* specified for offences* related to counterfeit pharmaceuticals set out in the medicines legislation (e.g. Drug Act/Public Health Act)?

5.   What are the legal powers of administrative inspectorates* as regards counterfeiting of medicines and counterfeit medicines?

Information on pharmaceutical counterfeiting and counterfeit medicines

6.   Are there legal provisions* concerning the reporting of counterfeiting and counterfeit pharmaceuticals to the health authorities?

7.   Are there legal provisions in the medicines legislation (Drug Act/Public Health Act) to ensure that information reported on counterfeiting and counterfeit pharmaceuticals will remain confidential?

8.   Is there a database system for tracking counterfeit pharmaceuticals?

9.   What is the number of new national cases* (incidence*) of counterfeit pharmaceuticals brought to the attention of the relevant health authority in each of the following years? Please give details in columns 3-5.

10.   What is the number of adverse effects* to national individuals caused by pharmaceuticals brought to the attention of the relevant health authority?

11.   What is the number of adverse effects to national individuals caused by pharmaceuticals with quality defects brought to the attention of the relevant health authority?

12.   Have near adverse effects to national individuals caused by pharmaceuticals with quality defects been brought to the attention of the Ministry of Health?

13. Do the health authorities have official powers to deal with counterfeit pharmaceuticals?

National co-operation

14. Is there a national network for co-operation against aspects of counterfeiting and counterfeit pharmaceuticals?

15. If such a network exists, which organisations and agencies take part?

International co-operation

16. Is your country a member of the World Health Organization (WHO) anti-counterfeit network?

17. Are national reports on counterfeit pharmaceuticals forwarded to the WHO database by the national WHO anti-counterfeit liaison person?

18. Does your Health Ministry have a rapid alert system (RAS) or similar arrangements in place to ensure prompt and effective co-operation and information exchange between countries?

B. Specific information

Production of pharmaceuticals

19. Are there legal provisions concerning the production of pharmaceuticals?

20. Are there legal provisions concerning the production of pharmaceutical packaging materials?*

21. Is a licence* required for the production of pharmaceuticals?

22. What controls are carried out by the health authorities on the manufacture of active ingredients?

23. Is repackaging* of medicines an important activity for manufacturers in your country?

Distribution of pharmaceuticals

24. Are there legal provisions concerning the distribution of pharmaceuticals in the domestic distribution chain?*

25. Is a licence required for the distribution of pharmaceuticals in the domestic distribution chain?

26. Are there legal provisions concerning the importation/exportation/transit of pharmaceuticals?

27. Is a licence required for the importation/exportation/transit of pharmaceuticals? Please specify activity:

28. Is the storage of pharmaceuticals in a bonded warehouse*/free zone* governed by medicines legislation?

29. Is it permitted to supply medicines to users by mail upon individual order?

30. Do you have legal provisions governing parallel import?*

31. Is the importation of unlicensed medicines in an amount adequate for personal use subject to specific legal provisions?

32. Do you have legal provisions governing unlicensed medicines other than for personal use?

33. Are there sanctions specified for offences to legal provisions governing unlicensed medicines?

34. Are there institutions/dependent bodies of the health authorities responsible to prevent the occurrence of unlicensed medicines in your country?

35. Do you have reasons to suspect that brokers* play a role in counterfeit trading?

Prevention, identification and testing of counterfeit medicines

36. Are there legal provisions in medicines legislation (Health Act/Drug Act) concerning the prevention of counterfeit medicines?

37. Who deals with the analytical testing of pharmaceutical samples suspected of being counterfeit?

38. Who has to bear the costs of testing?

39. The EC Regulation 1383/2003[1] specifies measures to be taken against goods found to have infringed certain intellectual property rights.

Prosecution of pharmaceutical crime including counterfeiting medicines*

40. Is there a definition of "pharmaceutical crime" in your legislation

41. Are there specialised police forces (or other enforcement bodies) which investigate offences in relation to counterfeit medicines?

42. Are institutions of the health authorities involved in actions against counterfeit pharmaceuticals? Do these institutions of the health authorities actively and systematically search for counterfeit pharmaceuticals?

Specific powers of health authorities (seizing, detainment, destruction)

43. What is the extent of the powers of enforcement* related to suspected counterfeit pharmaceuticals (active pharmaceutical ingredients, bulk product, finished product)?

C. Conclusions

44. Is there a need for international co-operation in order to successfully deal with counterfeiting of pharmaceuticals (active pharmaceutical ingredients, bulk product, finished medicinal product)?

45. Are the legislation and/or administrative structures adequate to prevent and prosecute counterfeit medicines?

46. Please list essential elements of good co-operation practices with the pharmaceutical industry and active ingredients' manufacturers:

47. Do the pharmaceutical industry and active ingredients manufacturers disclose covert and overt features* to investigators?

48. Are persons involved in the official distribution chain of pharmaceuticals adequately trained to detect counterfeit pharmaceuticals?

49. Please add comments and proposals.

---

1. Council Regulation (EC) 1383/2003 of 22 July 2003 concerning customs action against goods suspected of infringing certain intellectual property rights and the measures to be taken against goods found to have infringed such rights, 2 August 2003, L196/14, *Official Journal of the European Communities.*

2. Ministry for Internal Affairs – Police agencies: enforcement applicable to counterfeit medicines

A. General information

50. Are there legal provisions in criminal law* and/or specific legislation concerning counterfeits and counterfeiting applicable to counterfeit pharmaceuticals?

51. Is there a definition of counterfeiting and counterfeits applicable to counterfeit pharmaceuticals in criminal law and/or specific legislation (e.g. police laws)?

52. Are sanctions specified for offences applicable to counterfeit pharmaceuticals set out in the specific legislation (e.g. police laws)?

53. What are the legal powers of the enforcement authorities* as regards counterfeiting and counterfeits?

Information on pharmaceutical counterfeiting and counterfeit medicines

54. Are there legal provisions concerning the reporting of counterfeiting and counterfeits to the enforcement authorities applicable to counterfeit pharmaceuticals?

55. Are there legal provisions in the specific legislation (e.g. police laws) to ensure that information reported on counterfeiting and counterfeits will remain confidential?

56. Is there a database system for tracking counterfeit pharmaceuticals?

57. What is the number of new national cases (incidence) of counterfeit pharmaceuticals brought to the attention of the Ministry of Internal Affairs in each of the following years? Please give details in columns 3-5.

58. Have adverse effects to national individuals caused by counterfeit pharmaceuticals been brought to the attention of the Ministry of Internal Affairs?

59. If counterfeit pharmaceuticals are detected in the illegal distribution chain, where are they detected?

National co-operation

60. Is there a national network for co-operation against counterfeiting and counterfeit medicines?

61. If such a network exists, which organisations and agencies take part?

62. Does your Ministry of Internal Affairs have a rapid alert system (RAS) or similar arrangements in place to ensure prompt and effective co-operation and information exchange between countries?

B. Specific information

Prosecution

63. Is there a definition of "pharmaceutical crime" in your legislation?

64. Are there specialised police forces (or other enforcement bodies) which investigate offences in relation to counterfeit medicines?

65. Do these institutions of the enforcement authorities actively and systematically search for counterfeit pharmaceuticals?

66. Who deals with the analytical testing of pharmaceutical samples suspect of being counterfeit?

67. Are the analysis results from all official and private laboratories compiled centrally?

68. Who has to bear the costs of testing?

Special powers

69. What is the extent of the powers of enforcement for the enforcement authorities related to suspected counterfeit pharmaceuticals?

Coercive measures and special investigation methods

70. Are the following coercive measures and special investigation methods authorised in your country and applied to combating counterfeit medicines?

C. Conclusions

71. Are the legislation and/or administrative structures adequate to prevent and prosecute counterfeit medicines?

72. Please indicate essential elements of good co-operation practices with the pharmaceutical industry and active ingredients' manufacturers.

73. Do the pharmaceutical industry and active ingredients manufacturers disclose covert and overt features to investigators?

74. Are enforcement officers adequately trained to detect and prosecute counterfeit pharmaceuticals in the official or illegal distribution chain?

75. Please add comments and proposals concerning the legislation and administrative procedures applicable to counterfeit pharmaceuticals

3. Ministry of Justice – Jurisdiction – Prosecution – Civil and penal procedures

A. General information

76. Are legal provisions in criminal law and specific laws concerning counterfeits and counterfeiting applicable to counterfeit pharmaceuticals?

77. Is there a definition of counterfeiting and counterfeits applicable to counterfeit pharmaceuticals in criminal law and specific laws?

78. Are sanctions specified for offences applicable to counterfeit pharmaceuticals set out in specific laws pertaining to court?

79. What are the legal powers of the judicial authorities as regards counterfeiting and counterfeits?

Information on pharmaceutical counterfeiting and counterfeit medicines

80. Are there legal provisions concerning the reporting of counterfeiting and counterfeits to the judicial authorities applicable to counterfeit pharmaceuticals?

81. Are there legal provisions in the specific laws pertaining to jurisdiction to ensure that information reported on counterfeiting and counterfeits will remain confidential?

82. Is there a database system for tracking counterfeit pharmaceuticals?

83. How many new national cases of counterfeit pharmaceuticals have been dealt with by the courts (no pending cases)?

84. Have any of the national cases dealt with by the judicial authorities involved adverse health effects?

National co-operation

85. Is there a national network for co-operation against counterfeiting and counterfeit medicines?

86. If such a network exists, which organisations and agencies take part?

87. Does your Ministry of Justice have a rapid alert system (RAS) or similar arrangements in place to ensure prompt and effective co-operation and information exchange between countries?

B. Specific information

Administrative procedures/arrangements for settling cases

88. Are there procedures in law/administrative procedures for settling offences relating to counterfeiting or counterfeit medicines outside a judicial proceeding?*

89. Which authority takes the decisions in the administrative proceedings referred to in question 88?

90. What is the procedure for the administrative proceedings referred to in question 89?

91. Who deals with the analytical testing of pharmaceutical samples suspect of being counterfeit?

92. Who has to bear the costs of testing?

Legal action (criminal proceedings and penalties)

93. Which authority is responsible for criminal proceedings? Which specific bodies take the decisions in criminal proceedings?

94. Is there a specific prosecution policy for counterfeiters of medicines?

95. Is forfeiture* incorporated in the national prosecution policy?

96. Which general principles apply concerning the burden of proof?*

C. Conclusions

97. Are the legislation/and or administrative structures adequate to prevent and prosecute counterfeit medicines?

98. Please indicate essential elements of good co-operation practices with the pharmaceutical industry and active ingredients' manufacturers?

99. Do the pharmaceutical industry and active ingredients manufacturers disclose covert and overt features to investigators?

100. Please add comments and proposals – concerning the legislation and administrative procedures applicable to counterfeit medicines – concerning this questionnaire

4. Ministry of Finance – Tax and customs agencies

A. General information

101. Are legal provisions included in criminal law and specific finance/customs laws concerning counterfeits and counterfeiting applicable to counterfeit pharmaceuticals?

102. Is there a definition of counterfeiting and counterfeits applicable to counterfeit pharmaceuticals in criminal law and specific finance/customs laws?

103. The EC Regulation 1383/2003 specifies measures to be taken against goods found to have infringed such rights.

104. Are sanctions specified for offences applicable to counterfeit pharmaceuticals set out in the specific finance/customs laws?

105. What are the legal powers of the Finance/Customs Authorities as regards counterfeiting and counterfeits? Is there a legal obligation to investigate the case?

Information on pharmaceutical counterfeiting and counterfeit medicines

106. Are there legal provisions concerning the reporting of counterfeiting and counterfeits to the Finance/Customs Authorities applicable to counterfeit pharmaceuticals?

107. Are there legal provisions in the specific finance/customs laws to ensure that information reported on counterfeiting and counterfeits will remain confidential?

108. Is there a database system for tracking counterfeit pharmaceuticals?

109. What is the number of new national cases (incidence) of counterfeit pharmaceuticals brought to the attention of the Ministry of Finance (Finance/Customs bodies) in each of the following years? Please give details in columns 3-5.

110. If counterfeit pharmaceuticals are detected in the illegal distribution chain, where are they detected?

National co-operation

111. Is there a national network for co-operation against counterfeiting and counterfeit medicines?

112. If such a network exists, which organisations and agencies take part?

113. Does your Ministry of Finance (dependent customs authorities) have a rapid alert system (RAS) or similar arrangements in place to ensure prompt and effective co-operation and information exchange between countries?

B. Specific information

Import/export/transit

114. What controls are carried out by the finance/customs authorities on active ingredients in case of import/export/transit?

115. Is the importation of medicines in an amount adequate for personal use subject to specific legal provisions?

116. What controls are carried out on medicines, which are not licensed in your country in case of import/export/transit?

117. Are mail orders for medicines controlled? (Postal shipments of medicines to users upon individual order via the Internet)

Prosecution of counterfeiting pharmaceuticals

118. Are institutions of the finance authorities involved in actions against counterfeit pharmaceuticals?

119. Do these institutions of the finance authorities actively and systematically search for counterfeit pharmaceuticals?

120. Who deals with the analytical testing of pharmaceutical samples suspect of being counterfeit?

121. Are the analysis results from all official and private laboratories compiled centrally?

122. Who has to bear the costs of testing?

123. Do your customs authorities apply the methodology of customs risk analysis* applied by your customs authorities?

124. If one or more of above mentioned risk factors are present and known for an individual import/export/transit, does this give rise to controls?

125. Do your finance/customs authorities apply specific control measures in free zones and customs warehouses (bonded warehouses)?

Specific powers (seizure and detainment, powers of entry, etc.)

126. What is the extent of the powers of enforcement for the finance/customs authorities related to organised crime* and obtaining information?

127. Are there indications that in your country organised crime is involved in counterfeiting (pharmaceuticals)? (No confidential data required.)

128. Are there links of organised crime with organised crime based in other countries?

129. What other forms of criminality are linked with the traffic of counterfeit pharmaceuticals in your country?

C. Conclusions

130. Are the legislation and/or administrative procedures adequate to prevent and prosecute counterfeit medicines?

131. Please indicate essential elements of good co-operation practices with the pharmaceutical industry and active ingredients' manufacturers?

132. Do the pharmaceutical industry and active ingredients manufacturers disclose covert and overt features to investigators?

133. Are finance/customs officials adequately trained to detect and prosecute counterfeit pharmaceuticals in the official or illegal distribution chain?

134. Which influence on counterfeiting of medicines and the incidence of counterfeit medicines had the wavering of the European Union's internal border control by the customs authorities?

135. Does parallel trade of medicines facilitate the emerging of counterfeit medicines?

136. Do you have reasons to suspect that brokers play a role in counterfeit trading?

137. Please add comments and proposals.

5. Ministry of Economy/Trade: commercial laws including intellectual property rights (patent laws, trademark laws) (IPRs), copyright laws applicable to counterfeit medicines

A. General information

138. Are legal provisions in commercial laws including intellectual property rights including patent laws, trademark laws, copyright laws concerning counterfeits and counterfeiting applicable to counterfeit pharmaceuticals?

139. Is there a definition of counterfeiting and counterfeits applicable to counterfeit pharmaceuticals in commercial laws commercial laws including intellectual property rights including patent laws, trademark laws, copyright laws?

140. Are there criminal law sanctions (fine, imprisonment) foreseen for offences by counterfeit pharmaceuticals against commercial laws including industrial property rights and copyright laws, in particular patent law and trademark law?

141. What are the legal powers of the economy/trade authorities as regards counterfeiting and counterfeits?

Information on pharmaceutical counterfeiting and counterfeit medicines

142. Are there legal provisions concerning the reporting of counterfeiting and counterfeits to the economy/trade authorities applicable to counterfeit pharmaceuticals?

143. Are there legal provisions in the commercial laws including intellectual property rights including patent laws, trademark laws, copyright laws to ensure that information reported on counterfeiting and counterfeits will remain confidential?

144. Is there a database system for tracking counterfeit pharmaceuticals?

145. What is the number of new national cases (incidence) of counterfeit pharmaceuticals brought to the attention of the Ministry of Economy/Trade (its bodies) in each of the following years? Please give details in columns 3-5.

National co-operation

146. Is there a national network for co-operation against counterfeiting and counterfeit medicines?

147. If such a network exists, which organisations and agencies take part?

B. Specific information

148. Who deals with the analytical testing of pharmaceutical samples suspect of being counterfeit in the context of a violation of trade laws?

149. Who has to bear the costs of testing?

C. Conclusions

150. Are the legislation and/or administrative structures adequate to prevent and prosecute counterfeit medicines?

151. Please add comments and proposals concerning the legislation and administrative procedures applicable to counterfeit medicines.

Glossary of terms

Active pharmaceutical ingredient (API) (active substance)
See "medicinal product" (below).

Adverse effect
An unwanted effect produced by a medicine; it may be merely inconvenient, unpleasant, frankly dangerous or fatal.

A near adverse event or critical incident is an incident where a patient might have suffered harm and an undesirable effect without a medical intervention or treatment.

Anabolics (anabolic steroids)
A group of substances allied to the male hormone testosterone which have limited use in medicine but are misused to promote muscular development and hence achievements in various branches of sport.

Bonded warehouse (customs warehouse)
A secure warehouse authorised to hold goods which are not deemed to have entered the country and are therefore not subject to its laws, regulations and customs regime. A bonded warehouse may hold goods which may subsequently be released nationally (for example, medicines awaiting authorisation) or goods which are merely passing through in the course of transit shipment between third countries. See also free zone (below).

Burden of proof
The obligation to provide proof. In a cases of suspected criminal behaviour the accused is generally presumed to be innocent until the prosecution proves him guilty, that is the burden of proof lies with the prosecution. In certain circumstances, where the evident facts create an overwhelming presumption of guilt (for example, possession of large amounts of illegal substances or products) the burden of proof is in effect reversed and the accused will be required to prove that these facts did not amount to an offence.

Broker
(Commission) agent or middleman doing business upon order of a client.

Bulk
See "medicinal product" (below).

Cases
In the context of "new national cases" a case is any occurrence of a counterfeit product entering the market either imported or not irrespective of its batch or manufacturer.

Confidential purchases
See "controlled deliveries" (below).

Confiscation
See "seizure" (below).

Controlled substances
A group of substances mostly used as medicines but subject to additional and stringent controls, both nationally and internationally, because of the risks which they pose to society, especially because of dependence, addiction and misuse. Prominent members of the group subject to the highest levels of control include the opiates (morphine and allied narcotics) and the stimulant amphetamines.

Controlled deliveries
A means of obtaining evidence of illegal supply channels by placing orders for goods with these sources. Also known as "pseudo-purchases" or "confidential purchases".

Covert and overt features
Covert and overt features (of a product) are markers which are frequently used by the pharmaceutical industry to protect pharmaceuticals against counterfeiting. Overt features are visible (for example, holograms), whilst covert features can only be detected by analytical methods.

Counterfeit medicine
A counterfeit medicine is one which is deliberately and fraudulently mislabelled as to its origin and identity. The false information is intended to mislead the user, suggesting that it is a genuine product. In some cases the counterfeit is of lesser quality and does not contain the correct ingredients in the correct quantities.

As counterfeit medicines are not subject to control, they always present a danger to health. See also "medicinal product" below.

Criminal law
The legal provisions concerned with the trial and punishment of persons (or occasionally institutions) which have contravened the provisions of law and regulations in any field.

Customs risk analysis
Investigative method.

Customs tariffs
The rates at which import duties (that is, taxes) are imposed on goods entering the country. For example, a car imported into a country may be subject to a tariff of 23% of its original price.

Detention
Temporary deprivation of liberty. National laws make provision for a person suspected of a serious offence to be temporarily detained for a limited period while the possibility of bringing a charge against them is examined. At the end of his period they must be released or brought to court for a formal trial.

Distribution chain
The series of institutions through which a medicine passes on its way from the manufacturer to the ultimate supplier. These may include importers and exporters, wholesalers, community or hospital pharmacies or (for certain drugs) other authorised retailers.

Enforcement authority (enforcement agency)
Laws and regulations pertaining to a specialised field may create a special institution to ensure that the law is implemented and upheld, for example a regulatory agency to issue marketing licences for individual medicines and an inspectorate to examine the practice of factories, pharmacies, etc. This enforcement agency may have special powers of its own but will also work in collaboration with police, customs and other enforcement agencies.

Financial authorities
A general term for the government bodies charged with collecting tax and customs revenues.

Fiscal
Belonging to the tax system, tax legislation.

Forfeiture
- any kind of serious abuse of office by a civil servant or member of the armed forces;
- a felony committed by a public officer in the exercise of his functions;
- the fact of losing or becoming liable to lose (an estate, office, right, etc.) in consequence of a crime, offence, or breach;
- deliberate loss or deprivation, generally as a punishment. For example, a health professional who misuses narcotic drugs can be penalised by forfeiture of his right to practice.

Free zone
A circumscribed area of a country which for certain trading, taxation and customs purposes is deemed to lie outside the national area. The relevant legislation may, for example, decree that drugs may be manufactured in a free zone for export only without being subject to the

national taxation requirements or pharmaceutical laws relating to such activities. See also "bonded warehouse"(above).

Good manufacturing practice (GMP)
A set of internationally agreed standards ensuring that medicinal products produced are of consistent quality and controlled in accordance with appropriate standards. Many regulatory authorities require manufacturers to respect GMP. Recognition is obtained through the so-called GMP inspection which may lead to the issue of a GMP certificate.

Immediate packaging
The container or other form of packaging which holds the medicine in its physical (galenical) form (tablets, syrup, etc.).

Incidence
The frequency with which a new national case occurs. See "case" above.

Informant
An individual passing potentially incriminating information to the police or to an authorised enforcement agency, either spontaneously or by prior arrangement.

Infiltration
The process of obtaining access to known or suspected criminal circles in order to obtain first-hand information on their activities.

Inspectorate
A body of specialised officials (inspectors) authorised to examine and inspect persons, firms or institutions engaging in activities relating to certain commodities (for example, medicines) in order to verify their possession of an appropriate licence and their adherence to the terms of that licence. Specially qualified groups of inspectors deal with factories, others with trading institutions (for example, pharmacies).

International non-proprietary name (INN)
A non-commercial name given to a pharmaceutical substance, generally by the WHO, so that it can be readily recognised. It must be distinguished from the chemical name (which is used in science to describe the structure of the product, and which is often long and complex) and from the various trade names under which the product may be sold commercially.

Judicial
Belonging to the judge in court as well as to the prosecutor in certain contexts; judicial proceeding: court procedure (process).

Labelling
Labelling are all texts imprinted or attached to the immediate containers (for example, bottle) and outer packaging (cardboard) in which a medicinal product is supplied, providing the name of the medicine and information on its content, source, etc. In a broad sense including the package insert (leaflet).

Legal system
The complex of laws, regulations, ordinances, decrees and other official rules (legal provisions) which within a country are binding upon persons, firms and on the community generally. It is traditional to distinguish between:

(a) those legal systems in which all the essential rules are laid down in laws passed by the parliament (jointly comprising the country's "code of laws"); and

(b) those systems in which many rules originate primarily in rulings made by judges in individual cases, which then become binding on later cases ("common law").

In actual fact there is not a great difference between the operation of the two systems. In "code" countries the written law is subject to interpretation by the judges and thereby progressively modified, and developed, while in common law countries many of the rules originally made by judges have been incorporated into written laws passed by the parliament.

Licence
A permit issued by an authority to a given person or firm to engage in certain types of activity regulated by law. Examples include a marketing authorisation (a licence allowing a particular medicine to be on sale), a licence to import and/or export medicines, a licence

197

to operate a pharmaceutical wholesaling firm or pharmacy, a licence to trade in narcotic substances, etc.

Marketing authorisation

A medicinal product can be legally sold when a marketing authorisation has been issued by the competent (law making) authorities. The issuance of a marketing authorisation is subject to a favourable assessment of the quality, safety and efficacy of this medicine, according to legal standards performed by the health authorities.

Medicinal product (pharmaceutical)

A medicinal product, also known as a medicine or pharmaceutical product, is a substance or product which is used to prevent, alleviate or cure disease or to affect bodily function in some way (for example, an oral contraceptive). It may be designed and intended for human use or for use in animals ("veterinary medicine").

For practical purposes one needs to distinguish between an API (the active chemical or biological substance used in a medicine conveying the preventing, alleviating, curing or modifying effects), a BP (the active substance mixed with the other substances needed to make up the medicine before being packed in its final container and labelled) and the FP or finished dosage form (the final form of the medicine, ready for use in its final packaging and labelling including packaging leaflet).

In the context of this survey, "pharmaceutical" means API, BP, FP and immediate and outer packaging.

Narcotics

A traditional term for medicines with strongly addictive and sedative properties. Together with other substances demanding special controls because of the risks which they pose to society, they are better considered as members of the broad group of "controlled substances". Unauthorised use, manufacture or distribution is illicit.

Observation

Intensified ongoing examination of the behaviour of a person or group of persons suspected of illegal behaviour in order to ascertain whether there might be grounds for prosecution. Observation may be carried out personally (for example, by plain-clothes police officers) or by means of technical devices such as video cameras, microphones or tape recorders.

Offence

Any act which breaks the law or contravenes the regulations. In the area of medicines, a typical offence is engaging in certain activities without a licence, or without respecting the terms on which a licence has been issued.

Organised crime

(See United Nations Convention against Transnational Organised Crime – "Palermo Convention"), not yet ratified by all European members states: organised criminal group committing serious crime; serious shall mean conduct constituting an offence punishable by a maximum deprivation of liberty of at least four years or a more serious penalty.

Outer packaging

The cover in which the immediate packaging (container of the medicine, see above) is placed.

Packaging materials

Bottles, strips, boxes, etc., in which medicines in their final dosage form will be delivered to the user. These materials are not considered to be pharmaceuticals, though the law may set special requirements to ensure their quality when they are used to package medicines.

Parallel import

The importation of a drug other than through the holder of the marketing authorisation. Parallel import is widely practiced where a medicine emanates from a multinational producer and can be obtained more cheaply by buying it in a foreign country where it is on sale at a particularly low price.

Pharmaceutical

See "medicinal product" (above).

Pharmaceutical crime

All crime linked with pharmaceuticals.

Pharmacovigilance
Once a medicinal product is sold on the market, information on adverse reactions (see "adverse effects"), misuse and abuse, and consumption is collected and evaluated on an ongoing basis.

Pharmaceutical form
The physical (galenical) form of the final medicinal product intended for administration to the patient (for example, tablet, capsule, syrup or ointment).

Possession
Having direct control over a quantity of medicinal products, either by carrying them on the person or holding them in store in premises over which one has control, irrespective of whether the possessor has legal ownership of the goods or not. The term is applied particularly as regards the handling of unauthorised medicines or substances.

Proactive investigation
The intensive detection, collection, treating and recording of data relating to the acts of a person or group of persons suspected of illegal behaviour in order to obtain evidence which might justify criminal proceedings. See also "observation" above.

Pseudo-purchases
See "controlled deliveries" above.

Prescription medicine
A medicine which can only be supplied to the patient if a medical doctor or health professional has issued to the patient a medical prescription for the medicine.

Sanction
A penalty or punishment prescribed by the law in order to discourage improper behaviour.

Search warrant
An authorisation issued, generally only to police officers or specialised inspectors, to enter and search private or institutional premises to obtain possible evidence of unauthorised activities suspected of being carried on there.

Seizure
The taking and removal of goods or documents from a person or institution by a police officer, inspector or other authorised official. Seizure may take place in the course of a routine inspection or following entry on the basis of a search warrant. The law may allow goods to be seized where they are of a prohibited nature (for example, unlicensed medicines) or where they are in the possession of a person or institution not having a licence to handle them. Depending on the legal provisions concerned, the goods may be permanently confiscated or they may be held provisionally depending on the outcome of legal proceedings against the person or institution concerned.

Substandard medicine
A medicine which does not adhere to the standards laid down in the marketing authorisation applicable to it, due to unintended, deficient manufacturing by licensed manufacturers.

Tamper-proof packaging
A form of packaging for a medicine which has improved resistance against unauthorised interference with its contents before it reaches the user and makes such unauthorised interference evident.

Wiretapping
The monitoring of private (telephone) communications, generally as a means of observation. The process may involve the routine recording of incoming and outgoing telephone communications.

Appendix 3

Questionnaire for stakeholder survey –
Views on best co-operation practices, measures and experiences applicable to counterfeit (falsified or fake) medicines
Council of Europe Partial Agreement in the Social and Public Health Field, 2004

I. Description of the situation

1.   How many cases of counterfeit pharmaceuticals have been brought to your attention in the past few years? Please give the number of cases and indicate substance, pharmaceutical form and brand name, in so far as they are not confidential, for:

a. your company?
b. other companies within the pharmaceutical sector (including active ingredient manufacturers and wholesalers)?

2.a. If you cannot give a number of cases, please give your best estimate and indicate the basis for your assumption, if possible.

2.b. What are your estimates for the future (for example, following EU enlargement) and expected tendencies in regions or individual countries?

3.   What are your estimates (percentage) of the proportion of counterfeit pharmaceuticals on the market?

4.   Which types of pharmaceuticals are affected by counterfeiting? (Information: high price, known brand, high development costs, etc.)

5.   Which types of counterfeit practice have been identified in your country/other countries? (Example: illegal relabelling and repackaging of medicines for your market.)

6.   Do you think counterfeit pharmaceuticals appear in the legal distribution chain?

7.   Do you think that the Internet plays a role in the sale of counterfeit pharmaceuticals?

8.   Are you aware of a national/international database on counterfeit pharmaceuticals (trade, distribution, prosecution)?

9.   Is there a specific regulatory entity (authority) set up in your country to co-operate with the industry/wholesalers/pharmacists/traders in the field of counterfeit pharmaceuticals (for example, inspection, control)?

10. Do you think industry, wholesalers, traders and pharmacists know who should be informed, and which notification procedures should be followed?

II. Countermeasures to prevent counterfeiting and public health damage

11. What is needed to implement and improve the communication between industry/distribution/trade firms and authorities to take action against counterfeit pharmaceuticals (suspect or proven cases)?

12. Do you consider the current awareness of the authorities concerned, and their initiatives and systems (for example, inspection) are adequate to prevent/fight the counterfeiting of pharmaceuticals?

13. What should be improved in the current systems or provisions to effectively fight pharmaceutical counterfeiting?

14. EC Regulation 1383/2003 specifies measures to be taken against goods which have infringed certain intellectual property rights

15. Do you have your own security personnel to investigate counterfeiting of pharmaceuticals?

III. Conclusions

Please indicate your view on industry's best co-operation practices with the concerned authorities.

Please add any remarks, comments or suggestions, you wish to share.

Appendix 4

Questionnaire for survey –
National legislation on counterfeit and unlicensed medicines
Council of Europe Partial Agreement in the Social and Public Health Field, 2003

1.   Which specific national legislation is applicable in your country to protect the patient against counterfeit medicinal products?

2.   A case of a counterfeit medicinal product or otherwise illegal medicinal product has been identified or is suspected in your country. What specific national legislation is applicable in your country to take sanctions against the responsible criminal persons or organisations for (i) potential or (ii) proven health risks (penalties)?

3.   What national legislation is applicable in your country to prevent the spread of counterfeit medicines or unlicensed medicines to other countries?

Appendix 5

Council of Europe member state counterfeit medicine case reports (from survey – see Appendix 2)

Incidence of new national cases of counterfeit medicines brought to the attention of national authorities

Member state surveys 2004 and 2003

Member state/year	New national cases	API, BP or FP	Brand name or INN	Reported by institution/ organisation
Q9 (MoH/DRA)				
1				
2003	20-30	FP	Sildenafil tablets	Police, customs, manufacturer, own investigations, foreign counterparts
2				
1996	1	FP	Losec (Omeprazole)	Anonymous – not reported by any institution
1997-98	1	FP	Humatrope (Somatropin)	Police
2002	2	FP	Nubain (Nalbuphine Hydrochloride) Viagra (Sildenafil Citrate)	Industry Customs
2003	3	FP	Diazepam Beechams Powder Dettol	Police Anonymous Anonymous
2004	5	FP	Nubain (Nalbuphine Hydrochloride) Viagra (Sildenafil Citrate) Diazepam Lady Viagra (does not exist)	Anonymous Police Police Police
3				
2001	1	FP, Nigeria	Gboromo suspension	Unknown
4				
2004	Approximately 20 products	BP and FP	Various anabolics and injectable hormones	Still under judicial investigation (indictment secret)
5				
–	–	–	–	

Member state/year	New national cases	API, BP or FP	Brand name or INN	Reported by institution/ organisation
6				
2000	4 major international	FP	Amoxycillin capsules Halofanterin tablets Ciprofloxacin tablets	Customs
2002	4 minor national 4 major national	FP FP	Sildenafil tablets Anabolics (injections + tablets)	Customs + police
2003	8 minor national 3 major national 1 major international	FP FP FP	Sildenafil tablets Sildenafil tablets Ciclosporin capsules	Customs + police
2004	3 minor national 1 minor national	FP FP	Sildenafil tablets Anabolics injections	
7				
–	–	–	–	
8				
–	–	–	–	
9				
2000	14	API, FP	Broncholytin syrup Indomethacin tablets Cinnarizine tablets Spasmalgon tablets Sumamed capsules Solocseryl injections Nystatin solution Pentalgin-ICN tablets Ampicillin tablets Trihydrate tablets Trichopol tablets	
2001	8	API, FP	Reopolyglucon infusion and solution Nystatin tablets Salbey tablets	
2002	5	API, FP	5-Nok drops Festal drops Clotrimazole cream	
2003	8	API, FP	Sumamed capsules Pentalgin-B tablets Pentalgin-N tablets Nafthizine capsules Trichopol tablets Baralgetas injections and solution Viagra tablet	

Member state/year	New national cases	API, BP or FP	Brand name or INN	Reported by institution/ organisation
10				
–	–	–	–	
11				
2002	1	FP	Betamethasone Diprosone cream	
2003 and 2004	0	Only counter-feits of medical devices were reported		
11				
–	–	–	–	
12				
–	–	–	Nitrazepam	
15				
2002	3	–	–	
2003	5	API	Anabolic steroids (Nandolonc, Metandienone) Androgens (testosterone)	
Q58 (MoIP)				
3				
2003	20-30	FP	Sildenafil tablets	Police, customs, manufacturers, own investigations, foreign counterparts
6				
2003		FP	Viagra Aqua-T	Police from neighbouring country
2003		FP	Viagra	Police from neighbouring country
2003		FP	Sandimmum-Optorla Viagra	Police of another European state
2003		FP	Viagra Viagra for women	Police
11				
1995	1	FP (placebo)	Anti-meningococcal vaccine	MSF and MAH
1996	2	FP (API) FP (placebo)	Anabolic steroids Anti-cholera vaccine	MAH MAH
1997	1	FP (placebo)	Immunosupressants	MAH
2002	1	FP (placebo)	Sun block cream	MAH

Member state/year	New national cases	API, BP or FP	Brand name or INN	Reported by institution/ organisation
2003	1	FP (placebo)	Anti-eczema cream	Police seizure
2004	2	FP (placebo)	Anti-cholera vaccine Contact lenses	MAH DRA
Q84 (MoJ)				
No cases specifically reported to any MoJ (see other report sections)				
Q110 (MoFTC)				
2				
2002	3	FP	Viagra	Customs
2003	46	FP	Viagra	Customs
6				
2001	1	FP (579 kg)	Ampiclox Amoxyl Anti-malarial (Halfan)	
2002	None	None	None	
2003	65	FP	Viagra (299 388 pieces)	
11				
2004	1	FP	Viagra	

Appendix 6

Stakeholder counterfeit medicine case reports (from survey – see Appendix 3)

Cases of counterfeit medicines brought to the attention of manufacturers and wholesalers

Stakeholder survey 2004

Stakeholder/ year	API	FP	Country/ region affected
1			
A			
2003	Yes	–	UK
Comments General awareness raised by MHRA.			
B			
–	–	–	–
2			
A			
2004	Dozens or more cases, Nandrolone Decanoate, testosterone esters	Anabolic steroids and androgens	Most countries
2003	See 2004	See 2004	See 2004
2002	See 2004	See 2004	See 2004
2001	See 2004	See 2004	See 2004
Comments Our company has been confronted with the widespread counterfeiting of steroids and androgens for years. The products are very popular in the bodybuilder and sports scene. For this reason they are being extensively counterfeited throughout the world and offered in many sports schools and via the Internet.			
B			
–	–	–	–
3			
A			
2004	Finasteride	Propecia	Netherlands
Comments Source unknown.			
B			
–	–	–	–

Stakeholder/ year	API	FP	Country/ region affected
4			
A			
No cases	–	–	–
B			
No cases	–	–	–
5			
A			
2004		Geriatric Pharmaton capsules	Ecuador
		Asasantin 200/25 Retard	South Africa
		Buscapina Compositum	Argentina
		Bisolvon	Colombia
		Complegel	Colombia
		Buscapina	Colombia
		Macrodantina	Colombia
		Finalgel	Ukraine
		Buscapina Sup.	Ecuador
		Atrovent	Colombia
		Niflamin	Colombia
		Prodolina	Mexico
		Berodual	Colombia
		Berodual	Colombia
		Butazocea 200 mg x 10	Argentina
		Geriatric multivitaminic capsules	Colombia
2003		Mucosolvan compo solution	Guatemala
		Buscapina compositum	Colombia
		Buscapina compositum	Mexico
		Atrovent aerosol	Colombia
		Viramune tablets 200 mg	Mexico
		Mucosolvan solution	Mexico
		Finalgon	USA
		Pharmaton	Colombia
		Pharmaton	Mexico
		Dulcolax	Taiwan
		Geriatric Pharmaton capsules	Ecuador
		Asasantin 200/25 Retard	South Africa
		Buscapina compositum	Argentina
		Bisolvon	Colombia
		Complegel	Colombia

Stakeholder/ year	API	FP	Country/ region affected
2003		Buscapina	Colombia
		Macrodantina	Colombia
2002		OTC Pharma PF 30 capsules	Ecuador
		Buscapina compositum	Ecuador
		Dulcolax	Ecuador
		Perlutal ampules	Brazil
		Pharmaton Geriatric	Ecuador
		Mobic 15 mg, 10 tablets	Lebanon
		Bisolvon Linctus syrup	Colombia
		Berodual Solution	Colombia
		Buscapina compositum film coated tablets	Argentina
		Viramune tablets 200 mg	Mexico
		Mucosolvan compo solution	Mexico
2001		Ditec DA	Germany
		Berodual	Germany
		Buscopan compositum (Merk)	Nigeria
		Perlutal ampules	Colombia
		Neurocerebral H-Vitamin E	Colombia
		Bisolvon elixir	Thailand
		Atrovent aerosol	Colombia
B			
–	–	–	–
6 (see note iv)			
A			
2004		1 Product A Parenteral (NP)	Egypt
		1 Product B external packaging material	South America
		1 Product C solid (P)	Asia
		17 Product D solid (P)	Asia
		1 Product E solid (P)	Japan
		1 Product E solid (P)	Asia
		1 Product E solid/powder (P)	Asia
		1 Product E solid (P)	USA
2003		1 Product F solid (NP)	Eastern Europe
		1 Product G solid (NP)	South America
		1 Product E solid (P)	Asia
		11 Product D solid (P)	Asia
2002		1 Product F solid (NP)	Germany

211

Stakeholder/ year	API	FP	Country/ region affected
2002		1 Product H cream/ointment (NP)	South America
		1 Product C parenteral (P)	South America
		1 Product C solid (P)	Germany
		1 Product I solid (NP)	USA
		8 Product D solid (P)	Asia
2001		1 Product J solid (P)	Africa/Asia
		1 Product F solid (NP)	South America
		1 Product C solid (P)	South America
		1 Product D solid (P)	Asia
2000		1 Product C solid (P)	Africa
		1 Product K cream/ointment (NP)	Africa
		1 Product L solid (P)	Asia
1999		1 Product C solid (P)	Asia
B			
2002	–	Faked brand name (not company product)	South America
7			
A			
None			
B			
None			
8			
A			
–	–	–	Mexico
Comments No cases over the past years. The first case has now entered the legal process; Mexico is the affected country.			
B			
No information available			
9			
A			
None			
Comments We have not yet experienced a case.			
B			
Yes	–	–	–
Comments There are numerous reports of cases in the United States but none related to our suppliers or us. The NABP website has a listing of 31 drugs that are counterfeited.			

Stakeholder/ year	API	FP	Country/ region affected
10			
A			
2004		Yes	Bulgaria (1) China (50)
2003		Yes	Russian Federation (1) China (100) Vietnam (10)
2002		Yes	China (100)
2001		Yes	China (100)
B			
–	–	–	–
11			
A			
2004	6 cases investigated globally	3 major brands and 1 minor brand	USA, China, Nigeria, Venezuela, Egypt, Dominican Republic
2003	Approximately 20 cases investigated globally		For example, USA, China, Mexico, Colombia, Venezuela, Taiwan and Malaysia
Comments The number of cases quoted is based on the WHO definition of counterfeit products. All incidents investigated so far have been contained and dealt with locally. The legal/security and QA function were primarily involved – patient safety considered our highest priority.			
B			
–	–	–	–
Comments Numerous incidents throughout the world are known to us through literature in the public domain.			
12			
A			
2004	350 Tadalafil	350 Cialis 20 mg	Global – Source: China, Korea and Taiwan
2003	175 Tadalafil	175 Tadalafil	
Comments These are rough figures of where we are globally. They were obtained from live investigations using sources, patient complaints and Internet monitoring. The number of cases in Europe in 2004 is close to 75.			
B			
2004		1 Reductil	UK
2003		1 Lipitor	UK, USA

Stakeholder/ year	API	FP	Country/ region affected
13			
A			
2004		Glibenclamide (Daonil) tablets	India
		Furosemide (Lasix) tablets	India
		Metamizole Sodium (Novalcina) tablets	Colombia
		Naphazoline Hydrochloride (Colirio Moura) eye drops	Brazil
		Metamizole Sodium (Novalgyn) tablets	Paraguay
2003		Metamizole Sodium (Novalgina) tablets	Argentina
		Metalozone (Metenix) tablets	India
		Furosemide (Lasix) tablets	Thailand
		Phosphaditylcholine (Essentiale Forte) capsules	China
		Alimemazine Tartrate (Theralene) tablets	Vietnam
2002		Roxithromycin (Rulid) tablets	Russian Federation
		Pancreatin (Festal) tablets	Russian Federation
		Ofloxacin (Tarivid) tablets	Russian Federation
		Pentoxifylline (Trental) tablets	Russian Federation
		Ciclopyrox (Batrafen)	Russian Federation
2001		Cefotaxime Sodium (Claforan) injectable	Russian Federation
		Phosphaditylcholine (Essentiale) capsules	Russian Federation
		Metamizole sodium (Novalgina) tablets	Peru
		Metamizole sodium (Novalgina) tablets	Argentina
		Metamizole sodium (Novalgina) drops	Peru

Stakeholder/ year	API	FP	Country/ region affected
Comments Cases in the Russian Federation also involve lookalike and "legal" copies due to lack of patent protection.			
B			
–	–	–	
Comments Only publicly accessible information available.			
14			
A			
2004	0	82 (to end July)/ most actives and dose forms	China, Nigeria, India, Bangladesh, Lebanon, UAE, Egypt, Hong Kong, Indonesia, Pakistan, Sudan, Kenya, Russian Federation, South Africa, Brazil, Malaysia, Mexico, Philippines, Vietnam, Taiwan, Myanmar, Syria, Thailand, UK, USA
2003	0	151/most actives and dose forms	As above plus Germany, Bulgaria
2002	0	116/most actives and dose forms	As above
2001	0	50+	As above
Comments EU much less affected than developing markets, although counterfeit goods regularly transit it.			
B			
–	–	–	
15			
A			
2004	Cephalexin: imported from a manufacturer in the EU, labeled, etc. as an intermediate		Brazil
2003	Cephalexin: same as in 2004		Brazil
2002	1. Cephalexin: our company's labels and holograms were perfectly imitated; neither product nor packaging originated from our company. 2. Cephalexin: product from a		China

Stakeholder/ year	API	FP	Country/ region affected
2002	reputed Asian company had a very variable quality. The reason was that it was not manufactured by the company but purchased by them from other non-authorised producers and sold under the label, etc., of the reputed company		
2001	1. Cephalexin: same as above in 2002. 2. Cephalexin: same as above in 2002		China
2000	–	–	–
1999	Cephazolin acid: labelled, etc., as if from a well-known EU manufacturer but appeared to be Chinese material		Russian Federation

Comments

The detection of counterfeited API material occurs rarely and should be seen as the small tip of the iceberg. It, however, illustrates the types of practice taking place. Under "country/region affected" we have filled in the destinations of the API materials. It may well be possible that the countries where the final dosage forms are marketed are very different ones, including highly regulated markets such as the EU and the United States. The final markets are often not well known to API suppliers.

Our product package contains the API Amoxicillin Trihydrate. According to the results of various investigations (including those performed by the WHO) this is the most counterfeited pharmaceutical product in the world. At API level we have been confronted with various forms of counterfeiting of Amoxicillin and of our other antibiotics. The examples ranged from our company's drums/packaging/labelling being precisely copied and containing substandard quality products not originating from our company, to drums/packaging that did originate from our company but in which the antibiotic API product had been replaced by starch.

B			
2004	–	–	–
2003	Gentamicin: analytical finger-printing of gentamicin sampled from EU market leads to the conclusion that at least 33% of API samples are counterfeit, that is not produced by the labelled, registered manufacturers	–	EU

Stakeholder/ year	API	FP	Country/ region affected
2002	–	–	–
2001	–	–	–
2000	Gentamicin: at least 17 patients died from substandard gentamicin that contained API imported from China. As a result the FDA's upper management is summoned to appear at a hearing of the House Commerce Committee of the US Congress	–	USA
1997	Cefaclor (supplier: Biochimica OPOS in Italy). For example, consult: http://www.essential drugs.org/edrug/ archive/200110/ msg00077.php This is an example of how incredibly "refined"/thoroughly schemed counterfeiting practices can be. Even an FDA inspection almost failed to unveil that the API was not manufactured at the inspected plant at all (but in other plants in Romania, Italy and France using a process different from the one that was registered)	–	USA

Comments
As mentioned above, counterfeiting of APIs is believed to be a widespread phenomenon. What also makes it complex and difficult to tackle and to prove is that it partly depends on the regulatory requirements of a specific authority/country/market whether an API is a counterfeit. It must be re-emphasised that counterfeit APIs, even if their identity is correct, form a big threat to human health because of the possibility that highly toxic impurities may be present, the API's stability may be insufficient or its physical properties not suitable for manufacturing a safe and effective medicinal product. The examples included in the above tables are most probably only a very small tip of a large iceberg. And the iceberg itself is probably growing rapidly. We believe that counterfeiting of APIs is the least visible, most difficult to detect and prove, and most widespread (especially in Europe) form of pharmaceutical counterfeiting. It has the potential to result in health catastrophes of a large magnitude, and possibly is already causing severe but largely unnoticed damage to human health, also in Europe (see above point also).

Stakeholder/ year	API	FP	Country/ region affected
16			
A			
2002	Chemical intermediate for API	–	Origin of material was India
B			
–	–	–	–
17			
A			
2004	Dydrogesterone tablets		Philippines
2003	Dydrogesterone tablets		Pakistan
2002	Dydrogesterone tablets		Saudi Arabia
B			
–	–	–	–
18			
A			
2004	–	–	–
2003	–	–	–
2002	Diltiazem HCl	Cardizem	USA + ?
Comments Exotic source marketed under our company name and labels (detected by the FDA).			
B			
2004	–	–	–
2003	–	–	–
1999	Various	Various	Europe/Asia/Pacific
Comments Uncontrolled sources of APIs relabelled by a broker (Switzerland).			
19			
A			
?	Meloxicam (Metacam)	?	UK affected, France involved
?	Levothyroxine (Solokine)	?	UK affected, USA and the Internet involved
?	Ivermectin (Ivanec)	?	UK affected, Ireland involved
B			
–	–	–	–
20			
A			
–	–	–	–

Stakeholder/ year	API	FP	Country/ region affected
B			
–	–	–	–
21			
A			
2004		1 Tadalafil (Cialis)	UK, label and hologram
2003		5 Ciclosporin (Sandimmun)	Germany, packaging
		Fluvastatin (Locol)	Germany, packaging
		Nitrofurantoin (Urospasmon)	Germany, packaging
		Atenolol	Germany, packaging
		Codein (Codipront)	Germany, packaging
2002		32 Ciprofloxacin Stada 250 mg	Germany, packaging
		Ciprofloxacin (Ciprodura 250 mg)	Germany, packaging
		Fluoxetin Azu 20 mg	Germany, packaging
		Tinzaparin Natrium (Innohep 3500 Anti-XA 10 x 0.3 ml)	Germany, packaging
		Felodipin Stada 10 mg	Germany, packaging
		Furosemid Stada 500 mg	Germany, packaging
		Hypericum 425 Stada	Germany, packaging
		Certoparin (Mono-Embolex NM)	Germany, packaging
		Ofloxacin Stada Uro 100 mg	Germany, packaging
		Mesalazin (Salofalk 500 mg)	Germany, packaging
		Olanzapin (Zyprexa Velotab 5 mg)	Germany, packaging
		Olanzapin (Zyprexa Velotab 10 mg)	Germany, packaging
		Olanzapin (Zyprexa 10 mg)	Germany, packaging
		Omeprazol (Omeprazol Stada 20 mg)	Germany, Packaging
		Omeprazol (Omeprazol Azu 20mg)	Germany, packaging
		Sulpirid Stada 200 mg	Germany, packaging
		Clindamycin (Aclinda 300 mg)	Germany, packaging
		Clindamycin (Clindastad 300mg)	Germany, packaging
		Loratadin Stada allerg 10 mg	Germany, packaging
		Loratadin Azu 10 mg	Germany, packaging
		Roxythromycin Azu 150 mg	Germany, packaging

Stakeholder/ year	API	FP	Country/ region affected
2002		Roxythromycin Stada 150 mg	Germany, packaging
		Captopril (Acenorm 25 mg)	Germany, packaging
		Captopril (Acenorm 50 mg)	Germany, packaging
		Pravastatin (Pravasin Protect 20 mg)	Germany, packaging
		Amoxycillin + Clavulanate (Amoxyclav 875 125 mg)	Germany, packaging
		Amoxycillin + Clavulanate (Amoxyllat-Clav 875 125 mg)	Germany, packaging
		Molsidomin Stada 8 mg	Germany, packaging
		Ticlopidin Stada 250 mg	Germany, packaging
		Enalapril Azu 10 mg	Germany, packaging
		Enalapril Azu 20 mg	Germany, packaging
		Gemcitabin (Gemzar 1000)	Germany, packaging
2001		3 Fenoterol Hydrobromid (Ditec)	Germany, packaging
		Ipratropium Bromide (Berodual)	Germany, packaging
		Valproate (Orfiril)	Germany, packaging
B			
–	–	–	–
22			
A			
–	–	–	–
Comments No counterfeit medicines.			
B			
–	–	–	–
23			
A			
2004		Cialis (Tadalafil) 20 mg tablets	UK affected
		Reductil (Sibutramine) 15 mg capsules	UK affected, Spain involved
Comments Reductil still under investigation.			
B			
–	–	–	–
Comments No incidents reported in the UK since 1994, until Cialis and Reductil identified above.			
24			
A			
–	–	–	–

Stakeholder/ year	API	FP	Country/ region affected
B			
2003		Atenolol 100 comp (Heumann)	Germany affected
		Urospasmon (Heumann)	Germany affected
		Urospasmon sine (Heumann)	Germany affected
		Locol 20 and 40 mg (Novartis)	Germany affected
2002		Sandimmun Optoral 25, 50 and 100 mg (Novartis)	Germany affected, Switzerland involved
		Fraxiparin 0.3 (Sanofi Synthelabo)	Germany affected
		Ciprofloxacin AZU 500 (Azupharma)	Germany affected
2001		Berodual N Aerosol (Boehringer Ingelheim)	Germany affected
		Ditec Aerosol (Boehringer Ingelheim)	Germany affected
25			
A			
–	–	–	–
Comments As stated in introductory notes, no cases were reported.			
B			
Comments As stated in introductory notes, no cases were reported.			
26			
A			
–	–	–	–
Comments No cases.			
B			
–	–	–	–
Comments No examples.			
27			
A			
2004		Sibutramine Hcl (Reductil)	UK affected, situation still under investigation
		Tadalafil (Cialis)	UK affected, situation still under investigation
2001		Xenical (Roche)	–

Stakeholder/ year	API	FP	Country/ region affected
Comments Italy: no case brought. Norway: no problem in Norway yet. UK: both products have been issued with MHRA Class 2 recalls. Currently, both are still in recall phase.			
B			
2004		Surevue (contact lenses) Cialis	France Netherlands
		Sibutramine Hcl (Reductil)	UK affected, situation still under investigation
		Tadalafil (Cialis)	UK affected, situation still under investigation
2003		Sandimmun (immunosuppressive agent) Locol (lipid lowering drug) Zerit (anti-retroviral drug)	Germany Germany Germany
2001-02		Epogen Procrit Neupogen Nutropin Serostim (Serono) Combivir Zyprexa Gaminune	United States – 66 people died
2001		Artésunate (anti-malarial drug)	Cambodia, Thailand, Vietnam
		Viagra	United States
1999		Anti-inflammatory drug	France
1998		Anti-inflammatory drug	France
Comments France: in 1998 and 1999, the counterfeit anti-inflammatory drugs were confiscated by customs at the airport; none of them was sold to patients. Netherlands: brought to our attention by public news and telephone information (no specifics), no formal information. Spain: probably counterfeiting exists on the Internet. UK: both products have been issued with MHRA Class 2 recalls. Currently, both are still in recall phase.			
28			
A			
–	–	–	–
Comment The association does not know about cases of counterfeit pharmaceuticals.			
B			
–	–	–	–
Comments The association does not know about cases of counterfeit pharmaceuticals, including APIs and wholesalers.			

Stakeholder/ year	API	FP	Country/ region affected
29			
A			
–	–	–	–
Comments In our experience, we have never found counterfeit FPs.			
B			
–	–	–	–
Comments No cases in wholesale sector.			
30			
A			
2004	–	Cialis tablets	Detected in UK
B			
–	–	–	–
Comments Notified by EliLilly due to rapid alert by European regulatory authorities. No counterfeit medicine found in Norway.			

Notes

i. A – products from the responding company.

ii. B – products from other companies reported by the responding company.

iii. Respondents 1-14 = FP manufacturers; 15-18 = API manufacturers; 19 – veterinary product manufacturer; and 20-30 = wholesaler.

iv. Respondent 6's detailed response is as follows:

Year	FP	Formulation	Patent status	Country/ region affected
2004	1 Product A	Parenteral	Not patented	Egypt
	1 Product B	External packaging material		South America
	1 Product C	Solid	Patented	Asia
	17 Product D	Solid	Patented	Asia
	1 Product E	Solid	Patented	Japan
	1 Product E	Solid	Patented	Asia
	1 Product E	Solid/powder	Patented	Asia
	1 Product E	Solid	Patented	US
2003	1 Product F	Solid	Not patented	Eastern Europe
	1 Product G	Solid	Not patented	South America
	1 Product E	Solid	Patented	Asia
	11 Product D	Solid	Patented	Asia
2002	1 Product F	Solid	Not patented	Germany
	1 Product H	Cream/ointment	Not patented	South America
	1 Product C	Parenteral	Patented	South America
	1 Product C	Solid	Patented	Germany
		Faked brand name, not a product of the company		South America

Year	FP	Formulation	Patent status	Country/region affected
2002	1 Product I	Solid	Not patented	USA
	8 Product D	Solid	Patented	Asia
2001	1 Product J	Solid	Patented	Africa/Asia
	1 Product F	Solid	Not patented	South America
	1 Product C	Solid	Patented	South America
	1 Product D	Solid	Patented	Asia
2000	1 Product C	Solid	Patented	Africa
	1 Product K	Cream/ointment	Not patented	Africa
	1 Product L	Solid	Patented	Asia
1999	1 Product C	Solid	Patented	Asia

Appendix 7

Counterfeit medicine RAS reporting form (as proposed by the Council of Europe Ad hoc Group on Counterfeit Medicines)

Rapid alert notification of a counterfeited medicinal product Proposal from the Council of Europe Ad hoc Group on Counterfeit Medicines Status as of 13 October 2004

☞ Please fill out one form per product.
☞ If a choice of answers is given, please tick the correct answer(s), as required.
☞ In case information is missing, please leave the relevant point open.
☞ You can fill out this form elmectronically by switching between the shaded boxes with the "TAB" button.

To (agency):	**Fax number:**
(Please attach a separate list, if more agencies are alerted)	
Summary information	
Trade name of the licensed medicinal product, which has been counterfeited:	
Country from which this alert is sent:	
Summary description of the counterfeit:	
(Please see next pages for more detailed information)	

1. **Information on the licensed medicinal product, which has been counterfeited:**
a) **Brand/trade name:**   Country:
b) **INN or generic name:**
c) **Dosage form:**
d) **Strength:**
e) **Pack size and presentation:**
f) ❏ **For use in humans /** ❏ **For use in animals**
g) **Marketing authorisation holder:**
h) **Marketing authorisation number:**

2. **Information on the counterfeit:**
a) **Characteristics on the basis of which the secondary package can be distinguished from the licensed product:**

b) **Characteristics on the basis of which the primary package can be distinguished from the licensed product:**

c) **Characteristics on the basis of which the dosage form can be distinguished from the licensed product:**

d) **Batch or lot number shown on counterfeit:**

Identical with an existing batch or lot number of the licensed product?
❏ **Yes /** ❏ **No**

e) **Expiry date shown on counterfeit:**

If the counterfeit and the licensed product have the same batch or lot number, please indicate the expiry date of the licensed product:

f) **Content(s) of active pharmaceutical ingredient(s) in counterfeit (per unit):**
Name of active ingredient: **Content:**

Does/do the content(s) comply with the specification of the licensed product?
❏ **Yes /** ❏ **No**

g) **Special characteristics of the active pharmaceutical ingredient in counterfeit (for example, characteristic degradation products or any other information that helps to identify the counterfeit):**

Further details about counterfeit:

(If possible, please attach a photograph, showing the differences between the counterfeit and licensed product.)

3. **Risk of counterfeit:**
I   **The counterfeit is potentially life threatening or could cause a serious risk to health:**
❏ **Yes /** ❏ **No**
II **The counterfeit could cause illness or mistreatment (but is not potentially life threatening or is not likely to cause a serious risk to health):**
❏ **Yes /** ❏ **No**

4. **Information on the location where the counterfeit has been found and on the amounts which have been found**
Type of location: ❏ **Customs /** ❏ **Wholesaler /** ❏ **Retail pharmacy /** ❏ **Hospital**
❏ **Medical doctor /** ❏ **Other (please specify):**
Amount found:
(Please attach a separate list of locations where the counterfeit has been found, if more than one.)

5. **What has happened to the counterfeit medicinal product so far?**
    ❏ **The counterfeit is in the possession of the marketing authorisation holder**
    ❏ **The counterfeit is in the possession of the competent authority**

❐ Other (please specify):

6. If the counterfeit can not be distinguished from the licensed product, please indicate the distribution of the licensed product, including exports: ❐ Not applicable
Distribution: ❐ Wholesaler / ❐ Retail pharmacy / ❐ Hospital / ❐ Medical doctor
❐ Other (please specify):
Batch number/s:
Country:
(Please attach a separate list of recipients of the indistinguishable licensed product, including details such as name, address and country of recipient as well as batch number and number of packs delivered.)

7. Please indicate the action taken so far concerning the indistinguishable licensed product:
❐ Not applicable
❐ Recall of affected batches / ❐ Other (please specify):

8. Please list all other agencies that have been informed about the counterfeit
Type: ❐ Medicines agency / ❐ Police / ❐ Customs / ❐ Other (please specify):
Name:
Address:
Country:
(Please attach a separate list of agencies that have been informed, if more than one.)

9. Any further information?

10.a. This alert was issued by the following agency:	10.b. This alert was issued by the following firm:
Agency:	Firm:
Contact person:	Contact person:
Telephone:	Telephone:
Fax:	Fax:
E-mail:	E-mail:

11. Signature:	12. Date:	13. Time:

Attachments:
❐ List of recipients of this alert message
❐ Photograph, showing the differences between counterfeit and licensed product
❐ List of recipients of the original product that cannot be distinguished from the counterfeit
❐ List of agencies, which have been informed about the counterfeit
❐ Other (please specify):

Appendix 8

Major findings and recommendations concerning the Council of Europe surveys on counterfeit medicines. Presentation to the Council of Europe Ad hoc Group on Counterfeit Medicines by Jonathan Harper, 7 December 2004

1. Extent of the counterfeit medicine problem in Europe

- the problem of counterfeit medicine really does exist in Europe, despite eventual denials by some authorities and commercial organisations;
- indications are that it is on the increase (increase in cases reported by authorities and manufacturers);
- not all member states agree that they have a counterfeit medicine problem. However, they cannot deny there is a transit or source problem – if not an EU retail problem;
- the extent of the impact on public health is not entirely apparent (under reported) and thus reduces the perception of public health risk;
- there is a lack of differentiation of medicines counterfeiting from other forms of counterfeiting;
- major weaknesses in legislation, regulation and administration have been identified by survey respondents.

2. Types of medicinal products counterfeited

- every type;
- high volume (high level of prescribing);
- high price;
- known brand;
- "lifestyle"/non-reimbursed;
- blockbusters;
- all generics;
- parenterals (in developing world);
- off-label use drugs;
- short supply drugs;
- stakeholder responses indicate that all types are at risk, although the degree of risk is likely to depend on the particular local market characteristics;
- specific drug and therapeutic class examples quoted by respondents were:

  - developed world: particularly branded drugs for erectile dysfunction, weight loss and cholesterol lowering agents. Those mentioned included: Procrit, HGH, Viagra, Cialis, Reductil, Epo, Epogen, Neupogen, Lipitor, Augmentin, Sandimun Lescor and Anabolic drugs. The different types of drugs counterfeited in developed and less developed countries seems to be less pronounced now;
  - developing world: antibiotics, anti-malarials, vaccines and HIV drugs.

3. Counterfeiting practices identified

These are diverse; there is no shortage of creativity shown by counterfeiters.

A. Finished/intermediate medicinal product

- identical copy – identical packaging and formulation;
- pure counterfeit – lookalike (altered ingredients with similar packaging) (no/different/wrong dose of API or excipient);
- re-use of components (for example, refilling, re-use or replacement of components);
- false/illegal labelling/packaging (product falsely labelled as being from the original manufacturer). True counterfeiting is the copying of the primary and secondary packaging of the product involved by a third party, that is the product appears to be from the original manufacturer;
- "hybrid counterfeit" (genuine BP or packaging) and manipulated labels;
- illegal relabelling and repackaging (includes fake pricing label or fake labelling in general);
- illegal diversion and illicit trade of products, whether or not through the Internet (primary pack diversion with secondary counterfeit);
- Internet;
- unpackaged medicinal products;
- placing a non-licensed medicinal product on the market;
- false documentation (for example, granting a COS without auditing the given company or incorrect status on import documents);
- waste/expired product re-entering the market;
- combined counterfeiting (wide variety of combinations possible).

B. APIs (illegal production/distribution/diversion)

- use of (cheap) APIs from uncontrolled or non-GMP origins, and relabelling and repacking of APIs;
- ghost plant (APIs are sold by, but not manufactured by, the registered producer);
- ghost supplier (MAH purchases APIs from manufacturer not included in the MA);
- paper curtain (API manufactured by a process other than the one registered in the MA);
- authorised facades (manufacturer/trader with approved CoS or DMF supplies APIs from a large number of unauthorised manufacturers);
- unauthorised API material may also be shipped in containers labelled with the name of a different API;
- unauthorised API materials from obscure sources are blended with the registered API material;
- false MAA.

4. Major factors facilitating counterfeiting

- lack of awareness of problem/problem not perceived as serious (as regards the impact on public health);
- weak and unco-ordinated legislation (as regards regulatory gaps, enforcement and penal sanctions);
- regulatory gaps;
- weak and unco-ordinated administrative structures and procedures;
- distribution chain complexity (transactions involving many intermediaries);
- Internet pharmacy;
- high drug prices and pressure on reimbursement systems;
- organised crime sophistication in clandestine manufacture.

5. Legislative weaknesses

- no single satisfactory coherent national legal provision against medicines counterfeiting exists;
- large inconsistency between legislative provisions between states;
- weak inter-sectoral legislative co-ordination – possible provisions covered by different types of law:
  - law on medicines;
  - Penal/Criminal Code;
  - customs/trade law;
  - IPR law;

- absent supranational legislative/regulatory guidelines;
- absent definitions;
- inappropriate sanctions.

6. Specific regulatory weaknesses and gaps

- APIs;
- export and transit;
- parallel imports;
- traders/brokers;
- secondary wholesalers and wholesaling retailers;
- (re-)packaging/labelling and printing;
- Internet pharmacy;
- unlicensed medicines;
- testing and reporting systems;
- traceability systems.

7. Administrative weaknesses

- absence and lack of recognition of the problem (lack of priority for action);
- insufficient DRA resources;
- lack of inter-sectoral co-ordination (for example, between health and customs; and health and law enforcement);
- weak authority-industry co-operation (insufficient disclosure and reporting);
- weak reporting and database systems;
- weak inspection/enforcement (often lack of powers);
- difficult product traceability and security;
- absence of effective supranational co-ordinating function.

Recommendations for implementation

8. Important implementation factors

- political willingness to tackle problem is vital;
- necessary resource allocation (supranationally and nationally);
- multiple measures required;
- implementing/co-ordinating body and framework – who and what.

9. Supranational implementing structure

- clearly required – currently does not exist;
- avoidance of unnecessary duplication and ineffectiveness of effort;
- definition of the supranational body with responsibility for overseeing the co-ordination of proposed recommendations and their long-term management;
- definition of the supporting roles of the other relevant European and supranational organisations.

10. Strong recommendation 1 – Type of instrument

- highest legal basis for international co-operation;
- definition of supranational and national responsibilities;
- defining scope and content of strong instrument;
- codification of applicable member state legislation.

11. Strong recommendation 2 – Important definitions

- counterfeit medicinal product;
- pharmaceutical crime (illegal trading, falsification, health damage, etc.);
- traceability of a medicinal product (and product pedigree);
- trader/broker;
- bonded warehouse/free zone;
- parallel trade;

- risk to public health;
- others.

12. Strong recommendation 3 – Supranational tasks

- co-ordination of national authorities;
- co-ordination of industry (and wholesalers);
- co-ordination with other relevant supranational authorities;
- co-operation agreements and their supervision;
- public relations communication and monitoring (general public, authorities and health professionals);
- monitoring and database of medicinal products at high risk of counterfeiting (and those with a high public health risk);
- database of counterfeit medicinal products and counterfeit practices;
- database of legitimate and blacklisted brokers/distributors.

13. Strong recommendation 4 – National tasks

- RAS – integration into existing reporting systems?
- guidelines, for example good trade and distribution practice;
- inspection SOP (including sampling, testing and recall strategy);
- characterisation and monitoring of the pharmaceutical distribution chain;
- medicinal product traceability system;
- technology strategy for product security, traceability and product pedigree rules (based on a review of anti-counterfeiting technology used in other industries);
- definition of national tasks and national authority co-ordination procedures;
- regular forum with national authority and industry representatives;
- monitoring of results of strategy implementation;
- training support.

14. Strong recommendation 5 – Model legislative provisions (with emphasis on national tasks)

- import/export/transit licensing (emphasis on export);
- bonded warehouse/free zones;
- wholesaler and broker licensing;
- emphasis on API and excipient regulation and inspection;
- packaging and printing regulations;
- Internet pharmacy regulation;
- unlicensed medicine (compassionate use) regulations;
- industry reporting and disclosure requirements;
- national authority reporting requirements (both between authorities and to the supranational authority);
- customs procedures and risk analysis;
- risk management procedures;
- inspection and enforcement (powers of seizure and detention);
- penal sanctions (against pharmaceutical crime – as opposed to economic crime – and with a clear scale of infringement);
- authority resource allocation requirements (human, financial and systems).

15. Strong recommendation 6 – National tasks

- greater resources allocated to tackling the counterfeit medicine problem;
- definition of types of authority from different sectors to be involved and their respective roles;
- national authority co-ordination procedures;
- authority-industry-wholesaler co-ordination procedures;
- institution of specialised health police and related medicinal product customs officers;
- provision of reports to the supranational body.

16. What needs to be done by the Council of Europe

* determine report consultation process;
* obtain commitment by all member states to tackle the problem;
* determine resource allocation requirements;
* define legal instrument for international co-operation, if so desired;
* codify existing member state legislation;
* project extension to other member states – a tool for obtaining support for recommendations;
* training.

17. Council of Europe and counterfeit medicines: conclusions

* medicines counterfeiting is criminal, potentially life-threatening and undermines the health system;
* pharmaceutical crime/medicines counterfeiting has to be differentiated from other forms of economic crime/counterfeiting;
* now time to "get real" with counterfeit medicines in Europe;
* several reasons exist why medicines counterfeiting is prevalent;
* both authorities and stakeholders wish to see the issue comprehensively tackled;
* a European-level, multi-layered strategy and approach is required (as pure national approaches are likely to be far less effective and co-ordinated);
* instrument based on strong recommendations needed – should be in the form of the strongest legal co-operation possible;
* adequate resources need to be allocated to tackle the issue.

Appendix 9

Proposal for a model agreement on international and national multisectoral co-operation on counterfeit medicines

Introduction

This document outlines a draft model proposal in the form of an "instrument" for provisions to deal with medicines counterfeiting; at the level, firstly, of a European body tasked to co-ordinate regulations and policy and, secondly, the co-ordination of the relevant national sectoral authorities in the Council of Europe member states. Reference should be made to the recommendations in Sections 17.4 and 17.5 of the main report.

The type of "instrument" that is most appropriate should ideally be based on the highest legal form of co-operation possible between Council of Europe member states and its substance should be based on "strong recommendations" (as opposed to dictates). From a legal perspective, the proposed instrument can be any legally based document ranging from a convention to a co-operation agreement, depending on the political willingness and the commitment by the relevant parties to such a document.

The provisions of the proposed instrument should ideally not be placed just under the control of one sectoral authority (that is, not just under health), as satisfactorily dealing with the counterfeit medicine problem requires a co-ordinated inter-sectoral approach.

It is recommended that the proposed instrument should cover three principal areas:

(i) legislative/regulatory framework for dealing with medicines counterfeiting in member states;
(ii) European co-ordinating body (EU and international bodies) – roles and responsibilities;
(iii) national authorities – co-ordination, role and responsibilities.

Presented below is the draft outline of the proposed instrument. At this stage it should be viewed as a document for discussion and elaboration only.

Model provisions for an instrument on anti-counterfeiting

Title: Provisions to combat counterfeiting of medicinal products and pharmaceutical crime in the territory of the Council of Europe member states

Article 1 – General provisions, scope and application of the instrument

1.1. Introduction and background to the medicines counterfeiting phenomenon
1.2. Justification for creating the instrument
1.3. Constitutional, legal and agreement framework
1.4. Statement of policy objectives
1.5. Types of product (human and veterinary) and activities covered by the instrument

1.6. Legal instruments upon which the instrument is based (namely, Council of Europe Statute and agreements, and EU and other relevant international regulations and directives)
1.7. Codification of relevant member state legislation and regulations
1.8. Financing procedures for implementation of the instrument

Article 2 – Definitions and rules of interpretation

It is recommended that definitions and rules of interpretation should be based on existing EU terminology and meanings as far as possible. The following list is a proposal and not meant to be comprehensive at this point:

2.1. Medicinal product
2.2. Active substance/API
2.3. Excipients
2.4. Type of medicinal product: finished, original, generic, magistral, galenic, etc.
2.5. Counterfeit medicinal product
2.6. Pharmaceutical crime
2.7. Risk to public health
2.8. Intellectual property pertaining to medicinal products – data exclusivity, supplementary protection certificates, etc.
2.9. Legally and agreed transferable data (clear distinction between covert and overt features of any medicinal product)
2.10. Recognised pharmacopoeias
2.11. Pharmacovigilance terms and procedures (ADRs, etc.)
2.12. Manufacturer
2.13. Distributor
2.14. Retailer
2.15. Trader/broker
2.16. Possession
2.17. Unlicensed medicinal products and compassionate use
2.18. Internet pharmacy and mail order
2.19. Bonded warehouses/free zones
2.20. Parallel trade
2.21. Good pharmaceutical sector practices (namely, GMP, GDP/good trade and distribution practice, etc.)
2.22. OMCL
2.23. Labelling
2.24. Packaging
2.25. Traceability of a medicinal product
2.26. Medicinal prescription
2.27. CoS
2.28. EDMF
2.29. Import/export/transit licence
2.30. MA
2.31. Pharmacy licence
2.32. Wholesaler licence
2.33. Trader/broker licence

Article 3 – European co-ordinating body's tasks

Co-ordination tasks

3.1. Co-ordination of national authorities
3.2. Co-ordination of industry (and wholesalers)
3.3. Co-ordination with other relevant European-level and international authorities
3.4. Co-operation agreements (MoUs and MRAs, etc.) and their supervision

Technical tasks
3.5. Monitoring systems, databases and information bank (medicinal products at high risk of counterfeiting (and with high public health risk), counterfeited medicinal products

and counterfeit practices, diversion phenomena, recommended anti-counterfeiting measures, listings of legitimate and blacklisted brokers/distributors, listings of registered Internet pharmacies, successful legal actions, and international data on medicines counterfeiting from outside the European area)

3.6. Information provision to national authorities and stakeholders

3.7. Public relations communication and monitoring (differentiated between general public, authorities and health professionals)

3.8. Information disclosure system on suspected/known counterfeit medicines

3.9. RAS (integration into existing reporting systems?)

3.10. Risk management procedures

3.11. Guidelines (for example, good trade and distribution practice)

3.12. Inspection SOP (including sampling, testing and recall strategy)

3.13. Characterisation and monitoring of the official and unofficial pharmaceutical distribution chain, Internet pharmacy/mail order and the counterfeit medicine criminal business model

3.14. Medicinal product security and traceability systems

3.15. Technology strategy for product security, traceability and product pedigree rules (based on review of anti-counterfeiting technology used in other industries)

3.16. European-level suspected counterfeit medicines testing procedure

3.17. Elaboration and definition of the European legislative and regulatory framework on anti-counterfeiting (based on a full codification of existing EU and national legislation)

3.18. Definition of national tasks and national authority co-ordination procedures

3.19. Regular forum with national authority and industry representatives

3.20. Monitoring of results of strategy implementation

3.21. Public relations communication and monitoring (differentiated between general public, authorities and health professionals)

3.22. Training and educational support

Financing needs and procedures

3.23. Financing needs and procedures for functioning of the European co-ordinating body

Article 4 – National authorities' tasks

Tasks

4.1. Definition of types of authority from different sectors to be involved and their respective roles

4.2. National authority co-ordination procedures

4.3. Authority-industry-wholesaler co-ordination procedures

4.4. Institution of specialised police/interior ministry and customs authority liaison persons

4.5. National risk management procedures

4.6. National information and database systems

4.7. National suspect counterfeit medicine testing procedure

4.8. Reporting procedure and provision of reports to the European co-ordinating body

Financing needs and procedures

4.9 Authority resource allocation requirements (human, financial and systems)

Article 5 – Legislative and regulatory framework

The European co-ordinating body should have the task of ensuring that member state regulations are co-ordinated, consistent and effective in dealing with the counterfeit medicines problem. The Council of Europe co-ordinating body, while not having the authority of a regulatory body, should have the authority to make recommendations to member states concerning the following types of regulation. Whether it is decided if any specific dedicated legislation on counterfeit medicines is required has to be left to the discretion of national legislative bodies. The following outlines areas that may require specific co-ordinated legislation and regulations.

5.1. APIs and excipients manufacturing and distribution
5.2. FPs
5.3. Packaging, labelling and printing
5.4. IPR
5.5. Security and traceability systems
5.6. Broker/trader and wholesaler licensing
5.7. Import/export/transit licensing
5.8. Bonded warehouses/free zones
5.9. Internet pharmacy and mail order
5.10. Unlicensed medicines and personal/compassionate use
5.11. Regulatory authority, industry, wholesaler and pharmacy information sharing, reporting and disclosure requirements
5.12. National authority reporting requirements to European co-ordinating body (types of report to be provided and reporting procedure)
5.13. Customs procedures and risk analysis
5.14. Risk management procedures
5.15. Inspection and enforcement (investigation, seizure and detention powers)
5.16. Testing procedures (including payment) for suspected counterfeit medicines
5.17. Pharmaceutical crime and prohibited activities
5.18. Sanctions and penalties (administrative and custodial) for pharmaceutical crime (as opposed to economic crime, and with a clear scale of infringements)

Appendix 10

Council of Europe Partial Agreement in the Social and Public Health Field: medicines and the Internet – Model information for the Internet user

For information on the partial agreement's leaflet, please go to:

http://www.coe.int/T/E/Social_Cohesion/soc-sp/RD_E_InternetLeaflet.pdf

Sales agents for publications of the Council of Europe
Agents de vente des publications du Conseil de l'Europe

BELGIUM/BELGIQUE
La Librairie européenne
Rue de l'Orme 1
B-1040 BRUXELLES
Tel.: (32) 2 231 04 35
Fax: (32) 2 735 08 60
E-mail: mail@libeurop.be
http://www.libeurop.be

Jean de Lannoy
202, avenue du Roi
B-1190 BRUXELLES
Tel.: (32) 2 538 4308
Fax: (32) 2 538 0841
E-mail: jean.de.lannoy@euronet.be
http://www.jean-de-lannoy.be

CANADA
Renouf Publishing Company Limited
5369 Chemin Canotek Road
CDN-OTTAWA, Ontario, K1J 9J3
Tel.: (1) 613 745 2665
Fax: (1) 613 745 7660
E-mail: order.dept@renoufbooks.com
http://www.renoufbooks.com

CZECH REP./RÉP. TCHÈQUE
Suweco Cz Dovoz Tisku Praha
Ceskomoravska 21
CZ-18021 PRAHA 9
Tel.: (420) 2 660 35 364
Fax: (420) 2 683 30 42
E-mail: import@suweco.cz

DENMARK/DANEMARK
GAD Direct
Fiolstâede 31-33
DK-1171 KOBENHAVN K
Tel.: (45) 33 13 72 33
Fax: (45) 33 12 54 94
E-mail: info@gaddirect.dk

FINLAND/FINLANDE
Akateeminen Kirjakauppa
Keskuskatu 1, PO Box 218
FIN-00381 HELSINKI
Tel.: (358) 9 121 41
Fax: (358) 9 121 4450
E-mail: akatilaus@stockmann.fi
http://www.akatilaus.akateeminen.com

GERMANY/ALLEMAGNE
AUSTRIA/AUTRICHE
UNO Verlag
August Bebel Allee 6
D-53175 BONN
Tel.: (49) 2 28 94 90 20
Fax: (49) 2 28 94 90 222
E-mail: bestellung@uno-verlag.de
http://www.uno-verlag.de

GREECE/GRÈCE
Librairie Kauffmann
Mavrokordatou 9
GR-ATHINAI 106 78
Tel.: (30) 1 38 29 283
Fax: (30) 1 38 33 967
E-mail: ord@otenet.gr

HUNGARY/HONGRIE
Euro Info Service
Hungexpo Europa Kozpont ter 1
H-1101 BUDAPEST
Tel.: (361) 264 8270
Fax: (361) 264 8271
E-mail: euroinfo@euroinfo.hu
http://www.euroinfo.hu

ITALY/ITALIE
Libreria Commissionaria Sansoni
Via Duca di Calabria 1/1, CP 552
I-50125 FIRENZE
Tel.: (39) 556 4831
Fax: (39) 556 41257
E-mail: licosa@licosa.com
http://www.licosa.com

NETHERLANDS/PAYS-BAS
De Lindeboom Internationale
Publicaties b.v.
M.A. de Ruyterstraat 20 A
NL-7482 BZ HAAKSBERGEN
Tel.: (31) 53 574 0004
Fax: (31) 53 572 9296
E-mail: books@delindeboom.com
http://www.delindeboom.com

NORWAY/NORVÈGE
Akademika A/S Universitetsbokhandel
PO Box 84, Blindern
N-0314 OSLO
Tel.: (47) 22 85 30 30
Fax: (47) 23 12 24 20

POLAND/POLOGNE
Głowna Księgarnia Naukowa
im. B. Prusa
Krakowskie Przedmiescie 7
PL-00-068 WARSZAWA
Tel.: (48) 29 22 66
Fax: (48) 22 26 64 49
E-mail: inter@internews.com.pl
http://www.internews.com.pl

PORTUGAL
Livraria Portugal
Rua do Carmo, 70
P-1200 LISBOA
Tel.: (351) 13 47 49 82
Fax: (351) 13 47 02 64
E-mail: liv.portugal@mail.telepac.pt

SPAIN/ESPAGNE
Mundi-Prensa Libros SA
Castelló 37
E-28001 MADRID
Tel.: (34) 914 36 37 00
Fax: (34) 915 75 39 98
E-mail: libreria@mundiprensa.es
http://www.mundiprensa.com

SWITZERLAND/SUISSE
Adeco – Van Diermen
Chemin du Lacuez 41
CH-1807 BLONAY
Tel.: (41) 21 943 26 73
Fax: (41) 21 943 36 05
E-mail: info@adeco.org

UNITED KINGDOM/
ROYAUME-UNI
TSO (formerly HMSO)
51 Nine Elms Lane
GB-LONDON SW8 5DR
Tel.: (44) 207 873 8372
Fax: (44) 207 873 8200
E-mail: customer.services@theso.co.uk
http://www.the-stationery-office.co.uk
http://www.itsofficial.net

UNITED STATES and CANADA/
ÉTATS-UNIS et CANADA
Manhattan Publishing Company
468 Albany Post Road, PO Box 850
CROTON-ON-HUDSON,
NY 10520, USA
Tel.: (1) 914 271 5194
Fax: (1) 914 271 5856
E-mail: Info@manhattanpublishing.com
http://www.manhattanpublishing.com

————————

FRANCE
La Documentation française
(Diffusion/Vente France entière)
124 rue H. Barbusse
93308 Aubervilliers Cedex
Tel.: (33) 01 40 15 70 00
Fax: (33) 01 40 15 68 00
E-mail: vel@ladocfrancaise.gouv.fr
http://www.ladocfrancaise.gouv.fr

Librairie Kléber (Vente Strasbourg)
Palais de l'Europe
F-67075 Strasbourg Cedex
Fax: (33) 03 88 52 91 21
E-mail: librairie.kleber@coe.int

Council of Europe Publishing/Editions du Conseil de l'Europe
F-67075 Strasbourg Cedex
Tel.: (33) 03 88 41 25 81 – Fax: (33) 03 88 41 39 10 – E-mail: publishing@coe.int – Website: http://book.coe.int